Punctuated Equilibrium
and the Dynamics of U.S.
Environmental Policy

Punctuated Equilibrium and the Dynamics of U.S. Environmental Policy

Edited by Robert Repetto

Foreword by James Gustave Speth

Yale University Press

New Haven and London

Published with assistance from the Louis Stern Memorial Fund.

Set in Adobe Garamond and Stone Sans types by The Composing Room of Michigan, Inc.
Printed in the United States of America.

Library of Congress Cataloging-in-Publication Data

Punctuated equilibrium and the dynamics of U.S. environmental policy / edited
  by Robert Repetto.
        p.   cm.
  Includes bibliographical references and index.
  ISBN-13: 978-0-300-11076-0 (pbk. : alk. paper)
  ISBN-10: 0-300-11076-6 (pbk. : alk. paper)
    1. Environmental policy—United States.   2. Environmental protection—
United States.   3. Equilibrium (Economics).   I. Repetto, Robert C.
  GE180.P86 2006
  333.70973—dc22

                                                                    2005025917

A catalogue record for this book is available from the British Library.
The paper in this book meets the guidelines for permanence and durability
of the Committee on Production Guidelines for Book Longevity of the
Council on Library Resources.

10 9 8 7 6 5 4 3 2 1

Contents

Foreword

James Gustave Speth

This book grew out of conversations between Robert Repetto and myself regarding the failure of U.S. politics to come to grips with such global-scale environmental threats as climate change. In my book about these threats, *Red Sky at Morning*, I quoted extensively from Frank Baumgartner and Bryan Jones's *Agendas and Instability in American Politics* because they had given genuine analytical rigor to the impression we all have that policy progress is made not steadily but, as Repetto puts it, in fits and starts. If Baumgartner and Jones were right, their thesis offered hope that today's bleak political prospects for global environmental threats might rapidly change, giving way to the sea change of progress on global challenges that we saw on domestic environmental issues in the 1970s.

Given the seriousness of the global environmental threats, especially climate change, it seemed important to us to understand as much as possible about the workings of Baumgartner and Jones's "punctuated equilibria" in American environmental politics and policy development. Has this been the pattern followed to date? What factors lead to these periods of rapid change, when the status quo logjam breaks and rapid policy movement occurs? In particular, if we understand the dynamics of major policy change, might it be possible to hasten the day when it occurs?

Repetto took up this challenge, and support from the William and Flora Hewlett Foundation and the K. Vann Rasmussen Foundation made it possible to launch the investigation reflected in this admirable and important book. Robert Repetto is one of America's most accomplished economists working on environmental policy analysis. With great skill he assembled an outstanding team of social scientists—experts familiar with both political change theory and practical environmental affairs. Together they developed a study design and produced the insightful contributions collected here. Repetto's introductory chapter will surely whet the appetite for the excellent conceptual foundation chapters and case studies that follow.

The foundation chapters by Frank Baumgartner and William Brock explain processes that can lead to the political dynamics associated with punctuated equilibria in the policy domain and do so in a way that provides useful insights for those interested in understanding what brings about policy change. The case studies applying this framework are remarkable not only for the wide range of resource and environmental policy issues that they address but also for the fact that they analyze both issues that have undergone dramatic and abrupt change and those that have remained persistently blocked or stagnant. The use of punctuated equilibrium concepts to analyze policy change prospectively is one of this book's unique contributions.

Among those policy issues that have shown little progress in the United States, global warming is the most serious environmental challenge we face today or have ever faced. Some knowledgeable observers go further—Sir David King, the government's chief scientist in Britain, wrote recently in the January 9, 2004, issue of *Science* that "Climate change is the most severe problem that we are facing today—more serious even than the threat of terrorism." My own view is that King is right.

Are we near a tipping point in U.S. policy toward climate change? There are reasons to be doubtful. Since 9/11, advocates of preventive action on climate change have had to struggle even harder than usual to get attention from the public and politicians. Inattention to other issues has been part of the collateral damage from the war on terror and the war in Iraq. Evidence is rapidly mounting of the devastating consequences of the unchecked releases of climate-altering gases, but in 2004 America again elected national leaders in the presidency, and many in the Congress who have shown little evidence that they know there is a threat at all.

Wishing we were close to a major shift in climate policy in the United States does not make it so. I may be guilty of wishful thinking, but I do believe our national condition of denial is so fundamentally challenged by real-world events that the rationale for the established policy is, or soon will be, successfully challenged. When BP's CEO John Browne, former Secretary of State James Baker, former Central Intelligence Agency director James Woolsey, and many others from business and elsewhere outside the environmental community, including numerous state governors and attorneys general, advocate action to protect climate, we are seeing the emergence of a shared perception among stakeholders that business-as-usual is no longer feasible.

If this analysis is correct, a key question that emerges is what type of precipitating event will be the spark that sets off major change. Have the underpinnings of the status quo eroded so badly that small disturbances can have large consequences, shifting the system into a quite different behavioral path? Such a small disturbance might be the proposed establishment of a regional cap-and-trade program for reducing greenhouse gas emissions, involving the northeastern states, or a Stop the Warming March on Washington. Let's hope that we are at this stage. The alternative that would almost certainly set off a major transformation in policy would be a major transformation in the environment caused by global warming. The melting of the earth's ice at high latitudes and high altitudes may already be signaling an emerging calamity.

Robert Repetto and his colleagues have produced a volume that should have an important effect on how we view the development of environmental policy and on how we nurture that process. I am delighted that the Yale School of Forestry and Environmental Studies had a hand in facilitating this effort.

Acknowledgments

The editor gratefully acknowledges financial support for this book and the underlying research from the K. Vann Rasmussen Foundation and the William and Flora Hewlett Foundation. He also gratefully acknowledges editorial and research assistance by Nan B. Burroughs.

Chapter 1 Introduction

Robert Repetto

Nineteen-seventy saw the American environmental movement blossom. The first Earth Day brought millions of Americans outdoors to demonstrate support for environmental protection and resource conservation, a massive outpouring that surprised not only the Nixon administration and the Congress but also the corporate world and the old-line conservation organizations (Shabecoff 2003). The Environmental Protection Agency was created that year, bringing together many agencies and programs previously scattered around the executive branch. The Council on Environmental Quality was set up as a White House staff body to inform and coordinate environmental policy. Also in 1970, the enormously important National Environmental Policy Act was adopted, mandating environmental protection as an overarching national policy goal, providing for citizen access in protecting the environment and requiring environmental impact assessments for important actions and decisions by federal agencies.

In the months that followed, other important environmental laws were passed in rapid succession. Before 1970 was over, the Clean Air Act was passed, establishing mandatory air quality standards. So was the Occupational Health and Safety Act. In 1972 Congress passed the Federal Water Pollution Control Act, establishing goals for "fishable and swimmable" waters throughout the country and providing for large investments in municipal sewage treatment facilities. Then it passed the Noise Control Act, the Coastal Zone Management Act and the Marine Mammal Protection Act. In 1973 came the Federal Insecticide, Fungicide and Rodenticide Act, requiring safety testing and labeling of all chemical pesticides sold or used. Also in 1973, Congress passed the far-reaching Endangered Species Act, requiring the identification of threatened and endangered species and the development of recovery plans. Then in 1974, the Safe Drinking Water Act was enacted. In this brief period of time, most of the legislative framework for national environmental protection policy was created and the new Environmental Protection Agency, greatly expanded, was set to work devising and promulgating regulations.

Of course, the story didn't end there. In the subsequent years the Toxic Substances Control Act and the Resource Conservation and Recovery Act were passed, dealing with toxic substances and wastes, the Clean Air and Clean Water Acts were strengthened, and the Energy Policy and Conservation Act was passed in response to the oil shocks of the mid-1970s. The legislative and regulatory process has continued, producing other environmental and resource conservation laws at intervals. Nonetheless, that four- or five-year period was exceptional. In terms of public concern over environmental protection, political mobilization, and legislative consensus, there had been nothing like it earlier in American history and there has been nothing like it since.

Over the next twenty-five years, until about 2000, changes in environmental policy can best be described as incremental. Compared to those seminal years, change has certainly been modest. Environmentalists and business interests have skirmished in and out of court over regulatory issues. Contests have arisen in Congress over appropriations and legislative mandates. During the first Reagan administration there were strong ideological challenges to established policies for environmental protection, led by the likes of James Watt and Anne Gorsuch, but those assaults were met by strong opposition that forced the assailants to retreat with little lasting change in the policy framework. Neither the first Bush administration nor the two Clinton administrations achieved a great deal of change in the national environmental agenda one way or the other, though there were, of course, some achievements on the record. When environmentalists pushed for stronger action, industrial interests pushed back; when industry demanded regulatory relief, environmentalists and their allies resisted. The result has been a sort of rough equilibrium, with little sustained movement in any direction.

Indicative of the stabilization that took place after the initial ambitious burst of political energy is the fact that many of the goals set forth in those early laws still remained unfulfilled twenty-five years or thirty years later. At the start of the twenty-first century large parts of the country, particularly the urbanized parts along the east and west coasts, the Gulf, and the older industrial areas, still had air quality that failed to meet air-quality standards established in 1970. A large fraction of the nation's inland waters, a third of the rivers, and half of the lakes and estuaries remained impaired and unsuitable for swimming and fishing. Many parts of the nation dependent on groundwater still had unsafe drinking water supplies. Most of the pesticides in use when FIFRA was passed still had not been tested for health and safety and re-registered. Thousands of sites contaminated with toxic substances remained to be cleaned up. Most of the species identified as threatened or endangered were not on a recovery path and many more that were truly threatened had yet to be listed under the Endangered Species Act.

The contests that have led to this standoff or stalemate or equilibrium have been fought across many fronts. In the court of public opinion, environmental causes seem to have won people's support but not strongly enough to change their buying behaviors or their votes. Ideologically, the environment has been pitted against the economy and free enterprise. Scientifically, experts in the business and environmentalist camps have impugned each other's methodologies and findings. In the advocacy world, conservative and "green" groups have pushed forward their conflicting analyses and recommendations. In dealing with the government, the interest frustrated by a regulatory decision routinely takes the issue to the courts, and the interest frustrated by a court ruling routinely goes to Congress for relief. Battles lost on the legislative front are renewed in the drafting of implementing regulations and, if lost there, are taken up again in the course of enforcement and compliance. Every tactic devised by one side has been countered by the other.

The same pattern of prolonged stalemate interrupted once in a great while by abrupt bursts of policy innovation has been seen in the history of particular environmental and resource issues. This illustrates an invariance with respect to scale in this policy behavior: the same pattern can be found at the scale of individual issues as is displayed by the aggregate movement of environmental policy, although the timing differs. Three chapters later in this volume examine such experiences in widely different policy issues: the harvesting of old-growth timber in the national forests, the allocation of scarce California water among competing uses, and the introduction of market mechanisms in managing ocean fisheries. All three are marked by extended periods of policy equilibrium punctuated by episodes of sudden, discontinuous change.

Other examples can easily be found. In 1974 scientists identified an imminent threat to the earth's life-preserving stratospheric ozone layer. For the next thirteen years, industry and many governments resisted restrictions on the production or use of CFCs and other ozone-depleting chemicals while conferences, studies, and negotiations went on. Finally, in 1987, after the shocking discovery of an "ozone hole" over the Antarctic with an area greater than Brazil's, nations agreed to the pathbreaking Montreal Protocol phasing out those chemicals. In the ensuing decade, however, although phasedown did occur, the parties to the treaty continued to struggle with issues of noncompliance and enforcement and some industries renewed their resistance to the elimination of remaining ozone-depleting substances, such as methyl bromide and hydroflourocarbons (Benedick 1998). After the 1997 breakthrough, a pattern of stability and incrementalism was quickly reestablished.

Indeed, the statistical analysis in Frank Baumgartner's chapter, following this introduction, demonstrates that across the entire range of federal environmental policy decisions, as in other policy domains, patterns of budgetary change follow a similar pattern of incrementalism broken very infrequently by abrupt changes. The norm is stability from year to year. The infrequent exception is major change.

What explains this phenomenon? The policy science textbooks describe an almost linear progression in policymaking from "problem identification" to "formulation of options" to "policy analysis" to "decision" to "implementation" but, clearly, that is not the way the process works. Environmental policy has not progressed in steady incremental fashion but by fits and starts. On many issues the policy apparatus seems to be locked or frozen for considerable periods until, rather suddenly, it jumps ahead—or occasionally into reverse. Why does policymaking jam up even while the environmental problem persists or worsens? What builds up pressure for change? What triggers a release of political energy and resolve?

These questions are important because many important environmental and resource issues have been stalemated for considerable periods and remain so today. As a result, many domestic environmental goals remain unfulfilled, and a suite of global environmental challenges, first identified at least two decades ago, continue to worsen (Speth 2004). Whether one looks back twenty-two years to the U.S. Council of Environmental Quality's report, *Global 2000,* or thirty-two years to the Stockholm Conference on Environment and Development, one finds clear statements of urgent environmental challenges here in the United States and, globally, challenges that remain unmet.

- Tropical forests are still being cleared at an acre per second. Half these forests are now gone and developing countries are projected to lose another 15 percent of what's left by 2020.
- A fourth of bird species have gone extinct and another 12 percent are threatened. Also threatened are 24 percent of mammals, 25 percent of reptiles and amphibians, and 30 percent of fish species.
- Seventy percent of marine fisheries are now overfished, up from 5 percent in 1960, but most marine fisheries are still managed using approaches that have demonstrably failed.
- Perhaps most critical, greenhouse gas emissions and atmospheric concentrations continue to rise unabated. The basic physics underlying global warming has been understood for more than a century, and respectable scientific reports warning that the continued buildup of carbon dioxide and other greenhouse gases would inevitably alter the global climate have been appearing at short intervals for the past twenty-five years. Evidence of actual climate change has been accumulating: rising temperatures and sea levels; melting glaciers, permafrost, and sea ice; longer growing seasons, and other manifestations. Yet, the United States government position on steps to combat global warming is confined to research and voluntary actions by the private sector, essentially the same stance it took fifteen years ago. It has withdrawn from international negotiations on mitigation measures in the Kyoto Protocol.
- Although vehicular emissions account for a third of U.S. greenhouse gas emissions and a major share of urban air pollution, the United States government has maintained vehicle fuel efficiency standards virtually unchanged for twenty years despite the increasing percentage of trucks and sport utility vehicles in the fleet. This has led to declining overall vehicular fuel efficiency in the face of our increasing dependence on oil imports and the advances of automotive technology.
- An agricultural support policy that has persisted essentially unchanged since the 1930s results in overuse of chemical fertilizers and pesticides, overuse and deterioration of freshwater resources, and widespread soil deterioration.

Among the environmental consequences is an anoxic dead zone in the Gulf of Mexico at the mouth of the Mississippi River that is now the size of New Jersey.

What might break the domestic political deadlock? These first decades of this millennium are critical. Humans now impact hugely on natural cycles of carbon, nitrogen, sulfur, and water. There is little or no slack left in these natural systems. In order to avoid further decades of deadlock and delay in dealing with these long-standing and growing environmental challenges, new insights into the processes and levers of environmental policy change are needed. Invocations of "political will" are not enough. The underpinnings of these new approaches must be built on a deeper and more realistic understanding of policy change.

Grizzled veterans of the U.S. environmental movement puzzle over the reasons why progress seemed so easy back in the early 1970s but has been so grudging in later decades. They search for the sources of the spate of environmental legislation and regulation back then, hoping that that energy and consensus can somehow be recaptured. Surely, there were key antecedents to the events of the early 1970s, but none that seem decisive. Old-line organizations such as the Sierra Club, the National Audubon Society, and the National Wildlife Federation had been pushing a conservation ethic for many decades. The expanding and increasingly affluent middle classes were becoming less and less tolerant of the obvious pollution of their air and water. During the 1960s several path-breaking books warning of environmental threats were published, most notably Rachel Carson's *Silent Spring* and Barry Commoner's *The Closing Circle*. There were also dramatic milestone events that focused public attention on environmental issues, such as the ignition of the Cuyahoga River in Cleveland and the oil spill off the coast of Santa Barbara. Influential new environmental advocacy groups came into being in the period 1968–70 to pursue vigorous legislative, litigious, and populist tactics: the Natural Resources Defense Council, the Environmental Defense Fund, the League of Conservation Voters, and Greenpeace, among others. Do these developments provide a sufficient explanation?

America's travails and turmoil during the 1960s must also have a unique explanatory role. It was a time of social mobilization and unrest unlike any other since the 1930s, especially among students and other young people. Tens of thousands took part in direct civil protest and disobedience in support of civil rights for African Americans, and many more tens of thousands were inspired by those campaigns. Radical feminists railed against the dominance of the male establishment. Protests against the Vietnamese War became increasingly widespread, bitter, and violent as the decade went on, perhaps reaching a crisis of confrontation at the Democratic National Convention in Chicago in 1968, where the police rioted in full public view on national television. Youth organizations became increasingly radicalized as their demands remained unfulfilled and the Vietnam War escalated. Students for a Democratic Society gave way to the Student Non-violent Coordinating Committee, which was eclipsed by the Weathermen, the Black Panthers, and finally by the Symbionese Liberation Army. Riots in the inner cities were commonplace. By 1970 anti-establishment and revolutionary rhetoric pervaded the nation's campuses. Following the slaying of students by National Guardsmen at Kent State University in 1970, strikes took place at 30 percent of the country's colleges and universities, demonstrations at more than half of them, probably involving a million students. Thirty campus ROTC buildings were bombed or burned (Gitlin 1987).

The establishment was thoroughly discredited in the eyes of the most activist and vocal segments of the population. Both political parties were in disrepute for their pursuit of the war. Liberals in government were impugned not from the Right, as in the 1980s and 1990s, but from the Left. The corporate world, perhaps symbolized by Dow Chemical, a manufacturer of napalm, was under attack for its involvement in the military effort. Corporate prestige had already been undermined by public opposition to nuclear power and by the investigations unleashed by Ralph Nader's *Unsafe at Any Speed*. University administrators were denounced by their student bodies as collaborators in the Vietnam War and as sexist, racist pigs to boot. Those demanding peace, civil rights, equal rights, and protection of the earth were able to present themselves as the true defenders of American and universal values (Libby 1998).

Many of the activists from the civil rights, the feminist, and the antiwar movements signed on to the ecology movement, joining forces with the older conservation-oriented organizations and providing the new environmental organizations with aggressive, veteran tacticians. In this climate it is not difficult to see how Congress and the executive branch found it easier to give ground to popular demands on environmental issues than on the other pressing issues of the day. Passing environmental laws with ambitious goals to be achieved at future date uncertain, with implementing regulations yet to be written, with compliance deadlines well in the future and enforcement mechanisms still to be determined, was much easier for a national government under siege by many of its own citizens than ending the war in Vietnam, ending discrimination against women, or overcoming the racial prejudices of the South and of South Boston (Cahn 1995). Negotiating over these new environmental laws and regulations with clean-cut Ivy League–trained young lawyers was more manageable for the Establishment than dealing with the radical groups in the streets and at the police barricades.

The experience of the 1970s illustrates the path-dependence of the political process. For better or worse, the 1960s will not come again. Social movements are not produced wholesale or on demand, though they do share strong family resemblances (Tarrow 1998). Despite efforts to construct road maps for those who would promote social change (Moyer 2001), success is never assured. Some efforts collapse or peter out; others end in reform or repression and sometimes both. The emergence and fate of social movements are strongly influenced by the political opportunities available to them (McAdam, McCarthy, and Zald 1996). Social mobilization implies the positive-feedback political dynamics analyzed by William Brock in this volume, which may or may not result in the successful challenge to an older political rationalization by a new framing of the issue and which may or may not accumulate enough public participation and media attention for success. Fortunately, however, the case studies in this volume show that broad social movements are not necessary for policy punctuations to occur. Narrower coalitions of governmental and nongovernmental organizations can effect change.

In describing the phenomenon of stability and occasional discontinuous change, political scientists have borrowed a term from evolutionary biology: *punctuated equilibrium.* The idea in biology is that evolution apparently has not progressed steadily through a constant stream of mutation winnowed by natural selection but similarly through prolonged periods of stability interrupted by occasional but dramatic bursts of change. In adopting this phrase, the political scientists who initially analyzed the political phenomenon, including Frank Baumgartner, whose contribution initiates this volume, sought to emphasize the need to encompass both phases within the same analytical framework (Baumgartner and Jones 1993). Others had analyzed social movements and other processes that led to rapid political change; still others had focused on the political subsystems, "iron triangles," and political monopolies that promoted stability. Baumgartner and his colleagues sought a framework capable of explaining both. Such a framework might help explain why there is deadlock or modest incremental change in some arenas but sudden policy shifts in others. What forces provoke such shifts? Are they fortuitous or created by deliberate manipulation? When are policy arenas particularly unstable or susceptible to radical change? What are the bulwarks that lock in the status quo and how are they dismantled, if change occurs?

The punctuated equilibrium approach that has resulted recognizes the policy process as a complex dynamic system. Though developed in the physical and biological sciences, analyzing phenomena as complex dynamic systems has proven very productive in the social sciences as well. Within the past decade or so, there have been hundreds of applications in economics and finance, which have shed light on market-price fluctuations, oligolopolistic behavior, business cycles, and other economic phenomena (Rosser 2000). Studies of business behavior and organizational change have also made considerable use of this analytical approach (Bryson et al. 1996; Euell and Kiel 1999; Gersick 1991). There are also many examples of punctuated equilibria in the policy realm. A country may hold to a system of fixed exchange rates for many years and rather suddenly abandon it or undergo a massive devaluation. A country may hold to one economic system, such as socialism or communism, for many years and yet undergo an abrupt transition to a quite different system. Decisions to regulate or to deregulate particular activities have typically come about rather suddenly, after many years of resistance.

Another key feature of such systems is that under certain conditions small disturbances can have large consequences, shifting the system into a quite different behavioral path. For this to happen, a system must be near a critical point, just as a raindrop falling at the Continental Divide might flow to the Atlantic or the Pacific, depending on which way the breeze is blowing. The intriguing possibility is that a complex dynamic policy system might be highly sensitive to a small action taken at just the right time, despite long resistance to change.

In order to exhibit such features, the determinants of policy change must be characterized by both positive and negative feedbacks. Negative feedbacks would ensure that when a given policy is disturbed or threatened with change, forces emerge that drive it back to its original position. Clearly, if such forces dominated, then policy change would rarely, if ever, occur. Positive feedbacks would ensure that when a policy position is disturbed, forces emerge that reinforce that change, driving it even further from its initial position. Multiple equilibria are possible and policy can shift, sometimes abruptly, among or between them (Agliardi 1998). When both positive and negative feedbacks are at play in the policy arena, it is possible to observe the "punctuated equilibria" that seem to typify many policy areas.

Political scientists have identified many sources of negative feedback in the American political system. Some are structural and institutional; others are more behavioral. Together, they tend to impart a status quo bias to the political process. Among the more notable are:

- The separation and diffusion of power among political institutions in the federal system and among (and within) institutions in the legislative, executive, and judicial branches, which provide opponents of an action many avenues to block it and make it more difficult for proponents to maintain an effective coalition (Herzberg 1986).
- The heavy weight of precedent in judicial decision-making.
- The multiple constraints on bureaucratic actions due to relatively open administrative processes and onerous administrative procedures, which provide opponents many channels with which to intervene and make any action more difficult than inaction.
- The tendency of a multitude of organized interest groups to mobilize to defend their interests when threatened, often in opposition to other interest groups (Lohmann 1996; Grossman and Helpman 2001).
- The formation of policy subsystems and iron triangles: coalitions formed around an issue by interest groups, public management agencies, and political representatives, which can reward each other with favorable decisions, larger budgets, and reelection support to create a self-reinforcing cycle of support for a particular policy and to exclude opposing interests (Browne 1995).

Some political scientists have likened the results of this interplay of opposing interests and "countervailing power," operating through many political channels, to a political equilibrium, and, indeed, there is a great deal of stability in most policy areas. However, bad policies can persist as well as good policies and there is no implication that this interplay of forces operates, in any sense, to maximize the public welfare (Lowi 1969).

Since policies do change, often rather discontinuously, these negative feedbacks must be counterbalanced in the political realm with positive feedbacks, and several such processes have also been identified. Some have first been analyzed by economists in the context of market behavior but have close political analogues (Pierson 2000).

These include, among others,

- *Bandwagon effects:* Most politicians dislike being on the losing side of what appear to be popular issues and are more likely to support a policy, the more evidence there is of political support, creating a positive feedback.
- *Social contagion or social learning:* Many people, including politicians, form their opinions on an issue by consulting polls, other indications of popular opinion, or expert opinion; so, the more people hold a particular view, the

more convincing or compelling it will become to others, ultimate becoming "common knowledge" (Gavious and Mizrahi 2000).

• *Media mimicry:* Media outlets are more likely to "cover" a story that their competitors are covering. As a result, issues may either be largely ignored or afforded a great deal of media attention, at least temporarily.

• Political entrepreneurship: Politicians seeking to make a mark often seize on an issue that has gained media and popular attention, bringing to it new legitimacy, constituencies, and political initiatives. Combined with the preceding, political entrepreneurship reinforces a positive feedback (Mintrum and Vergari 1996).

A policy process characterized by positive and negative feedbacks such as these is capable of long periods of stability and abrupt, nonincremental changes. William Brock's chapter analyzes how such positive feedback mechanisms can lead both to policy lock-in and to discontinuous change at critical "tipping points." He shows how, at these critical points, policy is also potentially susceptible to relatively small influences. In addition, all policy processes are subject to outside events or "exogenous" disturbances that might create such a critical opportunity or tip the policy process in one direction or another (Frankel and Young 2000). Among such disturbances that have occurred in the past are:

• *New scientific information,* such as the discovery of the Antarctic ozone hole, which helped provoke an international agreement on control of ozone-depleting substances;

• *A shift in the underlying economic fundamentals,* such as the substantial rise in energy prices that prompted a shift in policy toward energy conservation and renewable energy sources;

• *A technological change,* such as the introduction of catalytic converters, which prompted a shift in policy toward vehicle emissions;

• *New information available to the public,* such as the Toxic Release Inventory or the publication of Rachel Carson's *Silent Spring;*

• *A change in the "macro-political" environment,* such as the election of a president with strong pro- or anti- views in a policy area;

• *An act of God,* such as the Three Mile Island accident, which changed public perception of nuclear power plant safety.

Such perturbations are not per se the causes of change. Oftentimes, as with the climate issue, new information arises but policy remains unaffected (European Environment Agency 2001). Advocacy groups often try to bring new information to bear on policy issues, but with mixed results. Technological changes can be diverted to serve other non-environmental objectives, as has happened with automobile manufacturing in recent decades. A new president may find it impossible to challenge some entrenched interests successfully, as Presidents Carter, Reagan, and Clinton discovered. Nonetheless, disturbances brought about by such exogenous factors may represent moments of opportunity when other interventions might have an enhanced probability of bringing about significant change because the policy system has been driven to a critical point.

THE CONTENT OF THIS BOOK

There have been attempts to build formal conceptual models portraying the environmental policy process as a complex dynamic system capable of nonlinear behaviors, although with limited empirical content (Brown 1994; Kline 2001). There have also been attempts to use this conceptual framework to describe and illuminate the history of some past environmental policy changes (Cowan and Gunby 1996). These efforts have succeeded in showing that insights can be gained by thinking about environmental policy processes in terms of complex dynamic systems.

The challenge that the research underlying this book accepted was to use this framework in a forward-looking approach to analyze policy areas that seem deadlocked and stalemated. Applying complex dynamic systems analysis to the policy process in a forward-looking way necessitates understanding the forces and mechanisms that hold a policy in place, understanding the forces that work to destabilize it, understanding what effects there might be from changes in these supporting and opposing structures, and understanding the forces that from time to time might act as strong disturbances to an apparent equilibrium, making policies unusually susceptible to change. If successful, such an analysis would provide insights into the most effective forms and points of intervention as well as the most promising times and opportunities for intervention. Even if the results of such analyses do not produce reliable predictive models, which are rare in the social sciences, a contribution to systematic analysis of the elements impeding and promoting change and the way they interact can still be enormously useful for policy analysts, advocates, and policymakers.

The book contains three parts. In the first part, a political scientist and an economist contribute the foundation chapters that provide conceptual underpinnings for the empirical analyses that follow and focus attention on key variables and processes. These two mostly conceptual chapters find many applications in the empirical case studies that follow.

Frank Baumgartner, the political scientist, is one of the originators of punctuated equilibrium theory as applied to the policy process. His chapter lays out the basics of the analytical framework. It identifies critical elements that often form part of abrupt policy change, including an institutional shift that opens the previously constrained decision-making domain to other interests and participants and a "reframing" of the issue that undermines the previous policy justification. Baumgartner's chapter also provides empirical support for the punctuated equilibrium theory. His analysis of data on year-to-year changes in federal budgetary appropriations for various environmental programs shows a frequency distribution that differs from a normal pattern: small year-to-year changes are more frequent but so are the rare large departures from previous spending patterns. Such "fat-tailed" distributions are consistent with an underlying punctuated equilibrium process. Baumgartner's chapter also explains the usefulness of the empirical case studies that follow in comparing episodes of rapid change and periods of stalemate and stability. This comparative approach adopted in the case study chapters helps in identifying key differences in the conditions that make for stability and those that allow punctuated change.

William Brock, the economist, contributed a chapter that emphasizes the dynamics created by the interdependence of choices and social or economic pressures to conform. These dynamics tend to arise whenever the positive feedback mechanisms mentioned above are present: bandwagon effects, social learning, or contagion, media mimicry, and the like. Brock shows how such dynamics can easily lead to policy "lock-in," even when the extant policy is recognized to be inferior by most decision makers. His chapter also shows how policy discontinuities and abrupt transitions can arise, especially when one participant's actions or decisions are conditioned by her expectations about what others will do.

Brock's chapter focuses attention on key variables, such as the costs to an individual of deviating from the norm, the amount of "noise" or experimentation in the policy domain that permits new approaches to intrude, and the way participants' expectations are formed. He explains how even simple "models" can explain not only the punctuated equilibrium pattern of policy outcomes but other commonly observed political phenomena as well: the tendency of compact special-interest groups to prevail against the broader public interest, the tendency of political advocates to use propaganda and disinformation campaigns to confuse voters on issues, and the ability of slowly changing conditions, such as the gradual accumulation of experience with a policy, to produce abrupt changes in support. The analytical framework developed in the Brock and Baumgartner chapters provides strong support for the empirical case studies that form the rest of the volume.

The second part of the book consists of three chapters that analyze important environmental or resource policy issues that have experienced the long periods of stability and the episodes of abrupt change that constitute punctuated equilibrium. These chapters were written by specialists who have followed those policy issues closely for many years but who are also familiar with the punctuated equilibrium approach to policy analysis. Each of these chapters explains the dynamics behind both the equilibrium phase and the discontinuous policy change, identifying key political and institutional mechanisms.

The first of this series, written by Helen Ingram and Leah Fraser, shows how a punctuated equilibrium framework helps in understanding the policy innovations introduced into long-standing California water management problems. For decades, urban and agricultural interests operated in a classic "iron triangle" to build and maintain a highly engineered infrastructure system to divert scarce water to themselves, co-opting or overwhelming environmental opponents. The authors describe the professional ideology, the path-dependency, and the political bartering used to sustain this system. They then analyze the events leading up to two remarkable innovations. The first was an institutional change that broke the previous policy oligopoly and admitted a broader range of stakeholder interests into policy and management. Accompanying this institutional change was a new commitment to an adaptive, learning-by-doing management approach. The second, even more innovative, was the introduction of a market mechanism, the Environmental Water Account, to ensure sufficient water for endangered fish species. This mechanism provided the Fish and Wildlife Service funding with which to purchase water rights for species protection, rather than continuing to challenge urban and agricultural allocations solely through legal or regulatory actions.

Examining the antecedents to these innovations, the authors identify two key developments that pushed the policymaking process to dramatic change. The first was a change in the policymaking venue to a multi-stakeholder group incorporating state and federal agencies, private interests, and public interest organizations. The second was the emergence of a shared perception among these stakeholders that business-as-usual was no longer feasible because of an imminent endangered species crisis (the "smelt-down"). This shift in shared expectations drove stakeholders along a decision path that generated its own momentum and led ultimately to a policy discontinuity, illustrating the positive feedback and interdependence mechanisms analyzed in the Brock chapter.

The second chapter in this sequence, by Robert Repetto and Richard Allen, investigates punctuated equilibrium in the approach to managing the nation's marine fisheries. For decades, even while resource conditions in most fisheries deteriorated and fishermen's incomes suffered, fisheries managers adhered to a management approach based mainly on input controls, ignoring more successful experience in other countries that limited the catch to sustainable levels through transferable harvest quotas—known as Individual Transferable Quotas (ITQs). After management councils in a few fisheries adopted the latter approach, a coalition of opposed interests secured a congressional legislative moratorium on any further development of such systems. This moratorium was renewed and sustained for six years, forestalling any further policy experimentation or innovation. Then, in 2002, without much significant change from the conditions prevailing in most fisheries when the moratorium was adopted, the moratorium was allowed to lapse. Two years later, ITQ approaches were embraced as government policy.

These fits and starts in fisheries policy demonstrate the importance of the "social trap" mechanisms at the heart of Brock's analysis. Fishermen, who play the decisive role in Management Council decisions, are typically conservative and risk-averse with respect to fundamental changes in the way their fisheries operate. They also constitute fraternities with the ability to exert social pressure on each other. Without concrete evidence that a new management approach would improve their own individual outcomes, fishermen are hesitant to change. However, unless some fisheries are willing to experiment with management innovation, such evidence cannot arise, "locking in" the traditional approach. The function of the national moratorium secured by ITQ opponents was to reinforce this impasse, preventing any further policy innovation. Erosion of support for the moratorium stemmed in large part from "policy learning" over a period of years from the remarkably successful experience with the ITQ system adopted before the moratorium in the Alaskan halibut fishery, which transformed a disastrous fishing situation into a highly successful one and demonstrated that many of the hypothetical drawbacks to transferable harvest quotas were avoidable. This policy learning altered the perceptions of significant numbers of fishermen, fisheries managers, and other key policymakers, undermining the policy dominance of the opposing coalition.

The third chapter in this section of the book, by Benjamin Cashore and

William Howlett, tests the punctuated equilibrium framework by examining changes in timber management and harvesting in old-growth forests of the Pacific Northwest. Their description of the abrupt drop in the timber harvest from national forests in the region in the early 1990s shows several strong parallels with that of water policy innovations further south in California. For decades, the Forest Service had been able to maintain a policy subsystem based on the ideology of scientific management, the professionalization of forest management, and a strong rent-seeking bond with the timber industry and congressional allies. It was able to use the discretion implicit in its multiple-use management mandate to give primacy to "getting out the cut" at the expense of ecological and economic considerations, just as the California water subsystem had been able to continue for decades its engineering approach to water diversion and supply. Also, as in California, the policy "punctuation" was precipitated by a change in venue and the "reframing" of the issue from one of commodity supply to endangered species protection. Environmental groups, bringing suit to force the Forest Service to protect the endangered northern spotted owl, were able to draw the federal courts into an active oversight role in harvesting decisions. The result was a dramatic reduction in the harvest from the national forests and a shift toward "ecosystem management" by the Forest Service.

Cashore and Howlett introduce a new element into the analysis, however, by comparing the response to the endangered species challenge on private lands in the Pacific Northwest, regulated by state governments, with the response in the national forests. On private lands, the response was at most incremental and led to no great reduction in timber supply. This comparison underscores the importance of differential policy opportunities created by different institutional settings. On federal lands, environmental laws created greater opportunities for interventions by public interest groups, and the Endangered Species Act and other laws governing Forest Service action imposed more stringent requirements on the federal agencies. On private lands, by contrast, there were fewer opportunities for intervention by environmental groups, stronger protections for private property rights, fewer requirements on private landowners for endangered species protection, and a regulatory apparatus more sympathetic to the timber industry. This comparison emphasizes the potential importance of institutional features in conditioning policy dynamics either to facilitate dramatic policy changes or to sustain a policy equilibrium.

The final section of the book contains three chapters analyzing issues that remain in policy equilibrium and have not yet experienced discontinuous change or punctuation. They assess the climate issue and two other deadlocked national environmental policy problems: the debate over vehicular fuel economy standards and the subsidization of environmentally damaging extractive users of the nation's public lands. These chapters analyze the sources of deadlock, the forces maintaining the status quo, and assess possible "triggers" that might lead to rapid change.

In the first of these chapters, Lee Lane examines the possibility that the United States will adopt domestic controls reducing greenhouse gas emissions and cooperate with other nations in constructing an effective international climate protection regime. As he points out, the obstacles are formidable. The economic costs of reducing emissions by enough to stabilize atmospheric greenhouse gas concentrations would be high in the absence of sufficiently cheap and plentiful renewable energy substitutes. By contrast, the damages that the United States would suffer from a changing climate are not evident even to experts, let alone to the average person, and in any case would be suffered decades into the future. This configuration of uncertain benefits and high costs is markedly different from those that supported decisions to reduce emissions of more conventional pollutants. Moreover, Lane points out, there is concentrated opposition to mandatory emissions reductions from well-organized and extremely influential energy industries. Finally, domestic U.S. action would be ineffectual without an international regime that constrained emissions from other countries as well, including especially the large rapidly growing countries in the developing world that put a very high priority on economic growth.

Lane's chapter is frankly pessimistic about the prospects for a breakthrough in U.S. climate policy, absent some dramatic manifestation of the risks of climate change, significant technological breakthroughs, a significant political realignment, or some combination of all these. He discounts the potential efficacy in triggering policy change of a new oil crisis, a widespread shift from coal to natural gas or state-level policy initiatives like those adopted in California and elsewhere. Instead, he sees hope in a more gradual approach to emissions reduction brought about by cost-effective market mechanisms, such as energy tax increases that could be politically justified partly as environmental measures and partly as revenue measures to address the serious federal budget deficits looming into the future. Should other industrialized countries move in that direction through a re-negotiated Kyoto Protocol or other international agreement, diplomatic pressures might help induce the U.S. government into a more cooperative policy stance.

In the next chapter James Dunn, Jr., takes up the related issue of vehicular fuel economy standards. When Corporate Average Fuel Efficiency (CAFE) standards were enacted in 1975, the automobile industry was the target of a punctuation in regulatory policy. In the mid-1960s, when Nader's *Unsafe at Any Speed* was published, the U.S. automobile industry was essentially unregulated. In the years that followed a cascade of technology-forcing regulations was enacted, addressing safety (seatbelts), emissions (catalytic converters), and fuel economy (CAFE standards). This burst of activity was fed by the more general enthusiasm for environmental legislation that arose in the early 1970s but was also enabled by conditions specific to the industry at that time. The sharp rise in oil prices in the early 1970s, which was then expected to persist, combined with the rapid market penetration by Japanese-made small sedans, persuaded car companies and their unions that consumers would accept more fuel-efficient cars and could offset any price increases with savings in fuel purchases.

Since then, there have been minor upward and downward adjustments to CAFE standards, carmakers have learned to live with them, and those who would strengthen them and those who would abolish them are essentially deadlocked. Political leaders have expended little political capital on the issue, preferring largely symbolic long-term research partnerships with industry. Meanwhile, the American car market has changed drastically. Faced with huge pension and health care liabilities and losing market share to imports, Detroit has become increasingly dependent financially on sales of high-margin SUVs and light trucks, which face much lower CAFE standards, if any. Technological advances have been ploughed into increased vehicle power and weight, maintaining fuel economy largely unchanged. Significant increases in CAFE standards that would imperil sales of these mega-vehicles or further increase the competitive advantage of the Japanese companies in the market for smaller cars would put Detroit in financial peril. The well-organized industry, the unions, and their congressional supporters in both parties would oppose such measures strenuously. Dunn sees hope for significant policy change only if driven by or at least consistent with altered market forces: significantly higher fuel prices produced by world supply constraints or the enactment of broader climate-related policies, or rapid penetration of hybrids into the U.S. market. Even then, in his view, a policy initiative with chances of success would have to combine higher fuel efficiency standards with financial incentives for the industry to produce and sell such vehicles. A specific example would be a gasoline tax with revenues dedicated to tax credits for purchases of acceptably fuel-efficient vehicles in all segments.

The final chapter in this section, by Charles Davis, assesses the prospects for significant change in policies governing livestock grazing on public lands in the West. He finds that the prospects are dim. Policies were developed as early as 1934 in the Taylor Grazing Act to ensure that ranchers' interests were well protected in the administration of the public lands by the Bureau of Land Management. Since then, the livestock industry, western governors, and legislators and the Bureau have been able to maintain an effective policy subsystem, repeatedly and successfully resisting efforts to eliminate grazing subsidies or the priority afforded to grazing and other extractive uses in management priorities. Attempts by environmentalists and others to construct a new policy image ("welfare ranching"), to push through legislative or administrative reforms, or to shift the policymaking venue to the courts have met with only limited success.

Despite the vast area administered by the Bureau of Land Management, Davis points out that nationally this is a low-stakes issue. The aggregate subsidy provided to livestock operators on public lands is a tiny fraction of the federal budget. Most of the semi-arid land in question is remote and of little value for grazing or anything else. Known as the "lands nobody wanted," they can readily be seen to be in generally poor condition. What is more difficult to imagine is that they could ever have been in good condition. Under these circumstances it has proven difficult to generate much national public, media, or legislative concern with which to overcome the entrenched defenses of regional interests. Davis sees the likeliest prospect for a policy punctuation to stem from the effects of a slow-acting variable: the changing demographics of the western states. Urban, white-collar households with recreational and environmental interests in the land are increasingly outnumbering households with traditional ties to commodity production on the land. The composition of elective bodies is shifting correspondingly. At some point the weight of regional interests may shift, fracturing that coalition and producing a national political configuration less deferential to ranching, mining, and logging interests.

LESSONS LEARNED

The data presented in Frank Baumgartner's chapter and elsewhere in this book show that the dynamics of environmental policy behave as the punctuated equilibrium model predicts. Stability and incremental adjustment are the norm. Abrupt policy innovations and reversals do occur, but rarely. This pattern appears across many environmental and resource policy issues.

The analysis in William Brock's chapter demonstrates that the reason for the manifestation of punctuated equilibrium is not just that things happen to disturb the status quo, although, of course, such things do happen. There is a more fundamental reason. Commonplace and widely recognized political processes create a dynamic capable of multiple equilibria, lock-in, discontinuous change, and other characteristics of punctuated equilibrium behavior. These internal dynamics may combine with exogenous events to trigger policy change if the system is close to a tipping point, but otherwise external disturbances may have little impact.

Punctuated equilibrium stems basically from the interaction of the positive and negative feedback mechanisms indicated above. These mechanisms are pervasive in the American political system. Though they are fully capable of explaining the observed patterns of stability and abrupt change, their workings are difficult to predict in particular policy struggles because of their complex interactions.

The infrequency of policy breakthroughs suggests that most efforts to bring them about will "fail." Entrenched interests and ideology will retain their dominance; challengers will be unable to gather sufficient resources, attention, and momentum. Nonetheless, such "failed" efforts may build a foundation for later success when conditions are more favorable by undermining the prevailing policy image, by mobilizing new interests, and by forming new coalitions. Even knowing that the odds are long, effective policymakers continue to work on their issues in order to be ready and primed when opportunities arise.

Timing is crucial. Many otherwise good campaigns have failed because they were launched when the campaign was ready to take on the issue, not when the issue was ready for the campaign. If public, media, and political attention are directed elsewhere, for example, it is difficult or impossible for a campaign to build the momentum necessary for success.

Across the broad range of resource and environmental policy issues, only a few, if any, are likely to have potential for significant change at any particular time. The ability to discern which ones these are is a vital strategic skill. Strategists must know how potential allies and opponents will react to a campaign before launching it; whether the opposing coalition is fractured or can be split; whether other developments have undermined or reinforced the rationale for the existing policy; and whether at the moment there is space on the political agenda for the issue.

For this reason, single-issue policy advocates are at a disadvantage, although they are likely to be intimately familiar with the politics of their own issue.

They push their own agenda in and out of season but most of the time their chances of success are small. To the extent that policy advocates or other change agents can coalesce to devote their combined resources to the issue or issues with the best chances for success at the moment, their prospects for bringing about change are greater. In this regard, larger, multi-issue organizations have the advantage of being able to shift resources internally in response to strategic opportunities. Their targets may change as the constellation of interest shifts, as the policy context changes, and as new information and policy entrepreneurs emerge. This has implications for foundations and other sources of funding for organizations involved in policy debates. Many already strongly encourage the formation of coalitions among advocacy organizations. Some provide flexible funding that can be shifted among campaigns opportunistically.

Flexibility is important because the interdependence of political choices and actions underlying positive feedback mechanisms can cause an issue to ripen suddenly. When political actors' decisions are conditioned by their expectations of what other actors will do, they may all move rapidly, as if coordinated, in response to some commonly observed signaling event that indicates which way the issue is likely to move. Even slow-acting demographic or economic trends can trigger sudden changes if they alter the position of a swing vote, a powerful committee chairman, or an important member of a coalition.

One such slow-acting variable is "policy learning," the gradual accumulation of experience with the performance of a policy compared to its alternative. In the "social trap" model analyzed by William Brock, learning about the alternative is inhibited by decision makers' reluctance to deviate from the majority position to endorse or to adopt a policy favored by only a minority in the absence of persuasive evidence that change would be beneficial. In such circumstances, Brock shows that policy lock-in can be combated by mechanisms that introduce some experimentation or randomization into the policy process. Disaggregation of decision-making responsibility is one such mechanism. As the chapters on water policy and fuel efficiency standards show, our federal system of government has allowed individual states to adopt policy innovations in advance of national decisions. As the fisheries case study also shows, the devolution of management authority to regional management councils allowed for important policy learning from the experience of a few innovative management regimes in particular fisheries and contributed to an abrupt policy reversal at the national level.

This supports Baumgartner's generalization that rapid change often occurs when the rationale for the established policy is successfully challenged and when new interests or decision-making authorities intrude on the entrenched policy monopoly or subsystem. The case studies provide repeated examples of these processes.

The six case studies in this volume prove the value of a comparative approach to the study of punctuated equilibrium dynamics. There are revealing contrasts between the issues that have experienced rapid policy changes and those that have remained in equilibrium. For example, in the fisheries case, there was significant policy learning from the experience with an ITQ program in the Alaskan halibut fishery to show that the program conferred benefits on participants and did not lead to the failings that opponents predicted. This helped bring about a change in national policy. By contrast, there have been no such opportunities for policy learning in the case of U.S. climate policy. As Lane's chapter points out, the high cost of reducing greenhouse gas emissions predicted by opponents of such action has been a stumbling block. This assertion has been controversial. Predicted economic impacts have ranged from disastrous through trivial to favorable (Repetto and Austin 1997). To date, there has been no official policy in place at the national or state level to show which prediction is closer to the mark. Intra-company voluntary emission reduction programs or limited trading on pilot carbon emissions markets do not provide valid benchmarks. In the absence of evidence to the contrary, opposing interests can continue to claim ominously that even moderate emission reductions would impose unacceptable costs on the American economy.

The water, forest policy, grazing, and climate policy cases also provide an instructive contrast. In the former two, there were action-forcing events, partly engineered by activists, that created high-stakes "crises," situations that would impose heavy costs on important interests if not resolved: water supplies to agricultural and municipal users in California would be interrupted; logging operations in the national forests of the Pacific Northwest would be shut down. These crisis situations led to presidential intervention in the forestry situation, gubernatorial and cabinet-level intervention in the water dispute to bring about policy resolutions. By contrast, in the grazing policy debates, there have been no such events and it remains a low-stakes issue unable to attract much attention. Similarly, nothing has happened with respect to climate policy to force the issue. Damages from climate change, however large or small they may be, are likely to manifest themselves decades in the future. Today's voters (and politicians) fail to grasp the issue's urgency. Moreover, since carbon dioxide, once released, remains in the atmosphere for the better part of a century, a greater reduction in emissions in the future can arguably be substituted for a smaller one today. Consequently, in the absence of an imminent and palpable threat, policymakers can avoid hard decisions and defer action.

The chapter by Benjamin Cashore and Michael Howlett draws another useful lesson from the study of forest policy in the Pacific Northwest by contrasting dramatic change in the national forests with much more incremental adjustment in the private forests regulated by state agencies. They show that institutional differences can create quite different policy opportunities. There were fewer entry points for environmental interests to intrude on the timber policy subsystem in the private forests and a weaker legislative mandate for conservation. Therefore, not only were conservationists less able to halt old-growth timber harvesting in private forests; most were discouraged from even trying. This illustrates Brock's analytical point that the supply of advocacy effort will be conditioned by expectations of potential success.

Among the many other lessons that could be drawn from the case studies, one final contrast will be mentioned, stemming from the history of CAFE fuel economy standards. In the mid-1970s, fuel economy standards could be adopted, even though the American auto industry and its unions were stronger than they are today, because industry opposition was muted. The sharp rise in gasoline prices during the first "oil shock" and the expectation that price increases would continue, together with the rising market share of Japanese imports, convinced Detroit that greater fuel economy was consistent with what the market demanded. By contrast, since gas prices have fallen and consumers have shifted en masse to SUVs and light trucks, which are highly profitable to the Big Three, Detroit's opposition to higher CAFE standards has been unyielding.

This history and that of the fisheries case both imply that policy change is much more likely to occur when the interests of opponents are taken into consideration and policies are designed to minimize their losses or to provide them with gains. A similar lesson emerges from the discussion of climate policy options, which include possibilities for compensating industries and interests that might otherwise suffer losses. As Brock's chapter points out, changes in the payoff structure to a political contest or "game" can engender a winning coalition where none had existed before.

Taken together, the chapters in this volume help in developing a deeper understanding of the forces for stability and for change in environmental policy. They support the punctuated equilibrium framework in the study of policy dynamics. They also provide insights for those who are concerned with lack of progress in the resolution of environmental policy issues and might hope to bring about change.

Chapter 2 Punctuated Equilibrium Theory and Environmental Policy

Frank R. Baumgartner

The environmental policy arena, like other areas of public policy, shows consistent patterns of stability and change driven by the dynamics of the policy process. New problems emerge, social movements form and mobilize, elections intervene, new scientific evidence accumulates, policy images change over time, institutions compete over jurisdictional control, and crises occasionally create the opportunity for dramatic new initiatives to take hold. For most issues most of the time, however, stable institutional structures, shared understandings of policy goals and available technologies, and a balance of power among interests ensure no dramatic shifts from the status quo. In this manner, environmental policymaking is no different from many other domains of public policy. How can we use the tools and language of punctuated equilibrium to help us understand the environmental policy arena? As subsequent chapters will show, a great number of precise applications show the value of the theoretical perspective to given policies, programs, and issues. In this chapter, I focus my attention on some broad themes of punctuated equilibrium as it relates to environmental policy.

A punctuated equilibrium (PE) perspective on the study of public policy reminds us to pay attention equally to the forces in politics that create stability as well as those that occasionally conspire to allow dramatic changes in public policy directions. While the punctuations may come only rarely, they can have long-lasting consequences. There are a number of ways to study public policies over time in order to assess whether a PE theory applies, whether a given policy may be ripe for punctuation, and what difference this all makes. In this chapter, I first review some of the major elements of the theory and evidence with a focus on assessing the applicability of the approach to the case of the environment. More importantly, I address some of the various methods that can be used to study public policy through a PE perspective. This allows others to do similar studies, but beyond that it points the way for more intensive case analyses to elucidate some of the dynamics within various policy communities that help to create the processes that we can trace over time with quantitative indicators. For example, the processes by which punctuations occur often appear to be related to positive-feedback processes that are inherently unpredictable because they involve the interactions of many different variables. That is, self-reinforcing processes are at the core of many policy punctuations, but, like the tropical depression that may or may not develop into a hurricane, we cannot tell which ones may develop and which ones may dissipate. So we need to study these phenomena in two manners: Find ways to study many policy areas simultaneously, using a probabilistic and even a stochastic approach to show the incidence of change and stability (but not predicting when individual occurrences will happen), and on the other hand study given policies in greater detail so that we can document the process by which critical positive-feedback processes take hold in some cases but not in others. My focus in the next section of this chapter is on the quantitative approach; subsequently I discuss the contributions that we can expect from more detailed case analyses; and in conclusion I lay out the merits of a combined approach incorporating both intensive and extensive analyses. Later chapters in this volume provide a number of detailed examinations of particular cases, illustrating many of the themes I mention here.

PUNCTUATED EQUILIBRIUM MODELS
OF PUBLIC POLICY

Bryan Jones and I borrowed from biology in our efforts to explain simultaneously both the long periods of stability that students of public policy have

noted to be characteristic of most public policies most of the time and the occasional bursts of policy innovation that come at the beginning of a new policy
or in its occasional restructuring (useful citations include Eldredge and Gould
1972; Eldredge 1985; Baumgartner and Jones 1991, 1993, 2002; Jones and
Baumgartner 2005; True, Baumgartner, and Jones 1999; Cashore and Hewlett
[this volume] also provide an overview of much of this literature). Most important to this general approach were several things: (1) a methodology of studying policies over long periods of time, typically several decades at a minimum;
(2) a focus on how complex public policies inevitably develop heuristic "short-
hands," which we termed "policy images" but which others have called issue-
definitions, frames, or causal stories; (3) attention to institutional venues as potentially variable, which implies that in order to study them as a variable one
cannot study only the activities of a given policy institution such as a government agency; and (4) the realization that positive feedback effects leading to
dramatic policy punctuations often stem from the rapid interactions of shifting
images and changing venues of policy action. (Stability, by contrast, often
stems from the ability of status quo defenders to avoid challenges to a dominant policy image or an established institutional venue with jurisdictional control.) Image and venue, we noted, often interact; where one changes, change in
the other becomes more likely. Where one is stable, stability in the other is reinforced. Some of the variables we pointed to, such as policy image, can be assessed through relatively straightforward content-analytic techniques; others,
such as institutional venue, need to be assessed in a manner that may be different for each study (though we have often focused on congressional committees
where comparable indicators can be used across a great range of policies; see
Baumgartner, Jones, and MacLeod 2000).

   In our original formulation of these ideas, our goal was simply to integrate
what had been two disjoint literatures: Most of the literature on public policy
focused on incrementalism and institutional analyses; these literatures shared a
common focus on the difficulties of creating dramatic policy changes. However, an entirely separate and quite vibrant literature focused on agenda-setting
and dramatic policy initiatives. Could we build a single understanding that
would incorporate explanations of both stability and dramatic change? In looking to biology for the answer to this, we realized that we were making a very
different decision than most political scientists, whose policy models and analytic techniques are more likely to come from economics or physics, where additive and linear-regression-type models are more commonly accepted. Most
importantly, punctuated equilibrium models focus on entire distributions of

outcomes, not single point predictions. That is, the goal in using a PE model is typically not to explain a single punctuation, because the causes of these are expected to be complex and sometimes literally random (as in the case of genetic mutations, for example, common in the biological literature). Rather, the goal is to understand a pattern of outcomes across large numbers of individual units (as when an evolutionary biologist would want to understand mutations in a population over time, not in a single organism at a single time). Of course, in the policy sciences, we typically want to understand both the overall pattern as well as the individual case, as we will see below.

In any case, our use of the PE paradigm meant that we wanted to explain what we termed positive-feedback processes (things that can create rapid self-reinforcing changes, destabilizing and explosive growth, for example) as well as negative-feedback processes (also called self-correcting, or homeostatic processes, leading to steady equilibrium-type behaviors over time). Normally, these processes are studied in isolation. Further, the self-limiting characteristics of the negative-feedback systems have two characteristics that have made them more common in the literature: (1) they are far more common than their counterparts, accounting for the vast bulk of the cases; and (2) they follow equilibrium rules, making them amenable for statistical analyses. Thus it is fair to say that the literature had been divided among those who used equilibrium-based analyses, often quite sophisticated ones, to study the steady-state functioning of operating policy monopolies, and those who were not able to use these techniques because they studied parts of the process that were out of equilibrium or involved in the initial creation of policy institutions that subsequently might allow the analysis of the ensuing equilibrium. Our goal was to study both processes, recognizing a paradox: most policies most of the time can be well understood by an equilibrium analysis, but virtually no policy can be fully understood, or understood over a long period of time, without an analysis of where the supporting images and venues came from. So we attempted to integrate the study of the inherently unpredictable punctuations that occasionally occur with the stable operation of a policy equilibrium that may well go on for many decades.

I can illustrate the possibility of dramatic shifts in a policy image with an example from our study of pesticides policy (Baumgartner and Jones 1993). Figure 2.1 shows the amount of media coverage toward pesticides and the "tone" of that coverage. Positive articles were those that mentioned such things as increased agricultural productivity, scientific advance, and the race to put an end to hunger (such themes dominated the early post–World War II discussion of

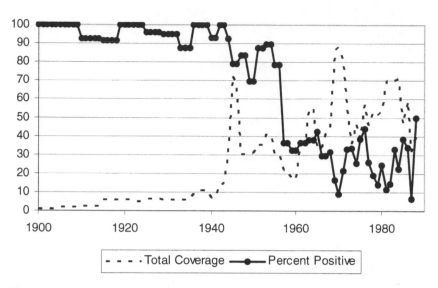

Figure 2.1. Pesticides coverage in the *Readers' Guide,* 1900–1988. *Source:* Baumgartner and Jones 1993, Fig. 5.3.

the development of the pesticides industry in the United States). Negatives are more familiar to us today: toxicity, danger, and environmental side effects such as fish-kills and threats to species.

Of course, there is no surprise that the amount of coverage of pesticides issues would have changed, often quite dramatically, over the years. Issues surge onto and decline from the agenda, and pesticides is no exception; it was the object of considerable attention in the immediate postwar years and again around Earth Day in 1970. After its initial surge into the national agenda in the 1940s, it never receded to its prewar levels of obscurity, again following a pattern that is relatively common.

The more remarkable element of Figure 2.1 is the dramatic shift in the tone of media coverage in a single year: 1956. Up to that year, the average percentage of stories coded favorable toward the pesticides industry was 95; it never declined below 69 percent positive during this period. From 1957 to 1988, by contrast, the average percentage of positive pesticides stories was 29, and the maximum was 50. In a single year, attention shifted from an overwhelming focus on the positives associated with the industry and its promise to the negatives brought on by toxic waste and environmental dangers. What caused 1956 to be the watershed year? Of course there were many reasons, as Jones and I discussed previously. However, the main point is that the industry itself did not change so dramatically in that one year; rather the policy image associated with it did.

A dramatic shift in the policy image associated with a major industry of course has many consequences, perhaps the most important of which is that it changes the political landscape. Political leaders who once rushed to promote pesticides as a way to help farmers, end hunger, eradicate diseases such as malaria, enhance exports of farm goods and agricultural products generally, and aid developing nations now saw growing public concern with the potential environmental fallout of too much industry encouragement. By the time pesticides were high on the agenda again, around 1970, the tone of public and governmental response had moved 180 degrees from the situation that prevailed in 1945. Clearly, these developments help explain shifting governmental responses to the issue, moving from encouragement and aiding of the development of the industry to increased regulation and focus on safety and environmental protection. These policy reactions are not visible in Figure 2.1, of course, but anyone knowledgeable about the history of environmental policies will note, for example, that the creation of the Environmental Protection Agency, in 1970, corresponds precisely with the surge in negative attention in the figure.

Studying individual policies over time is one major approach available to evaluate the PE perspective on policy change. When combined with case histories, it can be very effective. Another approach is more recently developed. An alternative to the PE perspective is one suggesting that public policies are simply incremental. Stability dominates most of the time even in the PE perspective, after all. Why not simply have an expectation that policies today are a reflection of policies yesterday, with some marginal adjustments? Bryan Jones and I have developed a further test of the PE approach that focuses not on longitudinal time series of a single case, as in Figure 2.1 above, but on the assessment of very large collections of data across scores or hundreds of policy areas and over long periods of time. The key question is the overall distribution of policy changes. A PE perspective leads us to expect a distinctive shape in this distribution, one noticeably different from the Normal curve.

Figure 2.2 shows the distribution of changes in annual federal spending across sixty-two categories of spending defined by the federal Office of Management and Budget (OMB), from 1947 to 2000. To make this figure, we first constructed historically comparable time series of spending data for each of sixty-two series from 1947 to 2000, or about fifty years for each series. Then we calculated the percent change for each series (with the effects of inflation re-

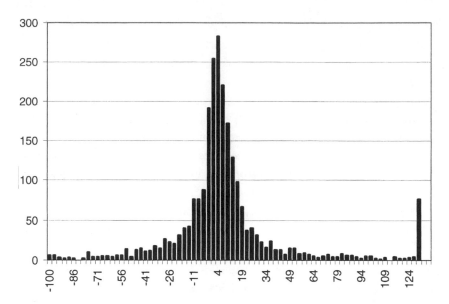

Figure 2.2. The distribution of annual percentage budget changes, 1947–2000. The data show the distribution of percent annual changes across sixty-two categories of federal spending, corrected for inflation, from 1947 to 2000. Entries of 130 percent and above are grouped together. Data are grouped in three-point intervals; for example, the leftmost column indicates that there are six cases with 98, 99, or 100 percent declines. *Source:* Policy Agendas Project (http://www.policyagendas.org/).

moved). Then we combined the sixty-two series into a single frequency distribution. So the resulting figure is based on approximately three thousand observations and simply shows the number of times that federal spending, in a given category, stayed the same, increased, or decreased by the amounts shown in the x-axis of the figure. Extremely high percentage increases are grouped together in the last bar at the right of the figure.

Figure 2.2 shows a distinctive pattern that is discernibly different from the Normal curve. Even disregarding for a moment the seventy-six outliers on the positive side of the distribution grouped together at the +130 point, the graph is leptokurtic. That is, it has a distinctively higher central peak than the Normal curve, weaker "shoulders," and a greater-than-expected number of extreme cases. Our PE theory leads us to expect just this: Little or no change in most policies in most years, but occasional positive-feedback processes that generate dramatic shifts in priorities, new programs being initiated, and entirely new programmatic priorities. These discontinuities in the policy process generate very great annual changes on both sides: sometimes policies are greatly expanded, other times they are abandoned or cut back sharply. Relatively rare in this process is moderate adjustment to changing realities. Rather than make continual adjustments at all levels of scale, we see that the system has an extreme status quo bias (reflected in the high central peak). This is because, we believe, the system often ignores new developments, sticking to a status quo policy until there is some often belated recognition that action is required; at this point large changes are common (see Jones and Baumgartner 2005 for more detail on this approach and our theory; see also Jones et al., 2003). In any case, the data in Figure 2.2, representing an overview of the entire federal budget over the entire post–World War II period, make clear that stability and dramatic changes do indeed coexist and that these cannot be explained simply by an incrementalist model since such a model would predict a Normal distribution of changes and we observe a leptokurtic distribution.

These analyses give us some ways of thinking of a process. However, while Figure 2.1 shows some evidence about a historical process that can be complemented with case histories, Figure 2.2 is completely ahistorical. That is, we purposefully take out of context there the various changes in policy direction that we have observed in different areas; our point is simply to demonstrate the relative frequencies of policy changes of different magnitudes. These approaches help to demonstrate the validity of a PE approach, but they do not exhaust what we can do, and to be complete they must be enhanced with more detailed case analyses. In the next section I focus on environmental issues in particular. How does the environmental policy arena compare to these general points, and how likely is it that a PE approach will be helpful there?

APPLICATIONS TO ENVIRONMENTAL POLICY

Does this general approach work well in the field of environmental policy? It is simple to see that the general trends apparent in the earlier section are largely mirrored in the environmental arena. First, pesticides policy itself is part of the environmental arena, and some of the most dramatic innovations in public policy in recent decades have been through the increased awareness of the need for environmental regulation and the aggressiveness of these activities. Any number of new policies can be cited, but the simplest is the creation of the Environmental Protection Agency in 1970. These developments can be tracked in two ways: first, federal spending on environmental activities; second, congressional attention to the environment.

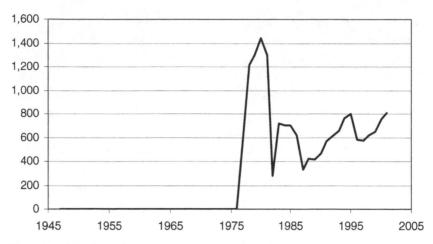

Figure 2.3. Federal spending on energy conservation, 1947–2001. The data reflect constant FY 2000 dollars, in millions; OMB category 272, Energy Conservation. *Source:* Policy Agendas Project.

Federal spending is available over time through the Policy Agendas Project for sixty-two categories of spending as defined by the OMB. Spending in many areas may have some environmental implications; however, two categories of spending are clearly indicative of environmental focus: Subfunction 272 (Energy Conservation) and 304 (Pollution Control). Figures 2.3 and 2.4 show inflation-adjusted spending on these topics.

Federal spending on energy conservation was zero from the beginning of our period of study until 1977 when it was established at $575 million and moved quickly to $1.2 billion in 1978. This is a clear example of a policy not being considered relevant to government until the oil price increases of the mid-1970s. Quite literally, we went from having no policy in this area to having a substantial one just two years later. Of course there was a lag between the initial oil shock and the establishment and consolidation of federal spending programs in this area. Still, Figure 2.3 shows a dramatic punctuation.

Figure 2.4 shows that federal spending on pollution control got a slightly earlier start, with spending initially established at the level of $3.8 billion in 1970 and quickly rising to almost $25 billion in 1973. There is no question about the "alarmed discovery" aspect of these two policy areas. We moved from a policy of no policy whatsoever to quite substantial spending in just a few years in each case. Subsequent histories of both spending series also show periods of substantial declines after an initial surge, and then a leveling off.

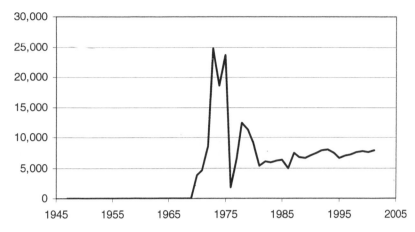

Figure 2.4. Federal spending on pollution control, 1947–2001. The data reflect constant FY 2000 dollars, in millions; OMB category 304, Pollution Control. *Source:* Policy Agendas Project.

Figure 2.5 takes the data from Figures 2.3 and 2.4 and displays them in a format similar to that shown in Figure 2.2 for the entire federal budget. That is, the figure shows the sizes of each annual percentage budget change for the two series.

While it is more difficult to see the overall shape of the distribution because there are only fifty-five observations in Figure 2.5 rather than three thousand— plus as in Figure 2.2, these environmental spending series display the characteristic leptokurtosis of a PE series (the kurtosis value for this series is 6.1). All in all, the data in Figures 2.3 to 2.5 make clear that dramatic punctuations are common in the environmental arena, at least as it concerns federal spending. Declines, not only huge increases, also occur. In fact, the series are particularly relevant because they both reflect the creation of new spending categories *de novo;* new programs and spending where none had existed before. Once established, these spending areas were quite volatile during their early years but more stable after some time.

Federal spending on the environment is not fully captured by just these two series. However, there is no question about the increased federal attention to environmental matters now compared to the 1950s, for example. Figure 2.6 shows congressional attention, measured by the number of hearings each year, on environmental matters. In contrast to the spending data, these hearings cover the full range of environmental concerns from air and water pollution to species protection to hazardous waste and indoor air quality.

Congressional attention to the environment more than doubled from 1968

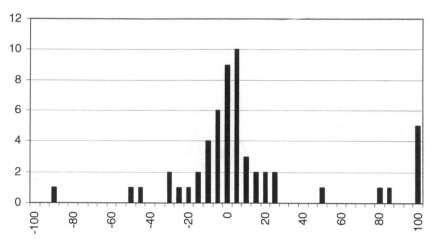

Figure 2.5. The distribution of annual percentage budget changes in federal environmental spending. The data reflect the annual percentage changes taken from the series reported in Figures 2.3 and 2.4. Five cases listed as +100% increases reflect those increases of 100 percent or more. The maximum increase in any single year was 266%. *Source:* Policy Agendas Project.

to 1969, reaching sixty hearings in that year. After this period the issue has never faded away from the congressional agenda, though the topics of concern have certainly shifted. We can also see a rise in attention again in the late 1980s with attention at levels three times as high as that in 1969, the initial peak. The environment clearly became institutionalized on the agendas of many congressional committees, with attention coming to environmental issues from many different angles and perspectives.

What can we say about the environment as an area for the application of punctuated equilibrium ideas and theories? First of all, compared to the range of policies across the entire federal government, environmental policies are new. Their histories are more recent. Relevant jurisdictional venues are less firmly in place. Institutional procedures are not as strongly rooted in tradition since they do not go back as far. Much of the period from 1970 to about 1985 was marked by the initial establishment and revision of a series of remarkable and major landmark policies, some of which were completely novel. So, do punctuations occur? Certainly in this area there have been a great number. What of the equilibrium part of the PE model? After the initial creation of these policies, like any others they have been justified by certain policy images and the creation of certain jurisdictional venues. These, however, remain subject to debate. As other authors in this volume will demonstrate, there are many

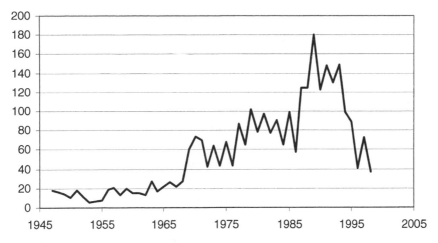

Figure 2.6. Congressional hearings on the environment, 1947–1998. *Source:* Policy Agendas Project.

cases of smoothly functioning environmental policies with relatively stable images and venues of action. In fact, Figures 2.3 through 2.5 showed many instances of little annual budget change for our two environmental series; this is typical of the budget in general across all areas. The environmental policy area may have a number of dramatic and high-profile policy initiatives, but not so many that it differs dramatically from the political system overall. Thus, it appears a fertile ground for the search for positive-feedback processes that can help to create new policy dynamics, upending status quo policies. As Figures 2.3 and 2.4 above should make clear, this volatility works both ways. Environmental policies are subject to change, and they are subject to challenge. Significant battles surround many environmental policies, and powerful images on the side of environmental cleanup and regulation coexist with powerful free-enterprise and economic growth images that often justify policies diametrically opposed to those sought by environmentalists. All in all, it is an area where attention to shifting policy images, like shifting venues, can help us explain some dramatic policy changes.

LESSONS FOR CASE ANALYSIS

The types of analyses presented above have the merit of allowing some systematic tests, applicable to the entire political system in some cases, allowing us to assess the value and attempt to disconfirm the PE approach to public policy.

However, these techniques must be supplemented with intensive analyses of the context and details of given cases if we are to understand the process completely. A combination of large-scale and small-N work is more powerful than either alone. It is particularly useful, however, if the two approaches are designed in a way to allow these complementarities to be apparent.

Perhaps the single most apparent element in the PE approach is that the processes that allow dramatic change are expected to result from the rapid interactions of positive-feedback processes. By their very nature, such processes cannot easily be predicted since they are highly sensitive to the interactions among variables, not simply additive combinations of them. Let me take an example from my own collaborative research to illustrate this.

In 1998 and 1999, the Environmental Protection Agency (EPA) considered and then adopted new standards for the amount of sulfur that could be in gasoline, reducing by 90 percent allowable levels, and establishing one of the most significant environmental advances of the Clinton presidency.[1] In early 1998 the EPA began reviewing these standards and considered a 50 percent reduction in sulfur levels, from 300 parts per million (ppm) to 150. Oil industry opposition could be expected, of course. The petroleum and automobile industries each sought to portray the other as the main source of difficulties: car companies want to show that cleaner gas would allow more efficient engines (see, for example, Alliance of Automobile Manufacturers 2000); oil companies do not disagree but point to the costs involved (see, for example, American Petroleum Institute 2000). Environmentalists and air pollution officials, of course, want whatever solution would work. In this case a jointly funded $5 million study pointed to sulfur content of gasoline as a particularly important element of this equation. Like many studies, this one gained little attention until a coalition of state and local air pollution officials began to make the rounds of environmental groups in Washington pointing to the importance of this study and urging pressure on the EPA to adopt a simple solution based on a much more dramatic standard: a 90 percent reduction. Congressional Democrats, including Senator Patrick Moynahan and Representatives Henry Waxman and John Dingell (no regular allies in other fights . . .), signaled their intention to introduce legislation requiring such a standard. Opposition from petroleum companies was present, of course, but this centered on small refinery operators mostly in the West, who pushed for a regional standard rather than a national one. The American Petroleum Institute did not actively attempt to discredit the study pointing to sulfur as the best solution to the issue, since it was a jointly funded project not easily attacked on technical grounds.

However, they argued that far more important problems had to do with encouraging greater energy production and distribution rather than reducing emissions, and pointed to cost issues saying that with energy costs so high these should not be ignored; finally they encouraged western refiners and the Western Governors' Association in their opposition to the proposal. In fact, many petroleum companies were relatively content with a policy that would raise costs for all, something much more manageable for large firms and that might simply have the impact of forcing some smaller suppliers out of the business. Environmentalists and air pollution officials were particularly helped by a widely used estimate that equated the decision to reduce sulfur down to 30 ppm to removing 54 million cars off the roads (see, for example, Sierra Club 2000). The combination of strong auto industry support, a consensus among environmental groups and local air pollution officials that this was a "winnable" issue, and an apparent split among petroleum interests allowed EPA Administrator Carol Browner to conclude that this was a good opportunity to enact a policy significantly more stringent than even the agency was initially planning. In the end, a 90 percent reduction was enacted, with President Clinton signing it in 1999. Petroleum companies vowed a fight if such a policy were next attempted on diesel fuel, which also happened in the waning days of the Clinton presidency in 2000. President Bush elected not to reopen either of these issues after coming to office.

Many elements combined to allow this dramatic shift to occur in this case. Perhaps most striking is the degree to which behaviors were driven by the expectations of the behaviors of others. Just as one might want to pick a winning stock, or choose which Democratic presidential contender might emerge from the primaries in 2004, the task is not to pick the one that one prefers so much as it is to pick the one that the greatest number of others will prefer. If all members of a community are thinking in the same way, then any initial momentum can be self-perpetuating (see Schelling 1972; Granovetter 1978; Crenson 1987; Kirman 1993; Becker 1992; Bikhchandani, Hirshleifer, and Welch 1992; Bak 1996 for more on this topic; Brock [this volume] also provides a good discussion of these issues). Further, even small initial differences in values can quickly lead to social cascades if relevant decision makers all make similar calculations about the relative merits of the options simultaneously. So, if decision makers are all attuned to the expected behaviors of others, and if those others are reacting to small differences in election results in a primary, for example, then small differences in these initial results can lead to great differences in outcomes; the initial differences, however, may be impossible to predict.

Similarly in the case of policy cascades, momentum can be self-perpetuating. As we saw in the sulfur example above, policymakers may be asking themselves whether a given policy is about to "move." If they simultaneously observe some event, whether that is the publication of some new scientific evidence, a journalistic exposé, a public statement by an important player, the decision by a committee leader to report a bill, or an oil spill, then policymakers can move en masse, and surprisingly quickly. The signaling event can be almost anything; the key is that many actors react to it. The characteristics of events that cause people to react to them are partly predictable—we know that a presidential initiative is more newsworthy than a senatorial initiative, for example. However, these processes are not fully predictable since they include agenda-crowding effects. A given event related to a given policy may garner considerable attention during a period when there is little other news; in a different environment, attention may be focused on some more prominent story or crisis. Thus, we cannot say for sure even whether a given set of events will be enough to cause a positive feedback process to kick in; it depends, among other things, on available space on the agenda.

In any case, policymakers inside of government, and advocates outside of it, want to spend their time on issues that are poised to move. If environmental groups have one hundred issues that they would be glad to see moved along, why would they not spend their time and effort on those issues that actually are gathering momentum and stand the chance of passage? Similarly, from the perspective of government officials (often the allies, not the opponents of advocates of change), do they want to spend their time on issues that garner no outside support, or given the choice would they prefer to work on issues that will generate broad alliances and have a strong chance of passage and implementation? Even in the case of those opposed to a given initiative, if there is a broad mobilization in favor, opponents may decide, as we saw in the sulfur case, to keep their powder dry, to take a defeat in one case in order to focus energy on those cases where more effective opposition can be mounted. In sum, the expectations of others matter in the policy process. The cascading, mimicking, and threshold-related behaviors that stem from this make prediction difficult, but the process can easily be observed as it happens.

A second element of the multiply interactive nature of these cascades is that efforts to create them should usually fail. Positive-feedback processes require the simultaneous combinations of several independent streams: policy images, technical evidence, political leadership, a consensus among relevant interest groups, a window of opportunity—all must be ready. Quite often, policy entrepreneurs will attempt to build a consensus but the window of opportunity will pass by, the technical evidence will be challenged, or political leaders will be entranced by a foreign war or some other preoccupation. Effective policy entrepreneurs certainly make many more efforts to achieve change than they succeed in; their batting averages do not count, however—only their occasional successes.

The two themes above may appear to be in contradiction: how can people be attuned to the behaviors of others, but usually fail to predict these things correctly? The difference is that no single actor typically controls the ultimate reaction of the entire policy community. From the perspective of the individual policymaker attempting to push through some new initiative, it is difficult to know whether others will see this as an initiative to support. Effective policy entrepreneurs, therefore, maintain many connections and many points of communications; these "weak ties" can increase the chances of knowing whether conditions are ripe for their issue to move (Granovetter 1973; Carpenter et al. 1998, 2004). Typically, however, conditions are not ripe as attention is focused on some other issue. Effective policymakers continually make efforts, knowing they will usually fail but that they must be ready if a window emerges to allow change.

From the broader perspective, not from that of a given policy advocate looking to push a favored new proposal, the process is more understandable. That is, we can predict that high-level attention will always be focused on something, that leaders will always want to be known for their policy initiatives, and that the distribution of policy outcomes will include many with little or incremental change but always a few with dramatic departures from previous policy. So the process is understandable and the distribution of outcomes is predictable. But the particular combinations of forces that must combine to create dramatic policy changes are so complex that we cannot tell ahead of time which cases will see all the elements fall together. (Think of a lottery: we know someone will win, but we don't know who that will be. Random processes have predictable outcomes at the aggregate level. They have unpredictable outcomes from the individual perspective, however.) The policy process, like the weather, genetic evolution, the establishment of particular towns as centers of commerce for a given industry, avalanches, or earthquakes, can be understood better in its range of outcomes—its distribution—rather than in its individual occurrences (for a range of examples from the physical and social world, see Bak 1996; Baumgartner and Jones 2002; Jones and Baumgartner 2005).

To say that these processes are unpredictable does not mean that they cannot be studied. However, we must know what we are studying: individual cases, or distributions of cases. It is particularly helpful in studying examples of policy change to study them over time and to note the differences between those efforts that succeed and those that fail; failed efforts to create policy change are rarely studied and yet they should be quite common. Often the difference between a successful and a failed effort to make a change may be only minimal because the process is expected to rely on the interaction of several variables, many of which are stochastic, beyond the control of any given actor. For the analyst, this means that we should pay attention to the differences and similarities among these failed and successful efforts to effect policy change. In the context of a case study, this simply means extending the time frame of the study and asking: what were these entrepreneurs doing in previous years? How many times was a similar proposal made but rejected before it was finally passed? What are the differences between the successful and unsuccessful efforts? If these differences are limited to elections and executive leadership, then we do not need a complex theory based on PE to understand it. But if the differences relate to the combination of factors present, not a single one in isolation, then we can move toward a better understanding of the interactive and multiplicative effects of the variables that contribute to policy change.

A further implication of this way of thinking is that distributional analyses alone can help us test the theory of punctuated equilibrium. What then, is the role of case analysis? It is to assess whether the processes that we observe are consistent with those expected in the theory. The full test is to know whether the predictions bear out across the full distribution of cases and if the observations and descriptions of particular cases correspond to the process described in the theory. But a single case does not test the theory. Case analyses could indeed disconfirm the PE approach to the study of public policy; the theory is fully falsifiable. For example, if a single element were systematically associated with successful examples of policy change, then we would not need a positive-feedback theory to explain it. But a positive-feedback process is interactive by its nature, so a simple test looking for the additive impact of separate variables studied in isolation would not be appropriate.

Analyses of selected cases of dramatic policy change can sometimes lead the analyst to expect these are common, or easy to produce. For example, in *Agendas and Instability,* Bryan Jones and I studied nine different policy areas, each of which witnessed a major policy change at some point in the period covered by our analysis. Any scholar of public policy can think of cases where dramatic reversals have occurred in other cases as well, and of course these stories are generally more interesting to tell than those relating the smooth functioning of a policy monopoly undergoing no particular threat. If a literature were developed solely on the basis of case studies of dramatic change, we might reach conclusions quite far off the mark, since we would have no estimates of how common policy punctuations are. Looking back at Figure 2.2 above, which covers more than three thousand observations of annual changes in budget figures, it is clear that most changes are marginal at best. In fact the overwhelming majority of cases show no change over any short periods. In the Public Advocacy Project mentioned above, we selected a random sample of 102 issues that were the object of lobbying; fewer than ten could be said to be the objects of dramatic shifts over a two-year congressional policy cycle; much more common are the marginal shifts, the failed policy proposals, and the routine efforts to revise a policy ever so slightly. As our literature develops based both on case analyses and systematic coverage, we need to develop stronger estimates of the relative strengths of those forces that promote stability and those that allow for the occasional occurrence of dramatic change.

If it is true that most policies most of the time will be relatively stable, policy advocates know that there is a constant threat of more dramatic change. This may be seen as either a danger or an opportunity. A major preoccupation of applied and theoretical work should be to identify those cases where dramatic changes are not only possible, but likely. From the theoretical side, no understanding of the development of policy is possible without explaining the causes of policy punctuations, even though stability dominates in most areas most of the time. From the practical side, environmental groups, foundations, political leaders, and businesses affected by environmental regulations should want to know how to create or avoid dramatic policy changes.

The discussion above concerning the mimicking and imitative nature of the policy process should make clear that the process by which positive-feedback processes get under way cannot be understood very well with a decision-theory structure. Rather, there are many players in the game, and the reactions of players B, C, and D are more important than the initial action of player A. Put another way, for both theoretical and practical reasons, it is important to know how opponents and allies will react to a given proposal before making it. Allies must be canvassed to know ahead of time whether a given proposal can perhaps gain their support. Opponents must be studied to know of their potential reactions. Will they counter with a rival policy proposal that may be more damaging (and successful) than the status quo, or will they be like the petroleum industry in the case of low-sulfur gasoline described above, barely reacting?

Clearly, a well-intentioned policy proposal made sincerely can easily backfire if allies are otherwise preoccupied and opponents are ready with a strong counterproposal.

Environmental policymaking, like many other areas of public policy, has extremely powerful symbols associated with policy outcomes on all sides. While environmentalists enjoy broad public support for saving species, reducing pollution, improving public health, and saving the planet, rival symbols are powerful as well. These include economic growth and jobs, local versus "outside" control over resources, and private property rights, to name a few. While it is not uncommon for powerful symbols to be evident on both sides of a debate, the environmental arena offers especially powerful ones. Further, in contrast to some other areas of policymaking where decisions may affect only small segments of the population, and where policy monopolies may develop, environmental policies in general tend to be conflictual when they arise. Business interests can be expected to mobilize in response to environmental initiatives. Partly, this is because the growth of environmental policies and regulations developed in reaction to the previous development of policy monopolies dominated by business and producer interests; environmental policies therefore came with ready-made opponents, the targets of the new policies. Across scores or hundreds of environmental policies, however, it is clear that greatly different levels of success have occurred. Some policies are widely accepted; others are severely contested; still others are barely proposed because of their lack of feasibility. Clearly, distinguishing systematically across many cases why some environmental arguments have been more successful than others is fundamental. Is it technical and scientific evidence? Social mobilization? Lobbying campaigns? Electoral politics? A consensus among a policy community? A lack of business opposition? Detailed case analyses, if done in a way that allows comparison, can tell us.

Attention to the reactions of opponents to environmental policies is important, and attention to the reactions of allies is as well. Will a given policy proposal become the object of a broad environmental consensus, or will other groups see their interests better served by avoiding association with the idea? Will allied groups combine their resources or will each work on different pet issues? It is clear that policy changes occur at every different level of scale, from the broadest to the most minute. Similarly, coalitions among like-minded interest groups, foundations, and policy advocates may be broad, narrow, or somewhere in between. Studying these processes systematically will allow a greater understanding of why some proposals "take off" whereas others fizzle; it can also help explain the differences in scale apparent in various policy changes.

Repetto and Allen (this volume) describe the type of "social trap" characteristic of the models that Brock (also this volume) explains conceptually. They show strong social cascade effects in the willingness of policy participants to adopt a new paradigm. In spite of evidence that each individually would be better off doing so, in many circumstances, groups of individuals will refuse to move from the status quo, unless large numbers of peers begin to do so. These analyses begin to show in greater detail than Baumgartner and Jones (1993) did how positive-feedback effects may or may not come into effect. In sum, even with powerful evidence that all might be better off with some new policy equilibrium, a status quo policy may be maintained only through the absence of a social cascade. A venerable tradition of studies of the "tragedy of the commons" and public goods problems more generally backs this up; a more recent but still robust tradition of studies showing how these common-pool problems can be overcome shows that these processes can be studied empirically and that their dynamics correspond with the ideas of positive and negative feedback mechanisms laid out here.

The question of the scale of policy change is related to complicated issues of levels of analysis, as Cashore and Howlett describe in their analysis of forestry in this volume. Levels of aggregation have long been a source of potential confusion in policy studies—do we study environmental policy, water quality issues, as in the efforts to clean up a given river system, or do we focus on a particular toxic site? None of these levels of analysis is the "wrong" place to study these dynamics, but studies at different levels of aggregation may sometimes be difficult to compare among one another. The lessons of the theoretical work and the distribution of policy changes across the entire political system described above lead one to expect that similar processes should go on at every level of scale, every level of analysis. At the higher levels of aggregation, changes should be relatively rare; policy changes based on new images or new policy paradigms should be easier to create, and more common, at lower levels of aggregation than at higher ones. But the processes that describe them should be driven by the same forces.

CONCLUSIONS

The environmental policy arena is a fertile ground for the use and further development of a punctuated equilibrium approach to the study of policy processes. In this chapter, I have laid out a series of systematic observations that should be applicable across the entire political system. I have also pointed to a number of things that can be learned only through detailed case analysis. Through the combination of broad, quantitative, and systematic studies of the political system along with case studies based on shared theoretical perspectives, we can further our understanding of environmental policymaking quite substantially. Further, these observations will have broader relevance beyond only the case of the environment.

In the first section of this chapter I reviewed some broad evidence about the punctuated equilibrium approach to politics and policy change. Looking across the entire political system and the full period from 1947 onward, I showed that policy changes follow a distinctive pattern characteristic of the PE approach; these broad patterns also are evident in the case of the environment. Generally, it is not hard to see that the broad ideas of positive feedback, negative feedback, and the impact of changes in policy images and venues on public policy have resonance in the case of the environment. The theory generally applies to the area. In the second part of this chapter I have reviewed a number of elements of the theory that cannot easily be observed across hundreds of cases at a time, but which must be the object of more intensive case analysis. Since this volume consists mostly of just such analyses, it is worth considering what we may want to look for in these analyses.

Perhaps the single clearest result from our theoretical discussions is that the process is highly interactive. Because of the role of the expectations of others, no single actor's behavior determines the outcome. Rather, social cascades can be put into action through the simultaneous reactions of many actors to what they see around them. These processes further imply that most efforts to create policy changes will fail, and that successful efforts may differ only in small ways from unsuccessful ones. Therefore it is worth studying in considerable detail what makes a given effort to create policy change succeed once where it may have previously failed ten times.

Ingram and Fraser (this volume) note that policy change can come in the absence of social-movement mobilization and indeed of much public involvement at all; water resources policy in California has gone through dramatic shifts in orientation and policy direction as networks of elites, not the mass public, have changed their understandings of the best policy solutions. Their analysis serves as a reminder that no single source, certainly not broad public opinion or even social movements, need be present for a positive-feedback mechanism to begin; dramatic policy change requires that those involved adopt a new policy image, but it does not require that this be done in the limelight or the headlines. Of course, dramatic policy changes often are newsworthy and have large effects and therefore draw substantial media coverage. But examples such as that described by Ingram and Fraser's discussion of water policy, like the "silent revolution" in divorce and family law in the 1970s, or of de-institutionalization of the mentally ill (see Baumgartner and Jones 1993 for these and other examples), make clear that these changes can also occur within communities of professionals without broad public involvement. Dunn (this volume) describes processes relating to the case of Corporate Average Fuel Efficiency (CAFE) standards that also make clear the importance of contingencies and interactions in the policy process. Cashore and Howlett (this volume) lay out the varieties and contingencies of how punctuations can occur; sometimes formal institutional rules are important elements of these changes, but in other instances informal social norms can be more important; there is clearly no single set of conditions, but rather a range of contingent and interactive causes.

Typically, conditions are not ripe for policy change for a given issue at a given time. However, the political system constantly produces policy changes; each year many dramatic changes occur in different areas of public policy. Welfare as we know it comes to an end, privacy rights are eroded in the fight against terrorism, global warming is recognized, new hybrid technologies enhance fuel efficiency, and foreign travelers are required to be fingerprinted upon entry to the United States, to pick some recent examples. Previous historical periods were perhaps even more volatile than more recent history (see Jones and Baumgartner 2005). So the political system as a whole harbors the opportunity, and indeed makes it inevitable that dramatic policy changes will occasionally occur, but these changes are rare for any given policy.

All this means that studies of only successful cases of policy change should be stretched out in time so that they cover previous or subsequent periods when policies were not changed. This can allow us to note whether the change was a simple reaction to changing contextual variables, or if indeed a positive-feedback process occurred. A combination of studies of many examples will lend more credence to the theory, and also help elucidate the process by which these positive-feedback processes are created.

Finally, this chapter should have some lessons for policy advocates as well. The theory of political change laid out here makes clear that dramatic reversals of policies are possible, but that the conditions that lead to these are highly contingent and difficult to predict ahead of time. This means that policy advocates should have a contingent theory of action. If a broad environmental agenda would have scores if not hundreds of policy goals worth fighting for, then one of the most important questions should be not which goal is more important than the others, but rather which ones have a realistic chance of being adopted. This set of "moveable issues" will change over time as new evidence arises, new social movements are born and fade away, new spokespeople develop who can articulate their claims well, and as business and government reactions to these proposals change. Is this process completely random? It need not be. Some efforts to help coordinate the actions of environmental groups so that they can spend time on issues that have a chance of passage can be very effective; self-reinforcing processes can be started up on purpose. This process will not always succeed, of course, but it can certainly be attempted.

In this chapter I have raised a number of broad issues relating to a punctuated equilibrium approach to the study of public policy and I have noted how these relate to the study of environmental policy in particular. Subsequent chapters in this volume will show whether these observations are helpful in developing theoretical and practical lessons for the study of environmental policies. Hopefully, these will be of interest to those with broad interests in the study of public policy, those with a theoretical concern with how environmental policies are made (and unmade) in the United States, and those with applied concerns about how to create (or avoid) the next major environmental policy punctuation.

NOTES

I gratefully acknowledge support from the National Science Foundation through grants SBR–9320922, SBR–9905195, SBR–011161, and SBR–0111224.

1. This example is more fully documented at the Lobbying and Public Advocacy Project Web site: http://lobby.la.psu.edu/024_Low-sulfur_Gasoline/frameset_sulfur.html. Data were originally collected by Frank Baumgartner, Jeff Berry, Marie Hojnacki, Beth Leech, and David Kimball through NSF grants SBR–0111224 and SBR–9905195.

Chapter 3 Tipping Points, Abrupt Opinion Changes, and Punctuated Policy Change

William A. Brock

Why is the political system sometimes so sluggish in dealing with environmental problems and at other times capable of very rapid responses? Why is the political system sometimes so slow when the capitalist system is so nimble? No one doubts that the creative dynamism of capitalism has benefited us tremendously, but growth and the continual introduction of new technologies rapidly increase the number and magnitude of negative externality problems that governments must control. Governments seem to be losing the race to create effective institutions to do this job. It is easy to find current symbols of this mismatch: (1) SUVs continue to multiply, endangering small car owners who collide with one of these behemoths; (2) McMansions continue to gobble up the landscape, spoiling other people's views; (3) use of lawn chemicals continues unabated though lakes are eutrophied and water wells are poisoned; (4) pollution from industrial agriculture and factory farms continues to increase, contradicting the notion that our food is cheap. One can go on with a depressing litany of similar situations where the problem is clear but action is lacking.

Since environmental goods are "free" until government gets organized to regulate and impose costs for using them, technical "progress" evolves to utilize these "free" inputs. Clearly, if there were no governmental (or other "social" controls such as "social stigma" and ethical norms) innovation would continue to economize on priced inputs and use non-priced inputs to the point where society itself might ultimately collapse under the weight of its own wastes. I call this process "Flat-of-the-Curve-Induced Innovation."

Indeed, Nordhaus (1992) lists this inability of the political system to react as a potential limiting factor to human progress that might be more serious than the usual limiting factors of exhaustible and renewable resources that capture the attention of ecologists and other natural scientists in debates about the "limits to growth." For example, in discussing potential limits to growth, he warned that wastes and emissions generated by economic activity could exceed natural assimilative capacity and raise pollution control costs disastrously high, or that societies might lack the political will to reduce environmental damages, even when possible at moderate cost.

Negative externalities from consumption patterns may even be more important than negative externalities from production patterns. Brock and Taylor (2003) report data on several major pollutants, showing that industry's share has dropped while consumption's share has risen. A major role for social norms, social stigmatization, and ethics is to check this process if government is not doing its job, but there is evidence that these social mechanisms are inadequate. For example, the owners of behemoth SUVs, which offload uncompensated risks onto other drivers, assume a right to drive them without paying compensation for the negative externalities they impose on the rest of the motoring public. Despite campaigns to instill stigma, norms, and ethics (for example, the "What Would Jesus Drive?" ads), the social mechanism of internalizing these externalities does not appear to be working.

The political system sometimes does act if the pressure is strong enough. Witness the nimbleness of Congress to act to protect the "Do Not Call List" as the courts kept throwing up roadblocks under the guise of rather generous interpretations of the Founding Fathers' intent to protect free speech. Congress knew that over 50 million people signed up for this popular list. But the mystery remains: Telemarketers had been annoying the public for a long time— why the sudden action by government at this particular moment? The problem was obvious to all for a long time. Then, suddenly, a rare bipartisan consensus of both houses of Congress as well as the executive branch rapidly "tipped" against an incredibly powerful special-interest group, the telemarketing lobby. Why did this abrupt change occur after a long period of inaction in the face of long-standing public frustration? I try to shed light on such abrupt changes in government policy responses to long-festering problems with the models developed in this chapter.

Natural and social scientists have worked hard to understand dynamic processes that produce punctuated equilibrium behavior. There are many kinds of models that do so: "sand-pile" models, "tipping point" models, "small world" models and other graph-theoretic models, "complex adaptive systems" models, and models that produce punctuated dynamics via a hierarchy of time scales.[1] Unfortunately, many dynamical processes that have little to do with complex systems processes produce identical empirical patterns. This problem is closely related to the well-known "identification problem" in econometrics: How does one use data to distinguish among observationally equivalent structures? Such an identification problem turns up in the attempt to use data to separate "true" social dynamics that produce punctuated equilibrium behavior from "spurious" social dynamics created by exogenous dynamics of unobserved variables.[2] This identification issue is especially important in deciding whether the sluggish political system acts suddenly because of "endogenous" emergence of pressure that "tips" it or whether it acts suddenly because an exogenous change acts on it, a change that may have little to do with the punctuated equilibrium dynamics of policy change discussed by Gunderson and Holling (2002).

In this chapter I present some simple models of the dynamics of problem recognition, the emergence of pressure from the public to do something about it, and the final tipping of the system into political action. I concentrate on modeling the self-emergence of pressure on the political system. Then I apply these models to some of the policy problems considered elsewhere in this volume. Though these models suppress institutional details, I fully realize that institutional structures can strongly influence outcomes in particular cases.

MINIMAL MODELS OF SOCIAL CHOICE DYNAMICS: THE "MEAN FIELD" CASE

This exposition uses ideas from discrete choice theory in economics and simple models of phase transition from statistical physics to model why social systems may get stuck in "social traps." The goal is not only to understand why a social system cannot move to a more efficient state but also to help find ways to break out of social traps.[3] The basic idea of discrete choice theory is that the preferences (Anderson, de Palma, and Thisse 1992) of agent i are stochastic and are composed of a deterministic part and a random part. Scheffer, Westley, and

Brock (2000, 2003) use discrete choice theory and build on the work of Brock and Durlauf (1999) in modeling abrupt paradigm shifts in science and Brock and Durlauf's (2001a, 2001b) general treatment of interactions-based models to model the emergence of new problems, followed by lagged recognition, followed by eventual action mobilization of pressure on the political system, followed by possible action by the political system.

This exposition shows the potential for abrupt change, bifurcations, hysteresis, and other dynamic phenomena, as does the work of Scheffer, Westley, and Brock (2000, 2003). "Bifurcation" refers to a relatively rapid change in a stable state of a dynamical system when a slowly moving parameter goes through a critical value that causes the stable state on the fast time scale to become unstable. "Hysteresis" refers to a behavior of a dynamical system such that a parameter slowly moving in one direction leads the dynamical system to shift to an alternative stable state rapidly when the parameter moves beyond a certain critical value, but that same parameter has to move in the other direction quite far beyond the critical value that triggered the shift in order that the dynamical system return to its original stable state. This is a phenomenon of partial irreversibility that is important in the analysis of ecological systems, such as lakes where oligotrophy and eutrophy are alternative stable states (Gunderson and Holling 2002).

Now consider a community of social agents, call them $i = 1, 2, \ldots, N$, facing two policy options, call them -1 and $+1$. Let the status quo be -1 and let the difference in utility for agent i between the two options be denoted by

(3.1) $H_i(t) = h_i(t) + n_i(t),$

where H is a random variable, h is its deterministic part, and n is its random part. Notice that both h and n can differ among agents and time periods. Using a standard model in discrete choice theory (Brock and Durlauf 2001a, 2001b), the probability that agent i chooses $+1$ in period t is given by

(3.2a) $P\{\omega_{i,t} = +1\} = P\{i \text{ chooses} +1\} = \dfrac{\exp(bh_{i,t})}{\exp(bh_{i,t})+1},$

where the parameter "b" increases to infinity as the standard deviation of n goes to zero (Anderson, de Palma, and Thisse 1992). We call "b" the "intensity of choice." Notice that the function

(3.2b) $f(x,b) = \dfrac{\exp(bx)}{\exp(bx)+1},$

where x stands in for h, is increasing in x, is ½ at x = 0 for all b, is ½ for b = 0 independently of x, and has a sharp threshold at x = 0 for huge positive values of b. That is, the probability that the agent will choose an option increases as its relative utility increases. The probability is 50:50 if both options are equally valued or if choices are purely random. The probability shifts quite rapidly in accordance with a relative preference if the intensity of choice is very high. To put it another way, as b increases from zero to infinity the function $f(x, b)$ goes from a horizontal line at ½ to a function that is zero for x < 0, ½ at x = 0, one for x > 0. As the intensity of choice increases from zero to infinity the probability that agent i chooses +1 when $h_i(t) > 0$ (+1 is "better") goes to unity as b goes to infinity. Equations (3.2a and 3.2b) give a convenient way to model increasing precision in choice as the random variability of an agent's preferences decreases. We shall see that the interaction between peer effects and precision of choice creates interesting social dynamics.

We can illustrate how this type of model works by using the example of scientific paradigms (Brock and Durlauf 1999). Let $v(+1)$, $v(-1)$ denote the deterministic parts of the utilities or values imputed by each scientist to theory +1 and theory −1 respectively. Assume first that these deterministic values are the same for all scientists. Bring in the peer effect within the scientific community by the following formulation,

$$(3.3) \quad du \equiv u(+1) - u(-1) = v(+1) - C(+1 - a(t))^2 - \left[v(-1) - C(-1 - a(t))^2 \right]$$

$$= v(+1) - v(-1) + 4\,Ca(t) \equiv h_{i,t} + 4\,Ca(t),$$

where

$$(3.4) \quad a(t) \equiv \frac{1}{N} \sum_{i=1}^{N} \omega_{i,t},$$

and $\omega_{i,t} \in \{+1, -1\}$ is the actual choice of agent i at date t and a(t) is the average choice of the group at time t.

Now the value of a theory to a scientist includes not only its intrinsic worth but also "C," the cost to a scientist who deviates from the paradigm currently held by most of the scientific community as reflected by its average choice. This cost is well known to any scientist who has tried to publish a paper in a journal whose editors follow the entrenched paradigm. Similarly, Courtney Brown (1995) discussed the role of such peer effects in creating non-linearities in changes of voters' feelings toward candidates.

Another important example arises in modeling party discipline and party loyalty in legislative voting. The cost "C" represents the cost to a legislator from deviating from the party line (which is represented by the average vote "a") on a particular piece of legislation. This cost could be imposed by the party leadership. The parameter "b" captures the intensity of the representative's position on the issue, for (+1) or against, (−1) a particular piece of legislation, whereas the deterministic part, $h_{i,t}$, captures the systematic part of the representative's preferences. For example, "b" could be quite large for a prominent issue about which the constituency cares greatly but "b" could be quite small for issues that are of little importance to voters or on which the constituency is evenly divided. Here, peer effects induced by party discipline dynamically interacting with issue dispersion within legislative districts could cause a legislature to exhibit punctuated behavior much like a scientific paradigm shift.

Let us reiterate the meaning of (3.3) and (3.4) in the context of scientific theory choice. The "systematic" difference in "utility" to scientist i at date t between theory +1 and theory −1 is the difference in v's adjusted for a peer effect where the scientist is "punished" for deviating from the average choice (3.4) of the scientific community. For example, if most of the scientists are choosing theory −1, the peer effect punishes scientist i for choosing theory +1. In this case scientist i will have to prefer theory +1 quite strongly to pay the price of breaking away from the scientific consensus. This peer effect creates a consensus that "tightens" as the intensity of choice b increases toward perfect precision of choice—that is, as b increases toward infinity. High values of b create "social traps" and historical "path dependence" even when the peer effect C is small and even when theory −1 is inferior to theory +1. A decrease in value of b can "open" the basin of attraction of a bad outcome and allow the dynamical system to "escape" such a bad basin of attraction. Here, the basin of attraction of a stable state of a dynamical system is the set of all initial conditions that carries the dynamical system's action to that stable state. I shall develop these ideas below.

There are several ways to formulate the dynamics of choice from this point on. One way is to assume that each agent i forms expectations about the average choice a(t), call it a(i, t), and chooses action according to

$$(3.5) \quad P\{i \text{ choose} +1\} = \frac{\exp\left[b(h_{i,t} + 4Ca(i,t))\right]}{\exp\left[b(h_{i,t} + 4Ca(i,t))\right] + 1}.$$

As before, the probability of an individual's choice will depend on his or her assessment of total value, which includes a peer effect estimated on the basis of the individual's expectations regarding the consensus position. This raises the issue of how to model the dynamics of expectation formation of a(i, t) for each agent. Some simple cases are

(3.6) $a_i(t) = a(t-1) + \phi a_i(t-1)$ (adaptive expectations), $0 < \phi < 1$

(3.7) $a_i(t) = a(t)$ (perfect foresight).

Let us illustrate by assuming $h_i(t) = h$ for all agents i and for all time periods t, meaning that there is perfect agreement about the relative merits of the competing paradigms. Assume expectations of all agents about the average behavior of the community are given by (3.6) with

(3.8) $a_i(t) = a(t-1)$.

That is, every agent i expects the community-wide average chosen next period to be the same as it was last period. Then, except for random variation resulting from very small communities,

$$(3.9)\quad a(t) = P\{i \text{ choose} + 1\} - P\{i \text{ choose} - 1\} = \frac{\{\exp[bh + b4Ca(t-1)] - 1\}}{Z(t)}$$

(3.10) $Z(t) = \{\exp[bh + b4Ca(t-1)] + 1\}$.

Call the difference

(3.11) $a(t) = P\{i \text{ choose} + 1\} - P\{i \text{ choose} - 1\}$,

the "net choice for +1." If the net choice is unity, all are choosing +1; if the net choice is zero, then ½ are choosing +1 and ½ are choosing −1; if the net choice is −1, all are choosing −1. In the science theory choice, context equation (3.9) says that the net choice in period t is deterministically related to the net choice in period t − 1, that is,

(3.12) $a(t) = g(a(t-1); b,h,C)$

for the deterministic function g given by (3.9) above. This is a difference equation that represents the dynamics of the consensus choice. The equation (3.12) has been written using notation that draws attention to the role of the three key parameters, the intensity of choice b, the difference in the systematic parts of the utilities, h, and the size of the peer effect, C. These three parameters determine the "shape" of the function g(a(t − 1); b, h, C) and the behavior of the dynamics.

The graph of g, Figure 3.1 below, depicts the function g on the vertical axis and a on the horizontal axis. It shows how the shape of the function changes as

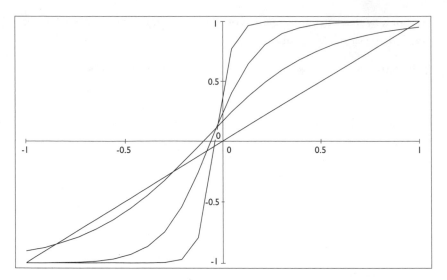

Figure 3.1. The function g( ) as a function of a for differing values of b and C.

the key parameters change. Notice how the graphed function looks like a low sloping grade for small values of b and C but assumes a steeper grade as b and C increase and finally becomes a sharp "cliff" as b and C become very large. It is this behavior that generates the alternative stable states, which are represented by points crossing the 45-degree line.

As drawn in Figure 3.1, there are two stable equilibrium points where $a(t) = a(t-1)$, one near a unanimous choice for -1, the other near a unanimous choice for $+1$. They are separated by an unstable equilibrium point near zero. The function g increases as $a(t-1)$ increases for all values of b greater than zero. An increase in h shifts the function up, and this generates a bias toward $+1$ as h becomes positive and increases. If both choices are equally valued, that is, if $h = 0$, an increase in b "twists" the function around the value zero and it becomes a sharp threshold increase from -1 to $+1$ as $a(t-1)$ moves from negative to positive no matter how small a move it makes. This implies that the consensus will stick at -1 or $+1$, depending on initial conditions. Also note that if $b = 0$, $g(a; 0, h, C) = 0$ for all a's so (3.12) just stays at the fixed point $a(t) = 0$ and the net choice is always zero. This makes sense: on the one hand, if each agent simply randomizes over the choices -1, $+1$ with no bias toward either of them, one would expect the system to settle quickly to a community net choice of zero, that is, ½ of them choosing -1, ½ of them choosing $+1$. By contrast, if choice is extremely precise, that is, b is huge and positive, then even a tiny amount of peer pressure, $C > 0$, can create "social traps" at both -1 and $+1$, even when h is positive. For example, if $a(t-1)$ is near -1, and

(3.13) $h + Ca(t-1) < 0,$

the system remains "stuck" at a point near -1 at date t, if $a(t-1) < 0$, even though choice $+1$ is preferred because $h > 0$. The dynamics of $a(t)$ given by equation (3.12) above can display alternative stable states that are "sticky" in the sense that once in a stable state, it is difficult to escape.

We sum up what we have learned so far as follows:

Result 3.1: If the group size N is sufficiently large and each member of the group always expects that $a_i(t) = a(t-1)$, then at each moment the average choice, $a(t)$, will always satisfy (3.12). If the group holds rational point expectations, meaning that they all share the same forecast of next period's $a(t)$ and it turns out to be correct, then all rational point expectations must satisfy the equation

(3.12.RE) $a^* = g(a^*; b, h, C)$, over all time periods.

This stable solution is unique if bC is small enough, meaning that either peer pressure or the precision of choice or both is small enough. It also is unique if the absolute value of h, $|h|$, is large enough, meaning that one or another theory is strongly preferred. It is one of two (locally stable) solutions of equation (3.12.RE) if the absolute value of h, $|h|$ is small enough and bC exceeds a

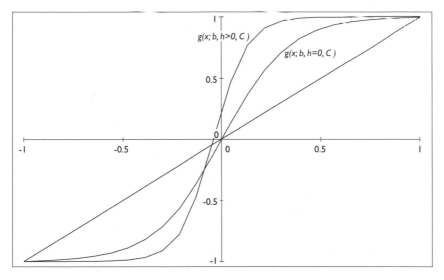

Figure 3.2. The function g(x) as a function of x for differing values of h.

threshold value. Then, though the intrinsic preference is small, peer pressure or the intensity of decision can push the consensus toward one or the other choice. This result is shown in Figure 3.2 above, which plots the function g(x; b, h, C) as a function of x, the average choice. Note the following properties:

1. The function g(x; b, h, C) increases in x first at an increasing rate, as the average choice approaches zero, then at a decreasing rate for all values of b, h, C;
2. The function g(x; b, h, C) is zero at b = 0, when choice is purely random, for all values of x, h, C;
3. At infinite b, when choice is precise, and h = 0, the function g(x; b, h, C) is zero for negative x, is equal to ½ for x = 0 and is unity for positive x. Then, initial conditions dominate. Thus, Figure 3.2 shows that for h = 0 the function crosses the 45-degree line at three points when b is large enough.

Therefore, if bC is large enough, there are alternative stable states for the difference equation (3.12) when h is close enough to zero. Consider the following example. Suppose h has been negative at a constant value for a while so that the current equilibrium is negative. Let now $h = h_t$ gradually increase, becoming zero for the first time at time t^* and continuing to increase for $t > t^*$. The social optimum is for a switch to occur at $t > t^*$, when the intrinsic value of decision +1 becomes superior. But it is easy to see from graphing the dynamics that the system is trapped (for the case where bC is large enough) in a negative stable state, in which the option −1 continues to be chosen. There are three fixed points of the dynamics (3.12). The middle one, the locally unstable one, blocks progress toward the socially desirable positive steady state because near that point, the consensus moves toward one or another extreme state. See Figure 3.3 below.

In the science paradigm case this outcome represents the sluggishness of the scientific community in adopting a better paradigm because of peer effects created by the past dominance of the old (now inferior) paradigm. The superiority of the new paradigm h(t) must increase to a rather large positive critical value before a "window" is opened up through which the dynamics can "escape" the low-level "trap" and evolve toward the better choice. This corresponds to the disappearance of the unstable equilibrium point when h increases sufficiently or bC diminishes. As h continues to increase the dynamics now move rapidly toward the positive alternative stable state. Once the dynamics are in the basin of attraction of the positive steady state, it will stick there even if a new paradigm appears to assume the role of +1 and the current newly established paradigm plays the role of −1. This type of dynamics requires a big push to get the system out of a historically determined, locally stable state toward an alternative that is now superior.

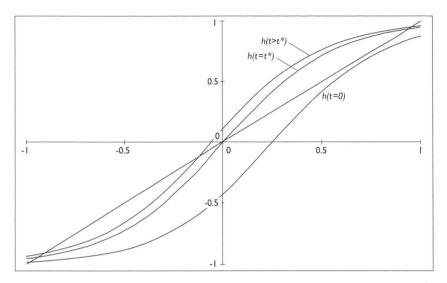

Figure 3.3. The function g( ) as a function of x for varying values of h(t).

I turn now to a type of dynamics that is not sticky but where the stable states satisfy the same equation as (3.12.RE).

STATISTICAL MECHANICS AND SOCIAL "PHASE TRANSITIONS": ESCAPE FROM "STICKINESS"

The second model takes into account the fact that a(t) is a random variable that induces correlations among the agents' choices because of the peer effects indicated by C. Interactions between these correlations and the intensity of choice b produce dynamics that differ dramatically from the previous ones. The first system assumed that, conditional upon expectations of a(t), which we denoted by $a_i(t)$, the choice made by agent i is independent of other agents' choices. This assumption ignores the fact that since a(t) is the average of all agents' choices and a(t) influences each agent's choice, agents' choices are correlated if there are few agents.

As a consequence, equation (3.12.RE) will be replaced by a result that gives the same equation for the stable states, a*, but will lead to different behaviors if there are multiple solutions of equation (3.11.RE). If h is not zero the steady state will be the one with the same algebraic sign as that of h. So, if h > 0, the stable consensus will favor +1 and if h < 0, the consensus will favor −1. If h is zero a mixture equal to ½ times the negative solution plus ½ times, the positive solution will be selected. Therefore, if h changes sign (no matter how small its absolute value) there will be an abrupt and truly discontinuous change that we shall call a social phase transition, using the language of statistical mechanics. The consensus will shift suddenly in response to a change in preferences, unlike the behavior produced in the earlier system. Some mathematical notation is needed to state and explain this result. Less mathematically inclined readers can just skip to the following verbal explanation.

MINIMAL MODELS OF SOCIAL CHOICE
DYNAMICS: SOCIAL PHASE TRANSITIONS

We can focus attention on a single point in time and drop "t" from the notation in order to simplify it. Then, we formulate a probability model:

$$(3.14) \quad P\{(\omega(1), \omega(2),...,\omega(N))\} = \frac{\exp[bU]}{Z},$$

$$(3.15) \quad U = \sum_{i=1}^{N} [u(\omega(i)) - C(\omega(i) - a^*)^2], a^* \equiv \frac{1}{N} \sum_{i=1}^{N} [\omega(i)],$$

(3.16) Z = a normalization factor

that makes the sum of P over all 2^N configurations of the N agent's choices between +1 and −1 equal to unity, as required in a probability distribution. Equation (3.14) represents the probability of a particular social configuration of agents' choices $(\omega(1), \omega(2),..., \omega(N))$. For example, it might represent the probability that all agents choose +1. Since each agent has two choices, −1 or +1, and there are N agents, there are 2^N of these possible configurations. As before, $C(\omega(i) - a^*)^2$ represents the "punishment" for deviating from the group average. However, now a* is the random variable given in (3.15), the sum of the probabilistic choices of individual agents, instead of a deterministic belief about the value of the group average. The quantity U sums the systematic parts of the values of each agent in the group, as a social planner acting for the group as a whole might do (Brock and Durlauf 2001a, 2001b). The intensity of choice "b" now refers to the random part of group preferences instead of the random part of preferences of each individual agent as before. The system (3.14) and (3.15) generates very different behavior as N increases even though the equation for the limiting behavior of the average is unchanged from that in the first model. Consider the simplest case, in which all agents have the same preference; that is,

(3.17) h_i = h, for all i = 1, 2, . . . , N.

Since $\omega^2 = 1$, whether the choice is -1 or $+1$, a little algebra can transform (3.14) into the form

$$(3.18) \quad P\{(\omega(1), \omega(2), ..., \omega(N))\} = \frac{\exp\left[b \sum_{i=1}^{N} (h + Ja^*)\omega(i) \right]}{Z},$$

where the normalization factor has changed but we still call it Z and J = 2C. Using this notation, it turns out that the limiting value of the group average, "a," satisfies,

$$(3.19) \quad a = g(a, b, h, 2J),$$

where g is the same function as in (3.12) above, and where the starred solution a* in that equation is now the solution of (3.19) with the same sign as h when there are multiple solutions of (3.19). That is to say, the stable consensus will reflect the group's preference.

The reason why the quantity "2J" appears in (3.19) instead of "J" as in (3.12.RE) is because (3.14) and (3.19) take into account the fact that each agent i impacts all other agents and each of those other agents also impacts i. The model considered in (3.12.RE) is like a noncooperative game in which each agent only takes into account the impact of the other agents upon his or her decision. Hence a "2" appears in (3.14) and (3.19), giving more weight to the costs of deviance than in the earlier model.[4]

The appropriate solution that satisfies (3.19) turns out to be the one that maximizes v(N) = V(N)/N, where $V(N) \equiv E\{\max U(\omega)\}$, the maximum expected utility over all configurations of possible group choices. This is analogous to the net benefit per capita criterion of conventional welfare analysis (Anderson, de Palma, and Thisse 1992; Brock and Durlauf 2001a). In this discrete choice case, however, randomness adds a new element. The maximum value collapses to the conventional welfare measure only if the intensity of choice, "b," is infinite, since then choices correspond to the conventional deterministic case.

For bJ > 1 the limiting inclusive value per capita has two local maxima, one corresponding to a negative group consensus and the other to a positive consensus. The global maximum shifts from the negative one to the positive one as h passes through zero from negative to positive. This corresponds to a dramatic change in dynamic behavior from the case above. In this present case there will be a sharp discontinuity in group behavior as preferences shift from negative to positive. We summarize the discussion up to this point by stating:

Result 3.2: Let bJ > 1 and let h ≡ h(t) slowly increase from negative to positive as t increases. That is, suppose h(t) < 0, for t < t* and h(t) > 0, for t > t*. Then a*(t) is the negative solution of (3.19) for t < t*, and a*(t) jumps to the positive solution of (3.19) for t > t*. Hence, for the case bJ > 1, the group consensus choice jumps discontinuously from the smallest solution of (3.19) to the largest solution of (3.19) the moment h passes from negative to positive. Similarly, if h slowly decreased from positive to negative there would be a discontinuous drop from the largest solution of (3.19) to the smallest solution of (3.19).

In the case bJ < 1 there is only one solution of (3.19) and no such discontinuity in the dynamics appears as h passes from negative to positive or vice versa. The system would "stick" indefinitely in whatever consensus represented its initial condition.

In terms of the scientific paradigm example, with sufficient peer pressure and precision of choice, this implies that as soon as the new paradigm had overtaken the older one in terms of its perceived intrinsic merit, the scientific community would immediately shift to a new strong consensus in its favor. This behavior contrasts sharply with the behavior in the initial model, even in the case of rational expectations. In that case, a*(t) is stuck at a negative solution of (3.19) until h(t), the perceived intrinsic merit, becomes so large and positive that the graph of (3.19) is lifted high enough so that the middle solution of (3.19) disappears to open a "window" so the dynamics (3.19) can "tunnel through" toward the desirable positive solution. See Figure 3.4 below, in which the two curves represent situations in which only one stable state exists, either negative or positive. To put it another way, the "dead hand" of history lies heavily on the dynamics in Result 3.1, but the dynamics of Result 3.2 escapes the "dead hand" of history and is able to react immediately to what is socially optimal currently. We call the dynamics of Result 3.1 "mean field" dynamics because these dynamics result from agents forming point expectations of the system-wide average, which is really a random variable. Point expectation formation shuts off the correlations in the Result 3.2 dynamics so the phase transition property of Result 3.2 is lost.

What explains the dramatic difference between Result 3.1 and Result 3.2? In the latter case, the correct choice of the solutions for a that satisfy (3.19) is the one maximizing the function v(N) (Brock and Durlauf 2001a, 257). Now call that function $W(\{H_i(t)\}, x; b, J)$ the limiting inclusive value per capita. Here x represents variable values of a, the group average. Consider the simplest case, in which $H_i(t) \equiv h$ for all agents for all dates, so that $W \equiv W(h, x; b, J)$. The function W has multiple local maxima in x when bJ > 1. As stated above, the average choice of the community, namely a*, will correspond to the global maximum of W. When $H_i(t) \equiv h = 0$ for all agents, and bJ > 1, this function, $W(0, x; b, J)$, has

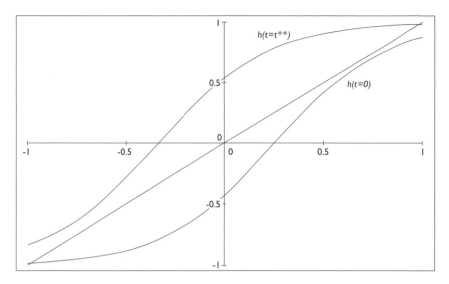

Figure 3.4. The function g(x) as a function of x showing negative and positive stable solutions.

two global maxima, one positive and one negative. Consequently, the limiting value of a* is a mixture with ½ of the probability on each of the two global maxima. When $H_1(t) \equiv h$ becomes slightly positive, the positive global maximum value of W becomes slightly bigger than the negative one, so the value of a* "leaps" from the equally weighted solution to one based solely on this positive and unique global maximum. However, should "h" become slightly negative, the new global maximum would now be the negative one, so a* "drops" discontinuously to the negative outcome. One can imagine an undulating surface with two local maxima, the larger of which is always chosen, as shown in Figure 3.5.

The lesson here is that correlation among agents' choices can lead to rapid shifts in the whole group in response to changes in underlying preferences. By contrast, the earlier model reflects behavior that can get stuck in a bad equilibrium or in a good equilibrium because of fixed expectations. Nonetheless, if parameters such as b or C slowly diminish so that the earlier system moves to a configuration that has only one equilibrium position, then rapid change can occur even in that system when multiple equilibria are replaced by a unique equilibrium. For example, suppose that while the party is in opposition to a measure that each agent recognizes to be worthwhile, the penalty for deviating from the party line diminishes. At some point, the cost of deviance becomes so small that each agent feels liberated to "vote his conscience," allowing a new,

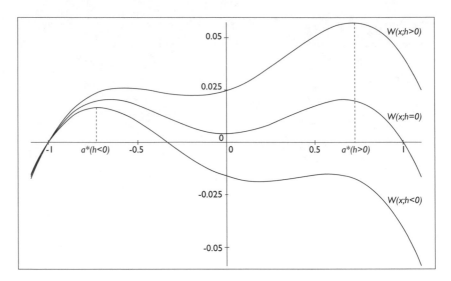

Figure 3.5. Stable values of g( ) for h < 0, h = 0, and h > 0.

strong majority to emerge. How might one be able to detect in practice the difference between a process governed by Result 3.1 and one governed by Result 3.2? Models of changing correlations that generate phase transitions rather than "mean field" models may better represent situations where conditional independence is replaced by dependence. Dependence can be created by "opinion leaders" (which could be media coverage rather than individual activists or policy entrepreneurs) who are exceptionally persuasive to individual agents and effective in coordinating their actions. Probability models of the form 3.14 and 3.15 are a useful way of capturing the effect of such leaders in increasing correlations amongst individual choices and also increasing b, the intensity or precision of choice. The implication is that effective leaders may be able to bring about rapid and discontinuous, even revolutionary, phase transitions. Think of Chairman Mao.

What evidence would reveal that a particular social process is more like Result 3.2 than Result 3.1? In the latter, each agent acts independently, after forming an expectation about what the group will do and the resulting peer effect on him or her, with the expectations being fulfilled in equilibrium. In the latter, the process unfolds as if some mechanism chose the configuration of group actions that optimized group welfare, respecting each agent's own objective but penalizing her deviation from the group average. In both cases there may be multiple equilibria, but in the latter, no mechanism is assumed that would lead to the best outcome. Possibly, we might expect a dynamic like Result 3.2 to operate when a leader can coordinate the preponderance of agents onto the best equilibrium but a dynamic more like Result 3.1 to hold when factional leaders compete or when no one or nothing plays the role of coordinator.

Also, could one use these results to help predict an emerging tipping point or another abrupt change, social phase transition, or regime shift? These questions are very hard to answer.[5] Attempting to predict a tipping point is rather like a doctor attempting to predict the exact moment a patient in bad cardiac health will have a heart attack. The doctor can only indicate that the patient has characteristics that suggest a heart attack will happen with high probability. He or she cannot say exactly when it will happen. Nonetheless, Result 3.2 suggests ways to make a social system more nimble and less sticky by strengthening the correlations amongst agents' actions.[6] This amounts to increasing positive feedbacks, perhaps by reducing random variability in agents' choices. For example, increasing the transparency with which agents make their choices might in some circumstances lead to increased correlation among them.

Results 3.1 and 3.2 shed light on what can happen as the result of gradual changes in $\{\{h_i(t)\}, b, J\}$. Recall that "b" measures the intensity of choice. A common strategy in policy debates appears to be one that lowers b and biases the h's away from the "truth" by sowing confusion about the issue and making false claims. Clearly, if such activity keeps $bJ < 1$ and $h < 1$, social action toward the desirable equilibrium will not crystallize and there will not be a phase transition like that of Result 3.2 to escape from a low-level equilibrium trap created because the system is in the basin of attraction of an inferior but locally stable steady state. For example, in the debate over manmade climate change, "scientists" working for special interests have muddied the waters by trying to direct attention toward other superficially plausible alternative causes, such as natural cycles, by questioning the measurements, or by contesting the consequences. The chapter by Lee Lane in this volume suggests that this seems to have happened particularly on the issue of global warming because the effects of climate change remain mostly in the future and hence are not evident.

On the other hand, transparency can be increased through dynamic and forceful scientific leadership and public education campaigns to clear away junk science and illuminate good science. Reputable scientific organizations like the National Academy of Sciences could play a major role in increasing "b" as well as removing bias in $\{h_i(t)\}$ if they could get their message to the public. Public media such as National Public Radio and the Public Broadcasting System could also play a key role here if they could overcome their tendency to seek "balance" by presenting equally extreme and distorted viewpoints on both sides of an issue.

If "b" is very large, even a very small amount of peer pressure (induced perhaps just by people communicating through their social networks) can cause bJ to be larger than unity. Politicians have begun using the Internet extensively to promote "meet-up" interactions among their "base" constituency in order to increase the correlation and intensity of choice. This cuts both ways. In the case of Result 3.2's dynamics, making bJ > 1 helps the system jump quickly to the preferred position. In the case of the dynamics of Result 3.1, increasing bJ can make the system more sticky, even at an inferior basin of attraction inherited from the past.

What observable indicators or signatures might tell us which dynamic is actually operating? One approach might be to look for direct evidence from surveys that ask people whether they have incentives to choose actions being chosen by others in the group and whether those incentives would change if the group chose opposite actions. A second is to look for indirect evidence such as observations of large variation of group outcomes across groups that seem homogeneous with respect to relevant characteristics.

In that context, now we will consider another result that will probably not be familiar to social scientists. Social scientists are familiar with normal distributions. Most social scientists are familiar with central limit theorems proving that a normal distribution is the limit for appropriately scaled sums of random variables as their number increases. But in settings like Result 3.2, limiting distributions with "fatter" tails than normal will sometimes emerge. Frank Baumgartner's chapter in this volume provides empirical support for this proposition, finding that extreme environmental policy events occur more frequently than would "normally" be expected.

Result 3.3 (adapted from Amaro de Matos and Perez 1991): Assume that bJ > 1 and that the variance of the distribution of $\{h_i\}$ across agents is always finite. We omit t in the notation but make the number of agents, N, explicit. We define a random variable X based on the average deviation from the group norm for each date t,

$$\frac{\sum_{i=1}^{N}[\omega(i)-a^*]}{N^{1/2}} \to X,$$

Here the random variable X is distributed as a mixture of normal distributions and the quantity a* maximizes an inclusive value expression analogous to that in the case where all h's are the same. The limiting behavior of this normalized sum of deviations from the mean is "unconventional" for the case $bJ > 1$. Not only does the "leaping" behavior of Result 3.2 emerge but also an unusual limit distribution of normalized sums. This limit distribution has fatter tails than the normal distribution, implying that extreme events are more frequent than would "normally" be expected. This result may lurk behind the common observation in social sciences of large variation in behavior across measurably similar communities and social groups. However, if $bJ < 1$, the limit distribution X is normally distributed.

We are now ready to ask what insights these models can offer in understanding the punctuated policy equilibrium phenomena discussed by Baumgartner (2003) and in building models that illuminate what Jones, Baumgartner, and True (1998) call policy macro-punctuations. Their analysis of a large dataset on federal budgetary changes found that in addition to the typical year-to-year fluctuations in program funding, which have moderated over the post-war years, there have been a relatively few large abrupt budgetary changes in response to some combination of internal dynamics and changing external circumstances. These macro-punctuations do not appear to be attributable to changes in partisan control of government, to surges in public opinion or to fluctuations in economic growth.

Suppose we model action on a particular item in the federal budget as −1 for the status quo and +1 for a change away from the status quo and let $H_i(t)$ denote the difference in preference for legislator i for this particular item at date t. Our first type of model (Result 3.1) produces alternative stable states by the internal dynamics produced by penalties from deviating from the group position. The same dynamics can result if one legislator's benefit is increased when more legislators take the same action. Since both mechanisms produce positive feedback, it is not surprising that they generate similar results. If such forces are strong enough and the intensity of choice is high enough so that the product, bJ, crosses a threshold, the status quo for the particular budgetary item or particular policy issue would prevail, unless the preference $H_i(t)$ changes dramatically away from the status quo for many legislators at the same time. Since such an event would be rare, macro-punctuations would occur infrequently.

Consider finding (b) above. The internal dynamics caused by $bJ > 1$ in our model tells us that there will be times when the status quo has been protected by negative feedback forces of conformity or complementarity, even as $H_i(t)$ trends up away from the status quo for a substantial number of legislators. Result 3.1 suggests that occasionally (possibly quite rarely) the basin of attraction of the smaller stable state, maintaining the status quo, is escaped by the dynamic process, at which point a macro-punctuation would ensue that might appear inexplicable by any dramatic change in the policy "fundamentals." Public opinion, "policy learning," or economic change might affect the preferences $H_i(t)$ of each legislator but it might surprise an observer to see the legislature as a whole respond dramatically, that is, a macro-punctuated response, to a seemingly small change in the $H_i(t)$, as the U.S. Congress did in dropping the ITQ moratorium, as recounted in the chapter by Robert Repetto and Richard Allen. But the interaction between internal dynamics together with external changes "driving" the system can produce these dynamics. Slow-moving variables, whether social, economic, or demographic, may drive the values of the $H_i(t)$ to a point where some kind of "threshold" is crossed.

Baumgartner (2003) discusses the following empirical signatures consistent with complex dynamics in policymaking processes:

a. The tone of media coverage of pesticides trended from mostly positive to distinctly negative, with a rather sharp drop in the 1950s when an upward trend in total coverage occurred.
b. Budgetary changes in the U.S. federal budget over the period 1947–2000 have thicker tails than a normal distribution would.
c. In a sample of issues in 1996, Baumgarter's team found that the number of lobbyists is highly skewed across issues, with one single issue occupying 17 percent of lobbyists.
d. The number of anti–death penalty stories showed no trend over the period 1960–98 but jumped up abruptly in 1999.

All such phenomena could be generated by appropriately parameterized versions of our models. Although it would be a full research project to build models that fully explain the findings of teams such as Baumgartner's in policy science, we hope to have indicated the potential usefulness of the kinds of models presented in this chapter.

CONCENTRATED SPECIAL-INTEREST GROUPS
VERSUS DIFFUSE GROUPS

Next, models are presented that focus on the structure of social interaction within groups in producing pressure on policymakers and political systems. The models discussed above are much too simple: most policy changes produce losers and winners but the initial models only had one group, winners, and the models explained how the system could get stuck in an inferior equilibrium. The much harder and more important problem is that of inducing policy change when the benefits to change outweigh the losses but the losers are better organized for collective action than the winners.[7] Fortunately, the simple, binary, discrete-choice models introduced above can still be used to model the movement of an agent i from a state of "latency" (which we denote by -1) to "entering the game" (which we will denote by $+1$). This leads to a "two-stage" game in which the first stage is the decision whether or not to enter the game, and the second stage is the choice of the magnitude of effort to expend after entry. The goal will be to understand the ability of concentrated special-interest groups to mobilize and to deliver more action than diffuse groups can.

A special-interest group is a group that is proposing to use or is currently using the government to obtain a benefit, b, where the cost to the whole society of giving this benefit is $c > b$.

Examples include: (1) tariffs, export subsidies, and other "protective" measures, where the cost of such benefits to the public is greater than the benefits received by the industries sheltered from competition; (2) subsidies to agricultural interests, where the costs to the public exceed the value of the agricultural subsidies; (3) the assignment of water "rights" to agricultural interests whose water uses are less valuable than alternative uses (Milgrom and Roberts 1992, 9); grazing rights and timber concessions on public lands awarded at subsidized rates, reducing public revenues and increasing ecological damages. The general pattern is that of "rent-seeking behavior," wherein one group uses the political system not only to take resources from the rest of society but also, in many cases, to impose deadweight losses on others that may even be larger than the value of the resources they capture.

Suppose we define politics as the authoritative allocation of value and economics as the competitive allocation of value. An interest group mustering political pressure faces the same structural problem as a group mustering the power to police its jointly owned common property or any group organizing to provide a commonly supplied local public good for itself. A key problem is that the group must be able to police free riders effectively to ensure that each member who potentially benefits contributes to the joint effort and bears a share of the costs. The superior ability of concentrated groups to wield political power might be due to characteristics of their livelihoods or communities that enable them to organize more effectively, to police free riders, and to muster resources to pressure the political system: Members of the group might be in a repeated economic relationship with fellow members. For example, local lobster fishermen deliver to the same markets, share the same docks, and work the same coastline. Also, members of the group might need access to a common joint factor of production for which there are no close substitutes. For example, surgeons need access to operating rooms at the local hospitals and the goodwill of fellow physicians for referrals. Real estate agents need access to the formal network of the Multiple Listing Service as well as their informal network (also known as "social capital").

This pressure-group problem has much the same analytical structure as the prisoner's dilemma studied by Axelrod (1984, 1997).[8] Organizing a political pressure group is structurally similar to self-organizing a group to provide a public good for the group to use or to manage as a common property resource. Ostrom's (1990) message is that, contrary to the metaphor of the "tragedy of the commons," many groups have successfully self-organized workable management of their commons without the intervention of a central authority. This optimistic message that groups can and do self-organize to solve commons problems implies that special-interest groups are also able to solve their own "commons problem" of self-organizing and applying political pressure to capture authoritative allocations of value. The general finding is this: groups that are compact, homogeneous, and whose actions are internally transparent are able to get political benefits that are less than their cost to the diffusely organized public. Therefore, only such groups are defined as "special-interest groups."

A simple way to analyze the contest between concentrated versus diffuse groups is to use "action supply functions" on both sides of the struggle.[9] Consider two groups, "gainers" (group 1) and "losers" (group 2) who supply pressure on the political system for and against policy at level $T(t-1)$ at date t according to

(3.20) $x_i(t) = F(S_i(t; T(t-1)), X1_i(t), Y1_i(t); a,b)$

(3.21) $y_j(t) = G(C_j(t; T(t-1)), Y2_j(t), X2_j(t); A,B)$

where $x_i(t)$ and $y_j(t)$ are individual contributions by gainer i and loser j at date t, $S_i(t;T(t-1))$. $C_j(t; T(t-1))$ are gains and losses to gainer i and loser j when policy is set at level $T(t-1)$. Also, $X1_i(t)$, $Y1_j(t)$ are member i's expectations regarding total contributions by the rest of group 1 and expectations of i regarding total contributions in group 2. Similar interpretation holds for Y2 and X2. Furthermore, a, b and A, B denote effectiveness and noticeability parameters perceived by individual members of groups 1 and 2. A member's contribution F is assumed to increase with the payoff S, increase with the expected contribution of other group members X1, and decrease with expected competing contributions Y1. The contribution F is also assumed to increase with effectiveness a and noticeability b even if S is small relative to the cost of individual effort for i. This last assumption captures the idea of "noticeability" of i by other members of the group. Similar properties hold for G. Assume that[10]

$$(3.20') \quad x_i(t) \text{ solves } \left\{ S_i(t;T(t-1)) \left[\frac{a}{(x + X1_i(t))} + \frac{b}{x} \right] = 1 \right\}$$

$$(3.21') \quad y_j(t) \text{ solves } \left\{ C_j(t;T(t-1)) \left[\frac{A}{(y + Y2_j(t))} + \frac{B}{y} \right] = 1 \right\}.$$

If one solves for Nash non-cooperative equilibrium to get reduced-form supply functions, then for a plausible set of game-theoretic structures, it will be true that if the total stakes for one side increase, that side applies more pressure. Also, if the total stakes on one side remain constant but its distribution among the group's members becomes more unequal (more concentrated), then that side applies more pressure.

This analysis can be easily extended to include cases where there is a slow-moving variable, such as a slow erosion of political power by one side of the struggle. The result can be an abrupt change in the outcome, related to shifts in the relative contributions of contending groups. This may be hard to link to observable "fundamentals," much like the "surprises" caused by a slow-moving variable in previous models. Empirical work in this area has had mixed success due to the presence of many confounding events and political forces that make it difficult to isolate the effects of interest-group pressure on the political outcome.

Building on the previous assumptions, the political system is assumed to choose the policy outcome T(t) according to

$$(3.22) \quad T(t) = P(T(t-1), X(t), Y(t))$$

where

$$(3.23) \quad X(t) = \sum_{i=1}^{N1} x_i(t), \ Y(t) = \sum_{j=1}^{N2} y_j(t),$$

Here the function P is assumed to increase in T(t − 1) and X(t) and decrease in Y(t). That is, the policy outcome is influenced by the magnitude of contributions of the two contending sides but there is an in-built momentum to policy decisions.

Assume that payoffs S and C are equal across all i and j respectively, assume rational point expectations, and use (3.20'), (3.21') to obtain

$$(3.20'')\ x(t) = S(T(t-1))\left[\frac{a}{N_1} + b\right], X(t) \equiv x(t)N_1 = S(T(t-1))[a + bN_1]$$

$$(3.21'')\ y(t) = C(T(t-1))\left[\frac{A}{N_2} + B\right], Y(t) \equiv y(t)N_2 = C(T(t-1))[A + BN_1],$$

$$(3.24)\ T(t) = P(T(t-1), X(t), Y(t)).$$

Social welfare at t is given by

$$(3.25)\ W(T(t-1)) \equiv N_1 S(T(t-1)) - N_2 C(T(t-1))$$

which we assume is optimal at $T = 0$. That is, we assume that the policy in question is an unwarranted and distorting government interference. Make the natural assumption that $S(0) = C(0) = W(0) = 0$. We obtain via substitution a "reduced-form" dynamic equation for the time path of policy outcomes,

$$(3.26)\ T(t) = F(T(t-1)) \equiv P(T(t-1), S(T(t-1))[a + bN_1],$$
$$C(T(t-1))[A + BN_2]).$$

Even though this formulation is simple, it is useful for focusing attention on what forces impede optimum policies. Optimal policy is $T^*(t) = 0$ for all t. Bad policy is positive T. We are interested in locating conditions for emergence of bad policy from a baseline of zero and eliminating bad policy once entrenched. These conditions are that good policy, $T^* = 0$, is an equilibrium state. However, the equilibrium is unstable, leading to bad outcomes, if $F'(0) > 1$. Then, whenever at the initial period there is some distortion, no matter how small (that is, $T(0) > 0$) the dynamic moves $T(t)$ toward increasingly bad outcomes. The optimum is locally stable if $|F'(0)| < 1$. Then, any initial distortion tends to be reversed. Assume instead that $F'(0) > 1$ and $F' > 0$ for all T. In order to prevent policy outcomes from becoming indefinitely worse once a single error is made, $F' < 1$ must hold for large enough T. It is plausible to assume that this is true because if special-interest distortions became large enough, the incumbents would be positioned so far away from the median voter that it would be easy for challengers to attack them. This would eventually hold true even taking into account the well-known incumbent advantage in U.S. electoral contests. Therefore, we assume $F'(T) < 1$ for T large enough, which means that if $F'(0) > 1$, so that bad policies get established, there will probably be at least one locally stable but "bad" equilibrium policy $T^* > 0$.

Consider, for example, an industry seeking a protective tariff T against imports. Because tariffs cause deadweight losses, $S(T) < C(T)$, the costs outweigh the benefits, so the socially optimal tariff is $T = 0$. Then why are there tariffs? Typically, the consumer group is very large with small losses for each household, so the noticeability coefficient "B" is plausibly zero for the consumer side. For example, no consumer is ever punished for failing to lobby against a sugar tariff that raises prices on all goods containing sweeteners. Free-rider problems loom very large for large diffuse groups, so the "perceived effectiveness" coefficient "A" is also plausibly zero. Hence, no lobbying against the tariff comes from the consumer side.

Things are quite different on the producer side. Not only is the producer group much smaller but the gains per firm are also much larger, as are the gains to workers from jobs at the producers' factories that might be lost without protection against imports. Hence, we might expect that "peer effects" on the producer side induce contributions from each member; that is, the "noticeability" coefficient "b" is likely to be positive. We might think of "b" as a representation of the effect of the peer-group parameter J in the models discussed above. Furthermore, the "perceived effectiveness" coefficient "a" is plausibly positive because, although free-rider effects will still be present, each factory or union looms large enough relative to the industry that it can be expected to perceive some effect of its individual contributions to the group effort. Thus, we expect a positive level T^* to be a locally stable equilibrium, and we expect $T^* = 0$ to be a locally unstable equilibrium that must be constrained by international agreements not to re-raise tariffs, once lowered. We used the tariff as an expository example because of its classic role in the economic analysis of pressure-group influence.[11] This analysis also explains why the only lobbying against protective tariffs is actually conducted by opposing industry associations that happen to use the imported commodity as a raw material or component.

The same analysis can be applied to environmental issues, since the pollution damages are usually spread out over a diffuse group of victims but the gains from being allowed to pollute are received by a concentrated group. In these cases, our analysis predicts more pollution than socially optimal. However, if the damages from pollution are concentrated on a local community and the benefits to industrial workers, customers, and shareholders of being able to pollute are diffuse, one might even have less pollution than socially optimal. This is the "Not In My Back Yard" (NIMBY) problem. One could approach NIMBY problems by allowing communities to "bid" in a "Willingness To Accept" auction on compensation levels rather than having the plant sited near some politically weak community, as seems often to have been the case. Although it may be more costly to site plants after paying the community enough to induce them willingly to accept the plant, that is good because it reveals the true cost of siting "nuisances" and forces consumers of the outputs of polluting facilities to pay their full social costs.

Leaving NIMBY problems aside, we focus now on cases where the issue is that well-organized, concentrated groups use the political system to extract resources (or impose costs) on poorly organized, and typically diffuse, groups. Several remedies are suggested by our rather trivial model: First of all, a heavy burden of proof can be placed on any distortionary policy. This would make T^* = 0 a locally stable equilibrium and induce a threshold at zero that would have to be crossed before the $T(t)$ dynamics could get into the basin of attraction of a locally stable positive steady state T^*. Already, for example, tariffs are "bound" by international treaties and cannot be raised without penalty except in special temporary circumstances. Omnibus legislation such as the National Environmental Policy Act (NEPA) constrains policy actions by the executive branch and subjects it to review. Other environmental legislation, such as FIFRA, prohibits the government from allowing new pesticides on the market without safety and risk-benefit studies.

Moreover, since the origin of the problem is the imbalance of power between concentrated and diffuse groups, steps might be taken to make the former more accountable to the latter. For example, corporations could be required to disclose their lobbying activities and positions on public policy issues to their shareholders, a much more diffuse group now including more than 43 million Americans, and gain prior approval for lobbying activities from a committee composed of independent members of the board of directors.

Creating a level playing field of "rules" ensuring that all groups will be equally able to create pressure for and against policy changes is also a key option, since lobbying success depends on the efficacy of action. This implies, for example, that processes are needed to ensure that groups on all sides of an issue should be afforded adequate opportunities to be heard during legislative or administrative proceedings.

A method sometimes used by group entrepreneurs to control free riding in diffuse groups is to offer a joint product consisting of lobbying combined with other desirable goods and services. For example, the AARP lobbies, ostensibly on behalf of seniors, and boosts its membership by offering all sorts of discounted services. The Sierra Club does much the same thing with environmentalists. Of course, competition among such entrepreneurs for members might induce one to "unbundle" the joint product, save money by dropping the expensive lobbying, and offer the services at a cheaper price than rival entrepreneurs. Then the free riding problem would reemerge.[12]

This latest model abstracts from the dynamics of the supply of pressure within each group. One could apply general theory of social interactions as in Durlauf and Young (2001) and Verbrugge's review (2003) to model the dynamics of group supply of political action (that is, pressure) on both sides of the struggle. The general outcome of this more sophisticated modeling would probably be insights into how the structure of network relationships' "social capital" for a group helps it to overcome its collective action problem.

SOCIAL CAPITAL

What is the role of "social capital" in allowing a group to solve its collective action problem in mustering more political pressure relative to other groups? Social capital is notoriously difficult to conceptualize or measure precisely, but the group that has more of it will be able to muster more political pressure.[13] Indeed, inequality across groups in the distribution of social capital is a major problem in democratic political systems and is a major reason why poorly organized public interests are so severely exploited by well-organized special interests. It also helps explain why the political system produces so much obvious deadweight economic loss. Indeed, increased political competition can produce results that reduce social welfare, unlike increased economic competition (Colander 1984; Magee, Brock, and Young 1989).

Consider, for example, state or city governments competing for new investments to generate jobs and growth. In each jurisdiction there are concentrated groups who stand to benefit if a project is attracted and a diffuse public that pays for the tax giveaways and other subsidies, as well as any other external costs. Therefore, the supply curve in each jurisdiction of incentives for new projects exceeds the social welfare optimum supply curve. This alone will create "excess development" in all such jurisdictions. Examples abound of states that "win" a factory paying many times more per new job created than the job pays itself. In such instances, the states could have saved lots of money by hiring new workers themselves. How can this be? Such results can be explained by adding to the political imbalance between special interests and the public in each locale the phenomenon of the "winner's curse" and sheer political myopia.

The "winner's curse" is that when the true value of the object being sought is uncertain, the winning bidder usually pays too much. Decisions on how much incentive to offer a potential development are based on economic impact studies that are subject to wide margins of uncertainty and bias. The state that happens to get a high estimate from their economic impact study will tend to bid high and, more often than not, will win, though to the detriment of its economy. It is notoriously hard for people to condition out this effect in preparing optimal bidding strategies, even for professionals like bidders on oil tracts and timber concessions, much less politicians and their staffs. Add to this the force of political myopia, the tendency of politicians to act to get benefits now and to push the costs onto the next person's watch, plus the imbalance of political pressure within each jurisdiction, and one has a sufficient explanation for the widespread destruction of America's environment by uncontrolled development.[14]

AMBIGUITY AVERSION, PEER EFFECTS, AND CHOICE INTENSITY: A REASON FOR "IRRATIONAL" INERTIA

"Ambiguity aversion"[15] expresses the idea that people react differently when facing situations in which objective probabilities cannot be assigned to possible outcomes. One of the simplest assumptions regarding such ambiguity is that people assume the worst-case outcome within bounds with a width that depends upon their knowledge about the possible outcomes. This idea can be applied to social systems like those analyzed above. Suppose that only one choice, -1, has been available for a long time. Let now a new choice, $+1$, appear at date $t = 0$. Assume that the objective systematic part of the utility difference is $h > 0$, implying that the utility generated by choice $+1$ is objectively better for all members of the community. Nevertheless, the intensity of choice, b, the peer effect, C, and the level of ambiguity can interact to deepen a social trap at -1 and make it harder to escape. Here's the idea: Suppose first that there is no ambiguity aversion. Let choice $+1$ now appear. If there are no peer effects, the difference equation (3.12) above has only one stable state, so it converges from the previous state, -1, to a new stable state that will be nearer to $+1$; the larger is b. The larger the intensity of choice, the more quickly and closely the community comes to the best choice, $+1$. Now introduce ambiguity aversion in the following way: let [h − B, h] be an interval that community members believe contains the possibilities for the systematic utility difference right after the availability of the new choice +1 appears. Assume that each agent hedges against possible misspecification of the systematic part of the gains from moving to +1 by imputing h − B, not h to the net systematic gain. This may describe how the emotional part of the brain reacts when facing a new alternative with which one has no personal experience, before the rational part of the brain has evaluated some accumulated experience. Whatever the explanation, this simple model shows how the intensity of choice b can interact with B to create a social trap.

If h − B < 0 and b is huge and positive, the dynamics, (3.12), is stuck near −1 and never escapes even though there are no peer effects. As the intensity of choice decreases, the stable state −1 becomes less resilient as its basin of attraction shrinks. Let B be a function B(a(t)) that decreases toward zero as a(t) increases from minus one. This could be a type of demonstration effect that reassures fearful agents once a few agents choosing +1 have been observed getting h out of that choice and not the feared h − B. Notice that a lower b would generate more experiments, so there are more observations of the outcome of choice of +1 available. This reduces B and causes yet more agents to choose +1, creating a positive feedback loop of escape from the bad choice −1 as b is lowered. This process is reminiscent of that described in the Repetto and Allen chapter of fishermen's groups choosing to adopt secure harvesting rights.

The reverse effect occurs when b is increasing and the system starts at the historically given choice −1. If b is infinite and h − B(a(0) = −1) < 0, no one ever chooses +1, so no observations of what actually happens to an agent who made choice +1 are ever available. In contrast, as b decreases, a few agents will happen to choose +1 even though h − B(a(0) = −1) < 0. Then, in the next period B is smaller, which makes it more likely that more choices of +1 appear. This positive feedback loop that was opened up by a reduction in the intensity of choice creates an avenue of escape from a bad social trap. In this context, peer effects just deepen the depth of a social trap because they place an extra cost on departures from the existing consensus at −1. Thus, peer effects cause fewer examples of +1 choice to appear and this keeps people fearful of the new choice, so they continue to assume a worst-case scenario.

This discussion can shed further light on the contest between concentrated special-interest groups and diffuse public-interest groups. Suppose that a concentrated subgroup stands to lose if the community moves away from −1, even though the community as a whole stands to gain from a move to +1. How might this concentrated group use its superior ability to muster resources and control free riding within its membership? It could muster and use resources to increase the size of B in the minds of the community, increase the intensity of choice b in the community, and increase the magnitude of peer effects C in the community.

The first strategy could take the form of inducing fear throughout the community by a disinformation (or less politely, a misinformation) campaign. Clearly, if a special-interest group, which could include a faction within the government, can use its resources to induce different media to propagate desired beliefs throughout the community, increase the intensity with which those beliefs are held, and create or strengthen peer effects that punish dissenters, it could effectively freeze public opinion in a bad choice and create a very resilient attractor of the social dynamics at the stable state -1.

SUMMARY AND CONCLUSIONS

This chapter shows how simple discrete-choice models of group dynamic choice can shed light on the ways group pressure on policymakers induces moves for or against the status quo relative to one or more alternatives. It has shown how the interaction of peer-group pressure dynamics within groups and the effect on the group effort of potential free riding by group members can produce abrupt policy changes that seem inexplicable in terms of observable fundamentals. The analysis has shown how policies can remain static for long periods in the face of changing underlying fundamentals and how, in contrast, slow or modest changes in those fundamentals can occasionally lead to abrupt and discontinuous policy shifts. This kind of analysis can help in understanding abrupt policy changes and improve ability to use observable facts to locate "lever points," where small efforts can be applied to escape policies that are "locked into" bad social states, so that endogenous social dynamics can move the system to better social outcomes.

NOTES

I thank Robert Repetto for essential help in editing and writing this paper. I thank Giacomo Rondina for excellent help with formatting and preparation of graphs. Neither are responsible for errors.
1. Accessible discussions that are precise enough to clarify the underlying science include Arthur, Durlauf, and Lane (1997), Durlauf and Young (2001), Colander (2000), and Gunderson and Holling (2002).
2. Durlauf and Young (2001) discuss this very difficult problem.

3. The modeling relies on some mathematics in Brock and Durlauf (2001a, 2001b) and Scheffer, Westley, and Brock (2000, 2003).

4. This is explained more fully in Brock and Durlauf (2001a, 2001b).

5. There is a close relationship between the problem of predicting the impending rapid shifts in social system dynamics that are the concern of this chapter and the problem of predicting regime shifts in ecology (Gunderson and Holling 2002). Ecological analysis stresses the role in producing rapid shifts of typically slow-moving drivers (our h's) as well as nonlinearities caused by positive feedback loops.

6. Mathematically inclined readers curious about the mathematical foundations of this result should consult Ellis (1985).

7. This is the classic Mancur Olson problem (Olson 1965), used by Magee, Brock, and Young (1989) in building a general theory of endogenous policy change.

8. It can also be modeled as a repeated game (Ostrom, Gardner, and Walker 1994). Alternatively, Magee, Brock, and Young (1989) model this problem as a Nash non-cooperative game and capture elements of Axelrod (1984) and Ostrom, Gardner, and Walker (1994) by using two parameters, "noticeability" and "perceived effectiveness." Noticeability measures the extent to which free riders can be punished later on by some group sanction (Axelrod 1997). Perceived effectiveness measures an agent's belief about the effectiveness of his contribution to the group's goal.

9. Here we adapt Magee, Brock, and Young's Mathematical Appendix (1989).

10. More elaborate functional forms that include the opposition's contributions are given in Magee, Brock, and Young (1989). They report empirical work using a "power index" (which is a product of the total sum of stakes and a concentration index of those stakes) to measure the effective supply of pressure by each group.

11. Indeed, in late 2003, at the time of this writing, steel tariffs were a top news story: steel users, including auto makers, were as concentrated and had a power index as large as the producers. The Bush administration had first catered to the producers and imposed steel tariffs. but users mustered strong pressure to remove the tariffs. A final threat from the rest to the world "tipped" the Bush administration into removing the tariffs. This illustrates a key point, that action to remove bad policies would be more feasible in situations where the "power indices" of groups for and against a current bad policy are roughly equal. Then, resources allocated toward "tipping" the system away from bad policies might be effective.

12. The model also illuminates why campaign finance reform in the U.S. political system is so difficult.

13. See Durlauf (2002) and Durlauf and Fafchamps (2003) for detailed reviews and discussion of the literature on social capital.

14. See Brock (2001) for a non-mathematical discussion of this and many other issues related to the topics covered in this paper.

15. Modeling ambiguity aversion, which is sometimes called Knightian Uncertainty, has recently attracted attention. We borrow here from models developed by Bewley (1986), Hansen and Sargent (2003), Brock, Durlauf, and West (2003).

Chapter 4 Path Dependency and Adroit Innovation: The Case of California Water

Helen Ingram and Leah Fraser

Water problems are today so serious and so generally evident that the issue should claim a prominent place on the national agenda and command dramatic policy change. Severe droughts have disrupted water supplies in many parts of the country in recent years. Besides such extreme events, growing demands for water press close upon supplies over wide areas of the country and the long-term sufficiency of this critical resource is uncertain. Moreover, water pollution including heightened levels of organics, toxics, and salinity, from a whole variety of sources, is worsening. Protection of aquatic habitat for fish and wildlife is increasingly difficult. On top of these experienced difficulties, models of global climate change and some observable evidence suggest that water troubles will further deteriorate in coming decades as temperatures rise and patterns of rainfall and snow pack change. Climate change experts predict there is likely to be more extreme flooding in some places and at certain times of the year, while less water is available during the summer irrigation season.

Continuity rather than dramatic change characterizes water policy, although momentous shifts in policy direction do occur. Instead of the highly visible national discussion of the issue that characterizes punctuated equilibrium in such issues as women's rights, human rights, and most environmental policies, significant change in water policy has tended to come at the sub-national level, with the federal government only one, and often not the most important, player. Further, administrative agencies, notoriously impervious to pressures for change according to theorists (Clarke and McCool 1996; Lindblom and Woodhouse 1980; Wilson 1995), are the locus of action rather than legislatures that are supposed to be more attuned to emerging issues.

This chapter deals with water policy changes related to the San Francisco Bay-Delta. This is the largest estuary on the West Coast, draining some 40 percent of the waters of the state of California, including the watersheds of the Sacramento and the San Joaquin Rivers. Federal and state projects in the Delta deliver water to both cities and farms. Two-thirds of the state's residents, the majority of whom are in southern California, receive some or all of their drinking water from the Delta, and it waters over two hundred crops that produce 45 percent of the nation's fruits and vegetables annually. The Bay-Delta also supports the state's largest habitat for fish and wildlife, providing a nursery and migration corridor for two-thirds of the state's salmon and contains Suisun Marsh, the largest contiguous brackish water marsh in the United States.

According to most accounts, a veritable revolution in the Bay-Delta decision process has occurred in a cascade of decisions over the past decade (Nawi and Brandt 2002; Wright 2001; Rieke 1966). Instead of gridlock and crisis between water contractors and environmentalists marked by interrupted water supplies and the taking of federal listed endangered fish species, the situation is marked by peace. An important element of the newly found amity is the Environmental Water Account (EWA). Because fish agencies acquire water reserves through markets, they can time the release of such purchased water so as to avoid conditions that could trigger the Endangered Species Act (ESA). Therefore, the water contractors, cities, and agricultural districts are guaranteed no surprises that would interrupt the reliability of water supplies and no additional costs. Not only has the EWA contributed to the prevailing peace among previously warring groups, it also represents a sharp change in water policy in that it uses market-like mechanisms to provide water for fish protection. This has replaced the previous reliance on government regulations, making the transfer of water a far more amicable process than it had previously been.

This chapter relies heavily on insights from the punctuated equilibrium theory to explain the changes observed in California Bay-Delta water policy (Baumgartner and Jones 1993; Baumgartner, this volume; Gersick 1991). Because water policy is largely dominated by stability, ideas from path-dependency literature are also useful (Pierson 2000). Since much of the action takes place within administrative agencies and their environs, new institutionalisms' concepts developed within sociological organization theory are exceptionally helpful in identifying the cultural conditions for the emergence of new organizational forms (DiMaggio and Powell 1991; Rao, Morril, and Zald 2000). We begin with the long-standing characteristics of water policy that make it so impermeable to abrupt policy change, contributing to path dependency in water policy. The narrative emphasizes the self-reinforcing mechanisms of policy image, institutions, and professionalization, as well as risk-spreading strategies that blunt attempts toward fundamental change. At length, however, these approaches to policy prove insufficient, allowing dissatisfied environmental participants to bring Bay-Delta water policy to a standstill.

The chapter then turns to the emergence of some conditions identified in the literature as necessary for punctuated equilibrium policy change. Beginning with the evidence of policy failure, conditions range from issues of reframing and social mobilization to shifting venues. The chapter sketches the outlines of some of the most important policy changes brought about in a series of actions leading up to the institutionalization of the CALFED Bay-Delta Authority in 2002. Arguably the most innovative policy change embraced in the process, at first only as an experiment, was the market-like water transfer mechanism, the Environmental Water Account. A detailed examination of how this new policy tool emerged as a viable idea and how it has been implemented suggests that what is in fact a sharp departure from past policy has been accepted seemingly as a permanent policy fixture, without much of the controversy that has surrounded rural to urban water sales in California. The chapter ends with some observations about sub-national policy change and reflections on the possibility of adopting astute and adroit policy changes even in path-dependent policy domains dominated by notoriously sluggish government agencies.

PATH DEPENDENCY AND WATER RESOURCES

Political scientists who have adapted the economic concept of path dependence to political phenomena emphasize the self-reinforcing characteristics or increasing returns aspects of successive policy steps. Once a policy domain begins to follow a particular track, the cost of reversal becomes very high. That is, the choice of other options—including some previously rejected alternatives—becomes less likely over time (Pierson 2000, 252). The application of these ideas to the large infrastructure-building approach long dominant in water resources policy is painfully obvious. A range of engineering technologies involving dams, diversions, locks, ditches, and channelizations was adopted throughout the first half of the early twentieth century to tame and put to productive use such large rivers as the Mississippi, Missouri, and the Colorado. Each big construction project involved large setup and fixed costs. Besides the enormous financial outlay involved in the initial construction, maintenance costs of water works are quite high because of the notoriously erosive powers of flowing water. The long time period involved in the authorization, funding, and construction of projects, currently averaging twenty-seven years, represents a sunk political cost as well. Politicians and agencies that might have been elsewhere occupied have their records tied into the perceived success of big water projects. Furthermore, water infrastructure projects are usually financed by loans to be repaid by user fees over a period of thirty or forty years. There is enormous reluctance to abandon a structure not yet paid off.

Once a project appears inadequate or flawed, it is more attractive to modify or add on to the project rather than to start anew. After an aqueduct is built, it is like a thirst that must be quenched continuously. Water users have made investments to connect to the aqueduct and depend upon it for vital supplies. There is an incentive to search farther and farther away from the immediate watershed to find new water sources to keep the aqueduct full rather than to manage demands for water so that moving water over long distances is no longer necessary. Environmental effects of infrastructure projects almost never lead to the early termination of projects. Instead, adverse consequences to fish are usually mitigated by additional construction of add-ons, like fish ladders, fish hatcheries, or tank truck portage of fish around dams. People forced to move away from bottomlands to be drowned out by planned reservoirs are compensated with resettlement aid and perhaps a promise of future water projects that would benefit them.

POLICY IMAGE

Something beyond the high exit costs from the policy trajectory underlies the continuity found in water policy. Crucial to the self-reinforcing mechanisms at work in water policy is the persistence of what is variously called the underlying master frame (Benford and Snow 2000; Gersick 1991; Snow and Benford 1992), policy image (Baumgartner and Jones 1993), or dominant causal logic (Schneider and Ingram 1997). Underlying all public water issues is a social construction of problems' causes and likely solutions. Therefore, in the water policy arena, there is a host of possible problems for which policymakers draw from a limited set of policy responses to solve. For most of the twentieth century, water was considered to be a product that is delivered through engineering systems that were managed to serve human values including municipal and industrial uses, agriculture, industry, and outdoor recreation (Blatter and Ingram 2001). Natural watersheds and river systems were denatured in the sense that they had to be modified to fulfill human desires. Variations in nature such as spring floods and summer droughts had to be controlled by dams that held back flows that were too large and stored excess water in reservoirs that could be drawn down later when natural flows were too low. The task of water policy was to routinize the irregular.[1] When supplies became unreliable, of undesirable quality, or overly expensive, an engineering solution was sought.

The notion of water as product was not just an escape from the irregularities of nature; it was also an uncoupling of water from places with distinctive climates, cultures, and geography. The All American Canal brings vast quantities of water from the Colorado River across the desert to serve southern California farms and cities. When it became clear in the early 1960s that upper basin states would not allow California unlimited access to the Colorado River, the State Water Project was constructed. The State Water Project tapped into the same Bay-Delta estuary that had previously been profoundly altered by the U.S. Bureau of Reclamation's Central Valley Project (CVP). The CVP is a system of dams, dikes, and ditches that encompasses an area four hundred miles long and one hundred miles wide, serving mainly to irrigate lands that were once ecologically rich wetlands. The State Water Project moves water through massive pumps from the Bay-Delta and conveys it 662 miles south. Thus, the waters nature intended to flow to the sea from the Sacramento and San Joaquin Rivers have been relocated. Through the wonders of water engineering, cities like Los Angeles and San Diego can bloom in landscapes that naturally could serve only very small populations.

INSTITUTIONALIZATION

The political institutions, particularly government agencies and their closely linked constituencies, in conjunction with water infrastructure projects, promote path dependency. There is a vast literature in water resource politics that chronicles how dominant interests in a particular historical context manage to perpetuate their dominance through institutionalization (Clarke and McCool

1996; Ingram 1990; Maas 1951; Reisner 1993; Worster 1985). The beneficiaries of projects prosper, grow in numbers and economic strength, and identify positively with the agencies and policies that constructed the projects and delivered the largess. Government agencies come to depend upon the vocal support of their constituents, the water users, in budgetary and legislative decisions.

Early and sometimes arbitrary success can shape subsequent actions (Powell 1991). For example, the success of Los Angeles in aggressively laying claim to and exploiting distant sources of water even before there was sufficient population to use it set a trend and trajectory for many other states and localities. The cleverness and foresight of William Mulhullond, an early water official, was largely responsible. Mulhullond rose to the top of city water administration mostly by accident when the city took over a failing private water company, and Mulhullond transferred to public employment because he was the only person who knew where all the lines of Los Angeles's far-flung water supply system ran. Early on, the city laid claim to the total supply of the Los Angeles River. The city, under Mulhullond's direction, declared war on upstream users and won a series of court victories. Mulhullond was the mastermind of the rather underhanded scheme to bring water through a mammoth aqueduct from the Owens Valley to Los Angeles to serve a population boom he and other city administrators hoped would come. The city quietly expropriated water rights and resident farmers were caught unaware (Lach et al. forthcoming). With Mulhullond's encouragement, agency expansion accompanied the acquisition of water. Los Angeles Water and Power combined with a number of other governmental entities in southern California to form the Metropolitan Water District (MWD). The MWD was a major player in securing the State Water Project and to this day is a major force in California water politics. Los Angeles's early success at producing water through infrastructure projects that moved water from far-distant places became the model for other western cities, and through its early victories Los Angeles was assured of a continuing reliable, cheap water supply.

PROFESSIONALIZATION

Path dependency in water policy was further legitimized by the emergence of a cadre of water professionals with a recruitment and reward structure that supported the prevailing ideas of water as the product of an engineered system. Hydrology and water resources experts are a global fraternity that arguably had its beginnings in the American West. While a diversity of academic disciplines are involved, it is generally accepted that water can and should be rationally managed. This brings experts from the physical sciences and economics to dominate the water policy arena. A number of universities, especially in the West, grant advanced degrees in water resources management. These graduates find their professional niche in governmental agencies and complementary organizational forms. In particular, engineering consultant firms including Dames and Moore, CH2M Hill, and others employ a large number of these graduates. Organizations like the American Water Resources Association and the American Geophysical Union publish important water journals, the contents of which shape organizational standards and routines. Water resource planning is highly rationalistic, involving large numbers of experts who simulate the vagaries of nature with highly sophisticated stochastic models. Water professionals nonetheless diagnose problems and prescribe solutions along path-dependent lines that are prone to exaggerate the benefits of projects and to underestimate adverse environmental consequences that are usually portrayed as "manageable."

BENEFIT AND RISK SPREADING

Beginning almost half a century ago, the concept of water as product, combined with the institutional arrangements that supported and perpetuated this conceptualization, came under heavy attack. To survive, policy strategies were developed to accommodate challengers without making fundamental policy change. One strategy was to generalize the beneficiaries. Supporters of prevailing policy were able to argue very effectively that the welfare of some was connected to the welfare of all. Linked infrastructure led to a coordination of effects. As a consequence of the huge service area of the MWD, the cities growing up around Los Angeles became junior beneficiaries in relation to Los Angeles Water and Power. As a result of the State Water Project, the level of snow pack in the Sierras became important to water availability and quality all over the state.

Preservationists mobilized early on to voice opposition to water infrastructure's damaging effects on the natural environment. The water resources community responded to these allegations by including more and more beneficiaries in their multipurpose projects, thereby increasing the political power and numbers of water development projects. In addition to farmers and urban water users, hydropower benefits and recreational facilities were added on to projects. To satisfy rod and gun clubs, fish hatcheries and wildlife sanctuaries were cobbled onto water legislation. Institutional arrangements were fashioned so that a risk to one was a risk to all. Fish and wildlife agencies got a large proportion of their budgets from water construction agencies that had to document project effects on fish and wildlife. As a consequence, many adverse effects were mitigated and few projects were halted outright. The overall consequences of these benefit- and risk-spreading strategies was the overbuilding of very expensive water facilities that were inefficient, complex, and prone to large, unanticipated negative effects.

NON-NEGOTIABLE CLAIMS AND DEADLOCK

For water interests concerned with the San Francisco Bay-Delta, the policy path came to an abrupt end in 1982. The voters decisively defeated the peripheral canal, designed to move water around rather than directly through the Bay-Delta. Residents in northern California opposed the loss of what they considered their water to the south. Environmentalists were not satisfied with the small number of environmentally friendly add-ons to the legislation. At the same time, farmers with agricultural interests in the San Joaquin Valley believed the deal included too many environmental restrictions. Further, the policy package designed to add numerous beneficiaries (who in the end did not support the legislation) became so expensive that voters suffered from sticker shock (Nawi and Brandt 2002).

Not only was water development brought to a standstill, the long-dominant interests lost some of their previous gains through court setbacks and other events. First the courts in 1986 and then the Environmental Protection Agency in 1990 disapproved of the state's water quality standards in the Delta. They ruled that the standards did not meet the requirements of the Clean Water Act. Cuts were made in the water entitlements of farmers in the Central Valley. The Central Valley Improvement Act allocated 800,000 acre feet a year of the project's supplies to fish and wildlife restoration. Even more ominous to the dominant interests, the Sacramento River Winter-Run Salmon and the Delta Smelt were listed as endangered. Because the pumps for both the State Water Project and the Central Valley Project damage fisheries and fisheries agencies are empowered by the Endangered Species Act to shut down the pumps if the "take" of endangered fish becomes too large, the reliability of water supply to cities and agricultural contractors was threatened. The lawsuits brought by environmental groups to implement the Clean Water and the Endangered Species Acts increased the uncertainty surrounding water resources.

EMERGENCE OF SOME CONDITIONS
FOR PUNCTUATED EQUILIBRIUM

Policy change theory anticipates the kinds of difficulties encountered in the Bay-Delta in the early 1990s. Institutions' resilience and self-reinforcing qualities can ward off change for long periods of time, but not indefinitely. Significant institutional and policy change does occur periodically. While theorists differ about the extent to which incremental (Hogwood and Peters 1983; Sabatier and Jenkins-Smith 1993; Kaufman 1976; Kingdon 1995) and continuous change occurs even during path-dependent periods, most theorists agree on the episodic pattern of larger innovative change (DiMaggio and Powell 1991; Baumgartner and Jones 1993, 2002). Punctuated equilibrium takes place when accumulated forces for change overwhelm path-dependent institutions, with the result that institutions and policies are displaced and superseded.

EVIDENCE OF POLICY FAILURE

The water resources community prizes low visibility. Researchers have described water utilities as very conservative institutions that measure whether or not they are doing a good job by their ability to stay below the radar of the press and politicians. They deliver a product that people expect to be reliable, high quality, and low cost. When water becomes a public issue, gaining notoriety by itself, it is taken by these conservative organizations as a sign of failure (Lach et al. forthcoming; Rayner et al. 2002). The actions by fisheries agencies, environmental agencies, and court suits by environmentalists involved the water community in a series of alarming headlines.

Matters reached a head in what was widely referred to as the "smeltdown." In June 1999, a story in the *Sacramento Bee* under the headline "Protection of Fish Puts Farm, Bay Area Water at Risk" quoted a high-ranking local water official as saying, "What has emerged in the last 48 to 72 hours is a real water supply crisis" (Stanford Law School). Numbers of endangered smelt had lingered around the pumping plants for weeks beyond what was expected, forcing operators to pump less than half the normal amount. Besides the fact that they were listed as endangered, little was known about the three-inch translucent fish that die when handled and are drawn through the protective fish screens of the big Delta pumps to be ground to death. Even environmental groups shunned such publicity because such an uncharismatic species had little hope of winning public sympathy in a water war between fish and people.

Yet, the issues raised were more fundamental than the headline suggested. Environmental and fish agencies have missions that fundamentally conflict with the water community, making it impossible to accommodate everyone using the benefit-spreading strategies described above (Rayner et al. 2002). Further, the underlying developmental values supporting the conception of water as a product of engineering processes were being drawn into question by these events. The citizens of California support environmental and lifestyle values and expect those values to be reflected in the state's treatment of water. Instead of decision-making processes that integrated environmental concerns, warring agencies were making directly conflicting decisions and policy statements. High levels of suspicion marked the relations between water agencies and environmental groups. The decades during which the water community had slighted the environmental consequences of policy, while at the same time claiming a monopoly of relevant expertise, had taught environmental activists to be deeply distrustful of water officials.

REFRAMING PROBLEMS

Despite its suggestive role, evidence of failure is usually insufficient to cause policy change. There must also be a new policy image, symbolic appeal, frame, or causal story to connect both the emergence of problems with institutional and policy failure and to link issues to possible alternative solutions (Snow and Benford 1992; Hojnacki and Baumgartner 2003; Rao 1998; Baumgartner and Jones 1993). Theorists sometimes use the singular in referring to the emergence of a new policy image (Baumgartner and Jones 1993). In an administrative setting, however, multiple logics often exist, providing different legitimating narratives for action (Morrill 1993). Such alternative concepts of water gained currency among the public and policy elites and supported sharp changes in policy direction.

Water as an element embedded in the ecology of specific places is an attractive conception to many environmentalists and life scientists (Blatter, Ingram, and Levesque 2001). Water in this perspective is viewed as inseparable from other environmental elements that make up a particular watershed or bioregion. The characteristics of water, including quantities, chemical composition, temperature, and turbidity are suited to the habitats in which it is found. Fish biologists note that at least part of the mechanism that returns salmon to spawn in the streams of their hatching has to do with the minerals flowing up through the gravel at specific stream sites. Small variations in stream temperatures that can be easily caused by impoundments, and return flows from irrigation can make a stream an unsuitable fish habitat.

Viewing water as a place-specific environmental element helps explain the unintended negative effects of some dams. To support the food chain, riparian areas depend upon organic materials picked up in spring floods. Less-turbid water released from dams deprives streamside plants of the silts essential for their flourishing. The irregular surges of water released from dams for hydroelectric power alternately wash out or strand the fish eggs laid in shoreline gravel and leave small fingerlings high and dry. According to the lessons taught by taking this perspective in contemporary water management, most water projects need to be re-engineered to reflect natural forces more closely. Ecosystems management requires that many environmental parameters must be varied in a flexible fashion to respond to species needs. Standard government regulation is too clumsy and inflexible a tool to serve the fine tuning that ecosystems require.

From a very different perspective, water can also be viewed as a commodity. This frame accepts the idea that water is a product that is portable from one place to another but asserts that the cost of water should reflect its productive value. Natural resource economists, particularly those associated with public choice theory, tend to see water problems not as questions of scarcity but of misallocation. Water problems would evaporate if it were simply allowed to flow to the highest-valued uses. Since water is worth a great deal more in urban households and industry than in farming, transferring water from farms to cities could solve California's water problems. From this point of view, many of the past water infrastructure projects found so objectionable by environmentalists and ecologists are also objectionable on economic grounds. Many projects are simply an unwarranted subsidy to agriculture. Furthermore, even growing urban water demands would be lessened and water conservation would be promoted if water were priced at its full economic value (Anderson and Leal 1991).

While these two partially conflicting perspectives capture much of the critical discourse about California water policy in relation to the California Bay-Delta, there are important political concerns that they both ignore. Both perspectives are highly rational and tend to view water instrumentally. The first perspective, water as a place-based ecological element, assumes that ecological processes can be understood and predicted and that ecological damage can perhaps be restored. The second perspective allows that there may be certain aspects of water that can not be quantified or monetized but asserts that even most environment values have a price that many environmentalists (if given the correct institutional mechanisms) would be willing to pay to preserve. Neither perspective is especially sensitive to the cultural values toward water often held by more traditionally oriented minority groups (Brown and Ingram 1987). Nor do they capture the socially constructed lifestyle values many contemporary environmentalists hold about water. For some, water is not instrumental but rather an end in itself, bound to notions of health and purity. Nonetheless, conceptualizing water either as a place-based environmental resource or as an economic commodity now represents the most dominant among the emerging frames in contemporary California water discourse.

ADMINISTRATIVE ENTREPRENEURSHIP
AND NEW MANAGEMENT PRACTICES

At the same time that frameworks for understanding water problems were undergoing change, ideas about ecological management systems were also in flux. The "smeltdown" was only one of a large number of similar clashes in which the Endangered Species Act directly threatened public comfort and economic well-being. As was often the case for endangered species, the science upon which administrative decisions were being made about the smelt was quite weak. Further, the application of the ESA was a draconian administrative action taken without public consultation and participation. Then Secretary of the Interior Bruce Babbitt was determined to take proactive steps to avoid the Endangered Species Act being repealed or modified by Congress during his watch (Doremus 1997). The Babbitt administration endorsed a new approach to wildlife species and watershed management labeled adaptive or ecosystems management.

Adaptive or ecosystems management is a vague concept best defined by Kai Lee (1993) in describing the Columbia River Basin. The practice is an explicit directive to incorporate new and evolving science into natural resources decision-making. It recognizes that under many circumstances decisions must be made and actions must be taken without precise knowledge about what may then occur. In such cases, policy formation is a matter of "learning by doing" in which experiments, replication, controls, and extensive monitoring are encouraged. Adaptive management envisions a very close relationship between scientists and managers, with management needs taken into account in setting agendas for scientific research and with managers closely tuned in to the latest scientific advances and also willing to modify practices in order to engage in controlled experiments.

This management strategy also recognizes that local habitats and watersheds can be enormously complex and that local residents often have invaluable knowledge and perspective. Adaptive management envisions incorporating locally based understandings along with more conventional science. Continuous collaboration between scientists, managers, and the public is promoted. The management strategy offered Secretary Babbitt flexibility and thus the potential to avoid damaging conflict. If managers and warring groups could come together under the legitimizing mantle of science to find ways to restore habitat and improve ecological conditions before endangered species were listed, then crises could be averted (Babbitt 1994b). The Department of the Interior followed this strategy in a number of settings, including the Habitat Restorations Program, the Everglades, and the San Francisco Bay-Delta. The ecosystems approach fit nicely the circumstances of endangered fish in the California Bay-Delta. Biologists recognized that regulations were not delivering the benefits to ensure fish survival. Regulations could not deliver water where, when, or in the desired quantity and quality needed to serve ecological requirements. Water needed to be available at particular times and places and at particular temperatures. Such flexibility required adaptive water management attuned to fish biology and changes in immediate climatic conditions.

VENUE SHIFTING

Policy change theorists see the emergence of a new venue as critical to the innovation process. A new venue can take the form of a government institution that is created, altered, or newly involved and endogenous to the policy process, (Baumgartner and Jones 2002). The sorts of new venues theorists identify are often court interventions, switching jurisdictions of congressional committees, or the involvement of a different executive department or agency (Baumgartner and Jones 1993). In the San Francisco Bay-Delta, the policymaking landscape was cluttered with administrative agencies at all levels of government and few of them were acting in concert. Further, agencies were being buffeted by conflicting constituencies of farmers and urban water utilities along with disaffected environmental groups that were critical of all the agencies. The arena here was administrative and most of the action took place between agencies and

interest groups. The insights of organizational theorists are helpful in understanding this kind of agency-centered policy innovation. New organizational
forms can emerge in the gaps or interstices among overlapping jurisdictions and
multiple organizations when the long dominant frames of reference no longer
seem to work. Interstitial emergence begins, according to theory, with pragmatic
innovation among a network of players responding to their shared perceptions
that conventional solutions have little promise for them (Morrill 1993).

Former Assistant Secretary for Water and Science in the Babbitt administration Elizabeth Anne Rieke testifies to interstitial emergence in the case at issue
here. She writes that the federal strategy for brokering a solution was "designed to
create an overlay of procedures and processes to compensate for the perceived in-
adequacies of the statutory mechanisms for agency cooperation, federal-state collaboration, and stakeholder participation in decision-making" (Rieke 1966). The
conditions for such emergence were set by clear indications of policy failure.
Rieke writes, "In the Spring of 1993, when I was first drawn into the Bay-Delta
conflict, California agricultural, urban, and environmental interests had been
fighting for more than a decade over the level of water quality standards needed to
protect the fish and wildlife resources of the Bay-Delta" (Rieke 1966).

Pressure to break the long-standing deadlock over water management in the
Bay-Delta was intensified on the Department of the Interior when Republican
Governor Pete Wilson ordered his state water quality board to withdraw its
most recent effort to set a water quality standard. He stated that the ESA "permits the federal government to preempt the state in its allocation of water resources" and piecemeal, uncoordinated implementation of the ESA made it
impossible to predict the total impact on water supplies, thereby creating enormous uncertainty for water users (Rieke 1966, 6). Secretary Babbitt responded
that the governor had chosen to abdicate his responsibility and that the federal
government would be forced to step in. To defuse some of the conflict and with
the blessing of Secretary Babbitt, Assistant Secretary Rieke took the initiative to
coordinate the activities of federal agencies including the National Marine
Fisheries Service, the Environmental Protection Agency, the Fish and Wildlife
Service, and the Bureau of Reclamation. Formally known as the Federal Ecosystem Directorate and more popularly as "Club Fed," the group negotiated
and published in the federal register a single notice in December 1993 on an integrated set of federal regulatory proposals to protect the Bay (Nawi and Brandt
2002, 12). The following June, the governor's Water Policy Council agreed to
join with Club Fed to coordinate activities in the Delta, particularly in setting
water quality standards.

There followed a series of semi-informal meetings that included not only federal and state agency people but also representatives of water contractors, farmers, and environmentalists. The science behind the water quality standards was of particular concern, so the group engaged a peer review process designed to overcome suspicions that federal science was driven by predetermined policy decisions. In December 1994, federal and state officials agreed to a number of actions that defused controversy and pledged that cooperation would replace conflict. The Bay-Delta Accord established a new entity: CALFED, a group of California and federal officials charged with continuing the collaborative effort. In May 1995, the CALFED Bay-Delta Program was charged with forging a long-term, comprehensive agreement. The federal government agreed to purchase any additional water beyond that provided in a month-by-month calculation of limitations on exports needed for ESA protections spelled out in the agreements. In exchange, water user groups agreed to assure monetary contributions toward non-flow measures for fish protection.

SOCIAL MOBILIZATION

According to policy theory, the mobilization of a challenging social movement motivated by new policy images and demanding change is a critical factor in policy innovation (Baumgartner and Leech 1998; Berry 1984, 1999; Gamson 1975; McAdam 1982; Meyer and Tarrow 1998; Tarrow 1998; Tilly 1978). Such mobilization is often accompanied by the rise of new interest groups attracting previously uninterested adherents and new coalitions among existing groups (Meyer, Jenness, and Ingram 2005). Interest group realignment, rather than very substantial outside mobilization, seems to be a critical ingredient in the Bay-Delta policy shift. While the public was alarmed about news stories of water crisis that threatened 20 million urban residents, the Byzantine architecture of water and endangered species policies eluded any simple and mobilizing portrayal. The specter, rather than the reality, of an aroused public insisting on a reliable water supply probably was a threat that kept all the parties at the table.

At the same time, particular policy entrepreneurs (Mintrom 2000) took steps to create public pressures for solutions. An array of well-organized interest groups were parties to water wars over the California Bay-Delta, and many of the same groups and individuals that fought the battle of the Peripheral Canal in the early 1980s were still at it nearly twenty years later. Three major collections of groups exist: agriculture, urban water utilities, and environmentalists. Overlaying these divisions are the long-standing geographical separation of northern and southern California, with northerners' fear of the loss of water and political clout to the fast-growing urban areas in the south. Strengthening ties across geographical divisions between urban and agricultural interests along with what some view as enlightened attitudes on the part of the environmentalists made agreement possible. Through much of the time groups were at loggerheads, but the principles of adaptive management, as well as political necessity, led agency officials to continue with broadly representative stakeholder meetings. Beginning in 1996, stakeholders met formally as a federally chartered Bay-Delta Advisory Council, but throughout the process groups met together in countless working groups and small meetings.

If California were a country, it would be the sixth leading agricultural exporter in the world. The agricultural industry sells an average of $20.8 million in farm exports daily to destinations far and wide (Nawi and Brandt 2002). Almost all of the agricultural production depends upon irrigation. Therefore, agricultural interests have significant political clout and economic might in the state. These interests also hold very senior and very valuable water rights. The Central Valley draws water from state and federal water projects, and San Joaquin farmers as well as other farmers south of the Delta depend on water that flows through the Delta. The continuing viability of agricultural water users of Bay-Delta water is dependent not just on water availability but also on water quality. Maintenance of the levees to prevent inundation of Delta farmlands, many of which are below sea level, is also an important water-related interest of farmers. A prolonged drought began in 1987, and this loss of water was worsened by what many farmers viewed as a "regulatory" drought stemming from cutbacks made necessary to meet standards of the Clean Water Act and the Endangered Species Act.

Urban water utilities, including the Metropolitan Water District, are the second significant group of interests. Among utilities the MWD was a goliath, with a staff and resources nearly matching the entire budget of the Bureau of Reclamation. A good portion of Silicon Valley receives water either directly or indirectly from the Delta and at the time the City of San Francisco also became involved. In 1993–94 urban interests took the lead in what was called the Three-Way Water Agreement Process, which included the environmentalists as well as farmers and which evolved a kind of consensus on water quality. Over time, this developed into a north-south alliance that included agriculturalists as well as urban interests but marginalized environmental groups. The urban/agriculture alliance was facilitated, perhaps, by emerging water markets. Gridlock in the Delta was a threat to voluntary water transfers from agriculture to urban use. As long as adverse impacts on fish populations led to restrictions on diversions, transfers of Delta water would be limited. However, all three groups did develop relatively constructive relationships with one another during the three-way consultations. Further, the seeds of new ideas such as the Environmental Water Account were sown in the Three-Way Water Agreement Process (Rieke 1966; Fullerton 1993).

Environmental groups constituted the third group of interests. These included national groups like the Natural Heritage Institute, the Environmental Defense Fund, and the Natural Resources Defense Council, among many others, as well as a number of groups focused primarily on the Bay-Delta, such as the Bay Institute of San Francisco and Save San Francisco Bay. The resources of these groups were dwarfed by a combination of both urban and agricultural interests. Their leverage was further eroded by internal disagreements. The survival of endangered fish was not always the first priority. For some groups halting the expansion of urban areas and urban water use was more important than the welfare of fish, and the ESA was only a means to slow development. For others, the human health of urban residents was a critical environmental issue, and water quality was of the utmost importance. Such divisions hampered the construction of coalitions through which influence could be pooled. Even without coming together, however, environmentalists had the advantage of the leverage of citizens' suits and federal laws. Authoritative commentators on the emergence of agreement noted that a strong incentive for other parties to come to agreement was created by lawsuits filed by environmental plaintiffs to enforce the Clean Water Act and the Endangered Species Act (Nawi and Brandt 2002). At the same time, environmental groups had much more influence in holding up the process rather than in shaping policy as agreements between urban and agricultural interests emerged.

The mobilization of interests outside the groups discussed above that did take place was designed to force agreement and to avoid gridlock. Assistant Secretary Rieke traveled around the state urging business interests to hold the feet of both federal and state officials to the fire. Urban water utilities, especially the MWD, also mobilized business interests. A letter to President Clinton and Governor Wilson signed by heads of BankAmerica Corporation, Wells Fargo Bank, the Federal Reserve Bank and San Francisco TransAmerica Corporation, Southern California Edison, Pacific Gas and Electric, San Diego Gas and Electric, and others stated that continued gridlock was simply unacceptable (Rieke 1966).

DECISION CASCADES AND MOMENTUM

Policy theorists point to the importance of the context in which decisions are made. Sometimes the innovations that might be impossible to accomplish if considered separately are swept along as other critical decisions fall into place (Baumgartner and Jones 2002; Hojnacki and Baumgartner 2003). Cascading has been examined in the policymaking literature recently as a component of positive-feedback processes (Baumgartner and Jones 2002; Hojnacki and Baumgartner 2003; MacLeod 2002). The momentum gains power over time. Originating within the economics literature under terms such as "lock-in" and positive returns, the concept of positive feedback served as the backdrop to threshold models and was applied to voting behavior theories in economics and political science (Baumgartner and Jones 2002, 15–20). The idea of cascades helps us to understand the process whereby dramatic policy change occurs after long periods of stability. This sharp change can be the result of a small institutional change that leads to changes in implementation, policy image, or myriad other changes that follow once an initial, often random, event starts the ball rolling. In the case of California water policy, the initial shift that began the cascade was a critical Bay-Delta water agreement that created momentum that ultimately transformed the way that California water is viewed and managed.

Each agreement struck on the management of Bay-Delta water built positive momentum for subsequent agreements. The resolution of each tough decision carried over to other policy decisions. The Bay-Delta Accord struck in 1994 led to a phased CALFED Bay-Delta Program. Phase two, the preparation of a comprehensive programmatic environmental impact review, reached a sticking point as Governor Wilson's term ended. Secretary Babbitt and Governor Wilson's chief of staff George Dunn staged a series of marathon meetings with stakeholders related to CALFED issues in the fall of 1998, but no agreement was reached on a preferred alternative for CALFED, although added support for the key idea of an Environmental Water Account emerged from those meetings (Nawi and Brandt 2002). The environmental group participants in the meetings endorsed the idea, intending it to be only a temporary buffer to protect endangered species while long-term arrangements were worked out between resource agencies and project operators (Bay Institute of San Francisco 2001). Governor Davis's administration proceeded cautiously, and although the CALFED staff held a number of stakeholder meetings, dispute broke out about the management and accounting of Central Valley Project water dedicated to the environment.

Secretary Babbitt had too great a stake in the process to allow it to languish. In the fall of 1999, a series of closed meetings took place between senior administrators at the Department of the Interior, Secretary Babbitt (at times), his representative David Hayes, members of the governor's cabinet, and Susan Kennedy, the governor's cabinet secretary. These high-level negotiations focused on a few key issues, including timetables, funding, and the Environmental Water Account. Based on these meetings, Secretary Babbitt and Governor Davis released a framework for action on June 9, 2000. In the next ten weeks, both the federal and state governments worked collaboratively on a final Environmental Impact Statement/California Environmental Impact Report and a federally required Record of Decision (ROD). The issuance of the ROD was the next successfully negotiated challenge. The preparation of the ROD included gaming exercises related to establishing the size of the EWA, an issue we will return to later.

The positive momentum has survived the transition to the Bush administration, an administration that is far less interested in California water and has not yet authorized federal participation (although it continues to do so informally). On January 1, 2003, the State of California authorized the California Bay-Delta Authority that is to include six state and six federal members (unauthorized), five members from regions affected by the Delta, two at-large members appointed by the state legislative leaders, and four ex officio members also appointed by legislative leaders.

Momentum in cascades of decisions operates across issues in packages as well as over time. This latitudinal momentum is important in explaining how the elements of the agreement could be stapled together. The final high-level negotiations included only a few key issues: setting out well-defined milestones for measuring progress in implementation; selecting storage options to pursue with site-specific environmental analysis; committing to program funding; and the Environmental Water Account. By the time negotiators got to the EWA, many difficult hurdles had been overcome and the EWA was not the kind of deal breaker that opponents could rally around. While it certainly had skeptics in the environmental and farming communities, neither group was sufficiently negative to carry the day against strong urban and business support. There were those in the fisheries agencies that were wary of staking the implementation of the Endangered Species Act upon the willingness of politicians to appropriate money for the Environmental Water Account. However, at this point the overall settlement had such a high public profile that no agency officials wanted the blame for the package falling apart laid upon them or their agency. Consequently, the very innovative idea of fisheries agencies using water markets to avoid damage to endangered species was adopted.

INNOVATIVE POLICY AND ASTUTE
POLICY DESIGN

The line between incremental and innovative policy is not easy to draw, especially in complex, multifaceted policies. There is a complex combination of positive and negative feedbacks at play within complex institutions (Baumgartner and Jones 2002). Certainly not all of the policy process and content adopted in the California Bay-Delta Authority is innovative. The pattern of benefit and risk sharing that marked path-dependent water decisions is still very much evident in the packaging of these agreements. The package includes a huge new commitment to habitat restoration, grants to watershed groups, aid to cities for water quality and water conservation programs, levee maintenance for farmers, as well as more traditional infrastructure items such as storage, water supply, pumping, and other improvements. There is practically no evidence of user fees, and government money, much of it gained through the passage of bond issues, supports this highly distributive program. At the same time, the California Bay-Delta Authority is a new entity. It has embraced and is currently attempting an adaptive management approach to water management. This new organization has legitimacy and greater public trust than the older water agencies with long records of disregarding environmental impacts. It is strongly committed to well-financed scientific research and intends to monitor actions and document lessons. The heavy emphasis on environmental restoration is a policy innovation but it could be argued that the program is a payoff to environmentalists given in exchange for new infrastructure and their agreement to allow exports from the Delta to grow. There continues to be a developmental tilt to the program, and the emphasis is upon making existing water serve larger goals than cutting back on water use (Public Citizen 2004). The process of decision-making has become much more peaceful and collaborative, but most participants agree that peace is not a sufficient measure of adequate change (EWA Science Review Board 2003).

The Environmental Water Account, which doubtless would not have been adopted except for its place in the complex, larger package, provides convincing testimony that meaningful change has occurred. As policy theorists have observed, great change may emerge from actions that at the time appear unremarkable. While not entirely clear at the time, the EWA signaled a backing away from the regulatory approach that had marked fish protection. Instead of simply mandating water releases and letting water contractors whose expectations of water supplies were disappointed bear the cost, fisheries agencies themselves were to own and manage water. The EWA involves voluntary water sales and contracts. It guarantees that environmental water will be available for fish without any uncompensated cost to the contracting agencies (cities and farms). It also modifies the role of fish agencies that were to manage the account, and requires a close working relationship with facilities operators not previously sympathetic to fisheries problems.

An integral aspect of EWA's innovative design is its dependence on water acquisition through voluntary markets rather than by governmental mandate. Water markets encounter considerable resistance even though most water resources academics and many environmental groups favor moving water to higher value uses through markets. There are concerns about the ancillary effects of water sales on agricultural communities. Further, markets make the allocation of water more efficient but do little to halt urban growth and development that many environmentalists oppose. Consequently, many water sales are quite controversial even though they regularly occur and have been taking place for over thirty years. The sale of water from the Imperial Valley to the City of San Diego that transfers 200,000 acre feet took nearly a decade and enormous political capital to accomplish. That transfer continues to have bitter enemies among some farmers and the Republic of Mexico, who will inevitably suffer negative indirect effects. In contrast, the Environmental Water Account, which in some years has moved almost as many acre feet, was negotiated in months and has a generally favorable public image.

GESTATION PERIOD AND
NETWORKED SUPPORT

In water policy as in many other areas, some ideas have a long shelf life. There are many water projects that remain as plans within construction agencies until some event or crisis produces the perceived problem for which the project is dusted off and presented as the solution. The idea of protecting the environment through markets is an old concept espoused by the Interior Department during the Reagan administration and favored by many California environmentalists. To some, however, the idea seemed wrongheaded. According to the public trust doctrine, the state was supposed to guarantee the use of water in the public interest of citizens, and if low flows were endangering fish, then diversions from the streams should be regulated. The citizens should not have to pay to purchase the welfare (adequate flows for fish) already guaranteed. Agricultural interests also had doubts. If problems were solved through markets, there would be less public support for the infrastructure projects farmers believed were essential. Further, many farmers felt that water sales might make individual farmers better off, but the farming communities would suffer as people moved off the land and no longer supported local businesses, schools, and civic enterprises. Further, water sales to city or state government raises both the demand and water prices, making water more expensive in local water markets among farmers. As a consequence, water markets have been talked about far more than they have been actively pursued until recently.

There is no consensus among authorities regarding the genesis of the Environmental Water Account. During the drought lasting from 1987 until the early 1990s, fifteen million dollars were allocated to help fish and wildlife. The money was used in a variety of ways, but at least part of it was used for the California Department of Fish and Game to buy water that could be used to improve habitat and flows for fish (David White, interview with author, 2003). While there was not a continuous fund like the Environmental Water Account, a precedent for using markets to buy water for fish was established.

In December 1991 an informal discussion process between urban, agricultural, and environmental interests began. Many of the ideas that found their way into the final agreement were discussed, shared, and gained broad support during what was termed the Three-Way Process. There were sixty members (twenty from each side) and an eighteen-member steering committee. The goal was to create a management structure that would be attractive to all sides. Among the key ideas was to create and fund the Environmental Water Authority (EWA) to purchase and hold water rights for in-stream flows. The idea was to satisfy environmental needs and avoid involuntary transfers that were opposed by agriculture (Fullerton 1993). However, governments were not involved in this discussion and the ideas were not yet concrete.

Moving an idea out of its community of core supporters and into another is a difficult proposition that often proves insurmountable. One of the major barriers to any proposal affecting the Bay-Delta was that concessions accepted by one side were rejected by another. The Three-Way Process provided a mechanism for networked support for the EWA. While the plans of the Three-Way Process did not come to immediate fruition as a result of federal and gubernatorial intervention, the goal of a package of proposals that appealed to all interests survived. For the first time, all interests came to accept an EWA in some form. In the words of one participant, "We had the concept. What we needed was the political support and the grease of public funding to make it go" (David Fullerton, interview with author, 2003).

CAST AS EXPERIMENTAL

To begin, the EWA was set up as a limited experiment with yearly evaluations and a thorough review planned at the end of four years. The temporary status of the program may well have quieted critics who were convinced that the failure of the program would bring on its own demise. In fact, quite the opposite has happened. After nearly four years of operation, considerable political momentum has built around the notion of making the program permanent, and perhaps providing a permanent funding base through user fees to be paid by cities and farmers. A crisis sufficient to shut down the pumps has not occurred in three years, lending stature to the program and building confidence among stakeholders. Further, as cities as well as the state-operated EWA scour the agricultural fields for year-to-year water contracts, agriculturalists have come to depend upon revenues available from water leases to help them in times of high costs and low agricultural prices (Fulton and Shigley 2003).

WELL-WORKED-THROUGH POLICY DESIGN

The most revolutionary aspect of the policy design is not so much the use of markets for ecosystem services, which are not new, but that fish management agencies should be given water to manage like every other user. Fish agencies are supposed to decide whether or not to spend their water assets on the basis of real-time information about fish movements. This was a marked departure from previous practice, in which pumping levels were set automatically at a low level during certain months even though fish might not be present during those months, but fish had no protection in other months except if endangerment triggered the draconian ESA requirements that curtail pumping operations. When endangered fish show up at the pumps at abnormal times, the release of environmental water is supposed to avoid any excessive take of endangered fish such as had occurred during the "smeltdown." Fish managers now must be water brokers, deciding whether to expend assets to address present fisheries management problems with a particular species or to save water for future problems that may arise with other endangered fish. According to one participant, a paradigm shift has occurred among fish agency managers who are now interested in how much water costs (David Fullerton, interview with author, 2003). Fish managers manage not just fish but also water assets and must consider risks to both simultaneously.

Careful analysis went into the determination of the size of the EWA and the source of its assets. Environmentalists were understandably concerned that the assets of the EWA would not be sufficient to protect fish, since a key part of the Bay-Delta agreement was that contractors in farms and cities could no longer be expected to bear any uncompensated costs to protect fish. A series of gaming exercises with the participation of important stakeholders was performed during the preparation of the Record of Decision on the EWA. The games, based on a fourteen-year hydrological sequence from 1980 to 1994, demonstrated to the satisfaction of some but not all stakeholders that the size of the EWA would be sufficient in all but a few years of extreme drought (Bay Institute of San Francisco 2001). According to participants very familiar with the legislative process in natural resources decision-making, the EWA was subjected to an unusual amount of scrutiny and policy analysis. A wide group of decision-makers and stakeholders participated in repeated gaming exercises in which parameters were changed to simulate effects of the addition of different infrastructures and variations in fish behavior (David Fullerton, interview with author, 2003; David Snow, interview with author, 2003; James White, interview with author, 2003).

A variety of options were provided for where and how the EWA could acquire fixed and variable assets. In addition, the EWA was to have a one-time asset of 200,000 acre feet. It could purchase water from willing sellers, borrow water from stored or contracted supplies, or acquire water by relaxing water quality standards or using excess operational capacity. According to the plan, fish agency personnel meet regularly with project managers, the people who run infrastructure facilities, to determine when to store, move, and release waters. The design envisioned that a good deal of learning would take place among operators who would come to understand fish needs and fish managers who would come to sympathize with operational constraints.

OUTSIDE EVALUATION AND LEGITIMATING

Another important aspect of the policy design was a mandatory review by a nationally recognized panel of scientists.[2] After the first year of operation, the lead scientist of the CALFED science program appointed a committee that has met each October, at the end of the season of greatest fish migration. Substantial problems were encountered during the first year when an unusually large number of salmon appeared at the pumps and substantially more than the 2 percent allowable take were killed. Rather than to use all the water in the EWA to save the endangered Winter-Run Chinook Salmon in February and March, the fisheries managers opted to save some water for the Delta Smelt that might cluster near the pumps later in the year. The loss of a large number of fish, 90 percent above that allowable under ESA standards, made the newspaper headlines. At the same time, 1991 was the first in several years that the allowable take of Delta Smelt had not been exceeded. The Science Review Panel studied the record and took statements from stakeholders, water and fish managers, and other experts. The panel report, though critical of a number of aspects of operations, especially research and the use of monitoring data, did not interpret the large loss of endangered fish as a failure. Instead they suggested that the method used by fisheries agencies to calculate the production of juvenile salmon had vastly underestimated the migrating population. The report suggested that if the estimate were correctly calculated, the take probably would not have exceeded the allowable limit. In all subsequent years, the juvenile production estimate has been calculated under the new methodology and mortality at the pumps has not been a problem. Had agencies simply switched to a new methodology without the blessing of the scientific committee, the fish agencies might well have been accused by environmentalists of lowering goals (California Bay-Delta Environmental Program 2001).

The requirement to prepare briefing materials and make presentations each year to the review committee has had a number of beneficial effects. Mid-level agency officials and scientists have learned to work much more collaboratively with one another. This has been particularly important in regard to the relationship between fisheries and water managers. Further, the review process has promoted learning from experience that allows policy to adjust to new science and changing circumstances. The science panel has urged with good results that the EWA managers develop expertise in water marketing. The public, formal review by the science panel is supplemented by periodic workshops on such things as fish predation, the operation of the gates at the Delta Cross-Channel, and salinity standards. Some members of the review panel and many stakeholders usually attend these workshops. The openness and transparency promoted by the review process has also served to pacify stakeholder groups. While the representatives of farmers' and environmental groups remain critical in different ways, the edge of the criticisms the first year has not carried over to subsequent years. Further, stakeholders' relations with one another have exhibited greater comity in recent years.

SKILLED IMPLEMENTATION

To succeed in water markets, special skills are necessary, involving knowledge about pricing, investment risks, and debt. These are not usually found in water or fisheries agencies. The EWA was blessed with skilled staff in its early years. David Fullerton, who was senior scientist at Natural Heritage Institute and was hired by CALFED to develop an analytical approach and computer model to make decisions about the types of water assets and quantities of water to acquire each year, was hired by the state and became the manager reporting to the scientific review panel. Fullerton managed the successful acquisition of water during the first year. Overpayment is very difficult to determine, however, since prices vary widely in newly opened markets. When Fullerton moved on to the Metropolitan Water District, Jerry Johns, who had previously worked for the State Water Resources Control Board and was chief of the Bay-Delta unit, took over. Jerry Johns managed to diversify the kinds of water acquired by the EWA, always searching for the cheapest water, whether it was located above or below the Delta. Johns engaged in long-term financial planning that suggested that it was useful for the EWA to carry forward some water debt. The financial analysis suggested that the EWA would have problems paying off debt, oddly, only if there were a string of very wet years.

Jerry Johns prepared and disseminated information and procedures aimed at prospective water sellers to expedite acquisition of water with a minimum of third-party impacts. The intention was to make the state an "enlightened consumer" of water through the EWA and other programs. The aim was to make purchases as environmentally and socially friendly as possible. Three principles guide the EWA: (1) no injury to other legal users of water; (2) no unreasonable effects to fish, wildlife, or other in-stream beneficial uses of water; (3) no unreasonable effects on the overall economy or the environment in counties from which the water is transferred (California Department of Water Resources 2002). These rules address the usual complaints about rural to urban water transfers and their enunciation and enforcement avoids possible difficulties.

The Environmental Water Account also profited by exceptionally able leadership at CALFED and its science program. Lester Snow and his successor as head of the CALFED program, Patrick Wright, were highly adept at getting agencies to work together and to honor the adaptive management principles of transparency and stakeholder participation. Sam Luoma, on leave from the U.S. Geological Survey, was the lead scientist during the first three years of CALFED operations. His impressive scientific credentials lent prestige to the program. The science program sponsored a large number of workshops and annual meetings, sometimes with hundreds in attendance. While it is not yet certain how much of the new science is finding its way into policy, a great deal more has been learned about fish behavior through CALFED science studies. Science is moving the management focus away from take at the pumps to the more general conditions existing in the total life cycle of fish. For example, it would seem that the pumps have less influence upon the survival of endangered salmon runs than was previously thought, at least if flows are above some threshold (James White, interview with author, 2003). Also, predation studies in Clifton Forebay, which is the pool in front of the pumps, and studies of the consequences to fish of the operations of the Delta Cross-Channel may eventually result in means for saving endangered fish that may be as or more effective than the old method of reducing mortality by shutting down the pumps.

It may be too early to proclaim the implementation a complete success after only four years. To some extent the relatively peaceful period in water management may be partially due to luck. There have been neither critical extremes in temperature and rainfall nor critical changes in the political landscape. New challenges are on the horizon. While the EWA has survived changes in political party control in the State House and in Washington, new leadership always requires renewing of commitments to both CALFED and the EWA. Money is bound to be more of a problem in the future. Up until 2004, the EWA was funded mostly by bond money, with some small federal contributions of water and money in the early years. Since then, the federal government has not provided financial support, and bond monies will become exhausted. The California state treasury is in terrible shape and it would seem a near certainty that some sort of user financing will need to be developed to make the EWA permanent and extend its operations into the future. While cities are generally willing to take on the burden, it is far less certain that agriculture will accept part of the costs of funding EWA. As the lessons of the past suggest, unless all three of the major interests, the environmentalists, cities, and agriculture, are in agreement, policy action becomes impossible.

Should EWA be authorized over a longer term, which at this point seems likely, there will be both additional opportunities and challenges. EWA will have additional flexibility to enter into long-term contracts that may bring lower water prices. However, it now will have to face the risks of inter-year expenditures of water. It may be too conservative in some years, resulting in unnecessary damage to fish, in order to save for a worse year in the future that may or may not come to pass (EWA Scientific Review Board 2003). In recent years, the EWA has had an opportunistic purchasing pattern that has cut costs, but has made EWA a strong competitor in the "cheap water markets" (David Fullerton, interview with author, 2004). This has been controversial to the agricultural water buyers. If users are expected to pay for the costs of EWA, they may insist on the imposition of additional burdens on EWA management that may or may not be good for fish. It is a testament to its successful implementation thus far that the Environmental Water Account is facing a future, however fraught with peril. The EWA becomes more and more accepted and institutionalized with the passage of time.

CONCLUSIONS

Punctuated equilibrium theory and organizational change literature are very helpful in explaining the conditions for policy change in the California Bay-Delta region. While it is difficult to predict exactly when change will occur, and as Frank Baumgartner (this volume) makes clear, the relative influence of change agents are context dependent, it is possible to identify certain causal variables. Evidence of obvious failure of the previous policy set the stage for the emergence of new policy images. Shifting to new venues also took place as action was shifted to arenas encompassing actors at different levels of government and involving all three principal water interests as well as the public. The political context of decision-making emphasized in punctuated equilibrium theory is also important here. The Environmental Water Account was swept along with other ideas in the package that became CALFED. No single item of the CALFED agreement could be removed without threatening the supporting coalition. Other theories related to organizational change also provide helpful insights, including the role of professionals and innovation through organizational adoption of ideas in good currency among professionals, in this case "adaptive management." The following factors were identified as important to this case study and to shed light onto other examples in the volume.

Positive Feedback for Change

Evidence of obvious failure of the previous policy disrupted the feedback that had long reinforced path dependency in water resources. It was no longer possible to continue with business as usual. Each new problem identified—endangered fish, poor water quality, and interrupted water supply—was interpreted as cause for new policy innovation. Together, these perceived problems accumulated, creating a momentum that brought the policy change abruptly and decisively.

New Venue

The movement of policy making from one agency, branch, or level of government to another is often identified as critical to large-scale policy change. In this case, the regional level became the venue where most significant change occurred. Although CALFED is a federal/state entity, and although participation at the federal level has not been formalized, the "Club Fed" or unified federal position led to state action and fostered federal/state collaboration. This highlights the importance of regional venues that are often overlooked in policy innovation. Often the exclusive focus on the federal or state level of policymaking steers us away from complex environmental issues that are often best dealt with regionally. The case of the EWA gives reasons for optimism to those who see very little hope for positive change in favor of environmental quality at the national level. Innovation in this case took place at the sub-national regional level. It may be that at a time when environmental policy is at a standstill or going backward at the national level, regions and states offer much more favorable climates for positive change. Further, the case suggests that administrative agencies are quite capable of innovation when it is in their organizational interests.

New Policy Image or Frame

Thinking about an issue in a new way is often important to the mobilization of new constituencies focusing on policy change. These new policy images or frames are reflected in changes such as increased press coverage, the use of different metaphors, and new causal theories. In the case of water, there were a number of competing frames that challenged the image of water as the product of an engineered production process. The case of the EWA indicates, however, that significant change can take place without a consensus on a new frame or image and without large-scale media coverage. Instead, policy elites came to agree upon an administrative concept, adaptive management, allowing different conceptions of water (as an economic commodity, or a place-based ecological resource) to coexist. Having coexisting frames that could be referenced by various groups kept all interested parties coming to the table with very distinct policy images. The master frame of adaptive management was able to encompass and override the importance of all other, potentially competing, frames.

Importance of Networks

The role of entrepreneurs is generally identified as quite important to policy change. In the case of CALFED, leadership was clearly plural. The various change agents involved created an elite network that became much more important than any individual in its support for change. While individuals in Secretary Babbitt's office in the Department of the Interior were clearly important, leaders existed in each of the three principal constituency groups, agriculture, cities, and environmental groups. During the long gestation period in which policy change was bubbling up, people were talking across organizational dividing lines about trying something new. This network was critical in the creation of the resulting policy innovation.

Whereas often policy change is seen as a function of social movements, in this case, the role of an elite network was clearly more critical. From the early 1990s and continuing for almost a decade there was continuous networked dialogue, and negotiation took place among many different parties and levels of government. Ideas about adaptive management with learning through science and the use of flexible policy tools were spread among water experts in agencies, environmental groups, municipal water utilities, and agricultural interests. This was not a case of building a new coalition that simply defeated the opposition. Instead, it was a sea change that occurred through the conversion of many into an adaptive management kind of thinking.

Adept Policy Design

Successful policy needs to appeal across ideologies. Both this chapter and the one written by James Dunn in this volume suggest that purist approaches fail to reach across boundaries of ideas and interest to include the necessary mobilization required to push through new policies. Successful policies have wide appeal that seems to make most everyone a winner. This policy was a clear example of carefully packaging different benefits to different interests. The EWA promised security for both cities and farms in terms of water reliability while at the same time promising more water for endangered fish. The policy was designed to reflect the goals of the network members, and no single item of this agreement could be removed without threatening the supporting coalition.

Cascades of Decisions and Momentum

The political context of decision-makers who are responding to each other and amplifying the effects of small changes is emphasized in punctuated equilibrium theory. This is important here because the Environmental Water Account was swept along with other ideas in the package that became CALFED. No individual or group wanted to be responsible for derailing the process of change. Also, there was substantial political cover available for those who went along with the CALFED vision. Since other agencies were taking similar positions at the time, the risk of being wrong was substantially lowered in the event that problems occurred.

Gestation Period

The particulars of this case also suggest that some amendments and adjustments to punctuated equilibrium theory are in order. There is the issue of change and the extent to which it is abrupt or continuous. This case would suggest that a great deal happens to promote change at a time when it appears that interests are deadlocked. While the adoption of EWA within CALFED was a sharp departure from the past, the concept had been discussed and broadly accepted within the discourse for years before it found its way into law. The process through which fisheries agencies came to believe that regulations were not providing the flexible, real-time management tool they needed took as long as five years. Agency officials also had to be convinced not only that the EWA might provide a better management tool but also that the officials could not continue to wield the Endangered Species Act regulations as they had previously done. Cities and farmers were insisting on greater security, and fisheries agencies could not afford to hold out. The water issue was of such high visibility for so long that no one wanted the blame for derailing agreement (David Snow, interview with author, 2001).

Role of Science

While science is often used as a rationalization, and new science alone seldom is sufficient reason for change, science is very important to understanding change in this case. From the early 1990s and continuing for almost a decade there was continuous networked dialogue, and negotiation took place among many different parties and levels of government. Ideas about adaptive management with learning through science and the use of flexible policy tools were spread among water experts in agencies, environmental groups, municipal water utilities, and agricultural interests. This was not a case of building a new, winning coalition. Instead, it was a process of conversion of many participants' mentalities to an adaptive management kind of thinking. Critical to change was the notion of best available science that could replace advocacy science where every interest group hired their own scientists to put their own spin upon data and conclusions. In fact, fish agencies were pressed to seek out new scientific ways to intervene on behalf of fish because of a limited EWA budget. Further, the hope for scientific advance displaces what otherwise might be deadlock between preservation and development.

There remains the issue of whether this significant change is enough. From the perspective adopted here, the EWA is a clear departure from the past because it changes the mindset of fisheries managers so that they are conscious of the price of water and the limits of their account. Water managers learn as well as they come to understand the needs of fish as they work with fisheries managers to plan EWA water releases. Clearly, water management is more informed, efficient, and environmentally friendly than before CALFED and EWA. However, for hard-core environmentalists who wish to see water scarcity set water limits to economic growth and human development, the EWA falls short. It assumes that with flexible and adaptive water management, water can be stretched to serve more purposes, including the survival and restoration of endangered species. From this more radical point of view, humans are already way out of balance with natural water supplies, and spreading water to serve more purposes simply pushes humans closer to what is bound to be cataclysmic water system failure. The EWA is definitely development oriented to the extent that it places no identifiable limits to California's continued population and economic expansion. It does ensure that endangered fish have a better chance of survival.

NOTES

The authors acknowledge the important contributions of Steve Rayner and Denise Lach, with whose collaboration many of the insights about water policy stability and change were developed. We also thank the UCI Study for the Center for Democracy and the UCI Newkirk Center for their support.

1. The authors thank Steve Rayner and Denise Lach for this turn of phrase.
2. In the spirit of full disclosure, it should be noted that Helen Ingram is a member of the review panel.

Chapter 5 On Social Traps and Lobster Traps: Choppy Waters on the Voyage Toward Fisheries' Harvesting Rights

Robert Repetto and Richard B. Allen

This chapter examines the halting progress in U.S. fisheries management toward the establishment of secure harvesting rights in marine fisheries through the establishment of Individual Transferable Quota regimes. After the adoption of ITQ regimes in a few fisheries, Congress imposed a moratorium in 1996 to block the development or approval of any more such systems in other fisheries under federal jurisdiction. This moratorium was twice extended and allowed to expire only in 2002. The imposition, extension, and ultimate removal after a six-year brake on policy development constitutes a policy history that illustrates the punctuated equilibrium policy behavior investigated in this book.

Analysis of the structural dynamics underlying this policy history yields strong evidence of the social trap described in William Brock's chapter. The trap operated as follows: Without actual experience demonstrating that shifting to an ITQ approach to fisheries management would make them better off, fishermen are reluctant to depart from the traditional modes of fisheries management. They also exert social pressures against those within their ranks who advocate change.

However, given the powerful role of fishing interests within the governing fisheries management councils, no ITQ system can be adopted in any fishery without the support of most of its fishermen. Without concrete evidence that change would improve their lot, fishermen won't approve change, but unless fishermen vote for change, such evidence cannot arise. Hence, fisheries continue with management regimes that have led and continue to lead to rent dissipation and inefficient outcomes. The moratorium on new experiments with ITQs functioned, in part, to preserve this social trap by preventing further evidence on the results of ITQ systems in practice from emerging.

The expiration of the moratorium in 2002 reflects, in part, the accumulation of actual experience with ITQs, especially in the Alaskan halibut and sablefish fisheries, whose fishermen benefited from a dramatic improvement after shifting to that approach. The experience led to a certain amount of "policy learning" that affected subsequent decisions in other fisheries and at the national level. As the favorable experiences in the Alaskan fishery accumulated and became more widely known in fishing circles, some of the claims made by ITQ opponents lost force.

In addition, the background to the expiration of the moratorium suggests the game-theoretic framework also developed in William Brock's chapter. During the period of the moratorium, changes occurred in the payoff structure of powerful interests that had blocked ITQ development, inducing them to moderate or drop their opposition and weakening the coalition in favor of preserving the moratorium. Changes in constituent interests and pressures were sufficient to alter the position of a few key congressional figures who held disproportionate power over the policy outcome.

THE DEMAND FOR SECURE FISHING RIGHTS

Economic historians have presented a great deal of evidence that property rights institutions come into being in response to economic stimuli. In studies of the exploitation of water, land, minerals, and other natural resources, historians have shown that when there are large and increasing potential gains from the creation or capture of economic rents through more secure and formalized property rights, those property rights institutions tend to emerge (Demsetz 1967; Anderson and Hill 1975; Dennen 1976; Libecap 1978; Lee, Eggertson, North 1990; Eggertson 1990; North and Thomas 1970). According to this theoretical and empirical literature on induced institutional change, when the potential resource rents are small, either because of inadequate demands for or

ample supplies of the resource, loose and informal systems of allocating and securing access to it will often suffice, and the costs of creating, monitoring, and
enforcing formal property rights may not be deemed worthwhile. However, as
potential rents grow, the conflicts over access and the losses from unrestrained
exploitation increase. At some point, the gains from property rights sufficiently
outweigh the costs of creating and maintaining those systems, and institutional
development becomes a worthwhile investment.

This process should surely be reflected in the governance and regulation of
ocean fishing. Prior to the twentieth century, fishing pressures on most commercial species were not large enough either to deplete stocks seriously or to de-
press the catch-per-unit effort substantially. (Commercial whaling was a notable exception.) Open access was the generally accepted approach to ocean
fishing. Many marine biologists believed that because of their high fecundity,
fish species could never be depleted by fishing pressures. However, the development of fishing technologies and the growth of harvesting fleets demonstrated
the falsity of that belief. Going back to Danish economist Jens Warmer writing
in 1911 or to Canadian fishery biologist A. G. Huntsman writing in 1949
(Warmer 1911; Huntsman 1949), the inefficiencies and rent dissipation resulting from open-access fishing have been explicated. In the absence of effective
access limitations, excessive effort and resulting crowding externalities dissipate
potential rents by raising harvesting costs and by increasing the unintended
damage to habitat and nontargeted fish populations. The lack of secure harvesting rights also leads to intertemporal inefficiencies in the form of growth
and recruitment overfishing, since no individual fisherman refraining from a
current harvest could be sure of reaping the larger harvest in the future (Gordon 1954). Unquestionably, there are large potential gains in the creation of secure fishing rights in marine fisheries.

The rent dissipation in fisheries without secure harvesting rights has been
not only explained in theoretical papers but also documented extensively in
empirical studies. Levels of effort far beyond those needed to harvest the catch
efficiently have been found in most such fisheries along with stock depletion
due to overfishing to levels far below those that would support economically
efficient catch levels (Bell 1972; Grafton, Squires, and Fox 2000; Crutchfield
1979). Consequently, the bulk of the resource rents from such fisheries have
been shown to be depressed well below the sustainable levels obtainable under
efficient economic management, if not eliminated altogether.

Correspondingly, an ample literature has emerged documenting the large
potential economic gains to be obtained if a system of secure harvesting rights

were instituted in conjunction with efficient overall limits on annual harvest limits (Shotton 2000; Squires et al. 1995; De Alessi 1998; Arneson 1997). These harvesting right systems in fisheries are generally described as Individual Fishing Quota (IFQ) or Individual Transferable Quota (ITQ) regimes. In such regimes recognized participants in a fishery are required to hold quota permits equal to their landed catch. Quotas are typically defined as percentages of the year's Total Allowable Catch (TAC). Recognized participants may include boat owners, operators, fleet owners, or even fish processors. They may acquire permits through an initial allocation based on their historical participation in the fishery or other criteria, through an initial auction, or by buying or leasing them from other participants. In such regimes, participants' ability to lease or sell their quotas encourages reduction of excessive effort. Participants' secure rights to participate proportionately in future increases in the value of the total catch discourages stock depletion and excessive harvesting of immature specimens. These economic incentives, if combined with appropriate limitations on the annual overall harvest, lead to large potential gains in resource rents in fisheries governed by IFQ/ITQ systems.

These gains have been demonstrated in countries other than the United States where ITQ regimes have been instituted. In New Zealand, which has converted most marine fisheries to quota management, rising permit values have provided evidence of increasing resource rents (Newell, Sanchirico, and Kerr 2002). The experience in Iceland, which has also installed ITQ systems in its major marine fisheries, also shows a reduction in excessive effort and overfishing and a rise in resource rents (Arnason and Gissurarson 1999).

A side-by-side comparison of the Atlantic sea scallop fisheries in the United States and Canada over the period 1984–99 demonstrated that the Canadian fishery, which operated a quota management system, achieved substantially greater increases in fishermen's incomes with less fishing mortality than did the U.S. fishery, which operated a regulatory system based on effort controls (Repetto 2001a). Comparable experience has been reported in other foreign fisheries as well (International Council for the Exploration of the Sea 1997).

Moreover, other approaches to marine fisheries management have not achieved similar improvements in resource rents nor have they been nearly as successful in reducing excessive effort or resource over-exploitation. Regulations limiting entry to a fishery, ending open access, have generally been imposed only after fishing effort has become excessive and overfishing has become evident. In these situations the size of the harvesting industry remains too large to achieve economic efficiency or conservation goals, so that further steps to limit fishing effort are usually required. Controls imposed on fishing inputs, intended to limit vessel capacity through restrictions on days fished, gear, crew sizes, and the like have generally led to compensatory changes in technology to maintain fishing capacity despite the controls, in a process known as "effort stuffing." This approach has usually raised fishing costs and reduced resource rents without resolving the underlying problems (Townsend 1990; Christy 1978; Christy 1996).

There have been ample economic incentives for institutional changes to create secure harvesting rights and thereby capture the potential resource rents in marine fisheries by eliminating excessive effort and overharvesting. The failures of open access and other fisheries management approaches and the potential successes of ITQ regimes have been documented. Nonetheless, progress in the United States has been halting and sporadic. Few fisheries or fisheries management councils moved to create secure harvesting rights. By the mid-1990s only three marine fisheries had adopted ITQ management approaches, and then only in response to near-crisis conditions. These three were the Atlantic Ocean quahog and surf clam fishery, the South Atlantic wreckfish fishery, and the Alaskan sablefish and halibut fishery (National Research Council 1999). In the Alaskan halibut fishery, for example, attempts to limit the catch by restricting the number of fishing days had reached such a point that the allowable fishing season was only a few days per year. Powerful vessels raced into the open seas when the season opened, whatever the weather, and fished around the clock until time expired. All vessels then returned to port simultaneously, dumping their catch on the market at once to create a temporary glut of halibut. This fishery adopted an ITQ regime partly to put an end to these dangerous "fishing derbies," which had led to numerous rescue missions and some fatalities in bad weather, and partly to correct the extreme market disruption and overcapitalization that characterized the previous approach (Pautzke and Oliver 1997).

In contrast, the ITQ program in this fishery allowed the industry to reduce the number of vessels fishing and to operate them throughout much of the year, lowering harvesting costs and allowing fuller utilization of capacity. The longer fishing season evened out the flow of fresh halibut to the market. As a result, more halibut could be sold fresh, bringing higher prices. More rational fishing also diminished gear losses and conflicts, reduced bycatch, and improved safety of operations. Most participants in this fishery, including some that were initially skeptical or opposed to ITQs, recognized the improvements.

Nonetheless, there was criticism of the program from those elements that thought that they had not received their fair share of the harvesting quotas and from local communities that felt that the volume of fish brought into their ports had declined. Similarly, in the ocean quahog and surf clam fishery on the mid-Atlantic coast, another early ITQ innovator, criticism came from those who questioned the allocation of quota shares and who objected to the subsequent consolidation of the harvest into the hands of fewer vessels and companies (Rieser 1999). Despite the successes of these early ITQ programs, these criticisms fed opposition to their replication in other fisheries.

Thus, when the Gulf of Mexico fishery management council developed and adopted an ITQ program for its red snapper fishery prior to the enactment of a congressional moratorium in 1996, it was specifically rescinded by that legislation, the reauthorization of the Magnuson-Stevens Act. Other fisheries, such as the Alaskan crab and groundfish fisheries, that had been considering ITQ systems, had their planning and development processes brought to a halt.

THE SUPPLY OF SECURE FISHING RIGHTS

In contexts other than fisheries management, observers have often pointed out the impediments and difficulties surrounding institutional change, even in the presence of strong economic incentives. "History is replete with examples of societies failing to change property rights at the optimal time" (Alston and Mueller 2002, p. 13). The impression created in some economic theories of a smooth response of institutions to changing economic needs and incentives is oversimplified in ignoring the impediments to institutional development. Many of these impediments are observable in the structure and governance of U.S. marine fisheries and have contributed to the slow pace of institutional change in the development of secure harvesting rights.

HIGH TRANSACTION COSTS

Harvesting quotas in fisheries managed in ITQ regimes become valuable assets. Although many regimes claim that quotas do not constitute property rights, they are bought and leased and are used as backing for commercial borrowings, so they have many of the key characteristics of property rights. Typically, as fisheries brought under ITQs recover from excessive fishing effort and overharvesting, resource rents rise and harvest quotas increase in value. Those who receive quota shares at the outset of the regime are likely to enjoy a significant capital gain, while those who do not have to buy quota at rising prices in order to enter the fishery. Therefore, the initial allocation of quotas among participants in a fishery, if quotas are not auctioned off by the government, is a matter of great consequence and is subject to intense negotiation. Any criterion adopted as the basis for allocation will favor some participants relative to others. Moreover, application of any allocation criterion, such as past catch history, is subject to interpretation, protest, and negotiation. Some participants may claim, for example, that the records of their catch in previous years are inaccurate or that their past catch was exceptionally low for reasons beyond their control.

Because so much is at stake, negotiations over the initial allocation of quota are inevitably difficult. Even though the adoption of secure property rights could make almost all participants better off, jealousies over the relative size of the gains among participants still fuel controversies. Even in fisheries with few participants, such as the Canadian sea scallop fishery, which had only twelve eligible participants at the time, the negotiation over asset allocation took more than a year to conclude. In larger fisheries, with hundreds of participants, the difficulties of negotiating an allocation rise exponentially. In the United States, where the fisheries management councils and the National Marine Fisheries Service manage some fisheries on a unitary basis over a large geographic area, rather than breaking them up into smaller regional subunits, the negotiations and transactions costs involved in changing management approaches are greatly elevated. The U.S. sea scallop fishery, for example, is managed as one fishery stretching from the Gulf of Maine to the mid-Atlantic coast, encompassing more than three hundred participants. At one time when an adjustment to declining stocks was needed, the scallop fishery rejected a proposal to consider an ITQ system as a management option on the grounds that negotiating quota allocation would take too long.

The transaction costs involved in adopting a different management approach are also elevated because of the structure and functioning of the regional fisheries management councils. These bodies include representatives of many of the federally managed fisheries in the region, onshore processors, state and federal officials, and sometimes environmental and other interests. Individual fisheries cannot autonomously govern their own fate. Even if a subcommittee for an individual fishery recommended adoption of an ITQ-like system, other interests on the council might object on the basis of possible repercussions on the constituencies that they represent or on other grounds. This structure complicates the negotiations over institutional change. Moreover, the decision process in the advisory panels that make recommendations to the fisheries management councils is not always clear-cut. In some cases, councils request that their advisers submit consensus recommendations rather than making decisions by majority voting. That process leads to prolonged discussion and debate in which interests outside the fishery can take an active role. Moreover, parties who are losing the debate within the fisheries management councils can and do shift the venue by trying to bring pressure to bear on the decision process from state and federal politicians, the courts, and the media.

Losing parties may also rally their constituencies to carry on the fight while the winners become complacent. An outcry from the energized losers sometimes stimulates the council to reopen the debate and reverse or modify its previous decision, setting the stage for another round of conflict. In the absence of any explicit allocation process, all of the conservation decisions made by the councils have allocational implications. Despite the protestations of many council members that the job of the council is conservation, not allocation, decisions are often influenced more by allocation arguments than by biological or economic considerations. All this increases the transaction costs involved in accomplishing a regime change in fisheries management.

"SOCIAL TRAPS"

During most of the period since Europeans first settled in America, marine fisheries were open-access resources, although perhaps not as free and open as the contemporary view of history may suggest (Higgs 1982; Acheson 1992; Johnson and Libecap 1995). Anyone with a vessel and gear could go fishing and bring home the harvest. Fisheries came under official management only when they showed unmistakable signs of stress. Some marine fisheries are still not actively managed. The tradition that anybody should be able to become a fisherman still resonates strongly in coastal communities and among established fishermen who, at some earlier point in life, decided to go to sea and don't see why their nephews and sons-in-law shouldn't be able to make the same choice. This attitude is especially strong in the New England states, where fishing was a pillar of the economy and trade in colonial times and thereafter, up until the time that a manufacturing base was established.

This bias against excluding people from within the community persists even as participants in stressed fisheries have reluctantly been forced to accept restrictions on their allowable fishing days, their gear and vessel capacity, and even on the total allowable catch. Ninety percent of fishermen consider themselves to be "above average in ability," like the children of Lake Wobegon. Consequently, they think that in an open-access situation, if they were just freed from limitations on catch or effort, they would make out better than their rivals would. The people in a fishery are those who have survived. Overoptimism and overconfidence are typical among Americans generally and seem to be especially characteristic of fishermen, whose occupation is entrepreneurial, opportunistic, and individualistic.

Fishermen traditionally sought to limit competition from "outsiders" through intimidation and residency requirements. Maine's "lobster gangs" and recent campaigns of intimidation against Gulf shrimp fishermen of Vietnamese origin are examples. However, during the last half of the twentieth century these traditional access limitations became less effective. As people became more mobile, traditional access limitations became a double-edged sword—they might keep fishermen from doing what they wished as well as keeping the competition at bay. Most residency requirements were struck down by the courts, bringing the state to the aid of interlopers who might previously have been driven off by vigilante enforcers. Some fisheries were also overfished to the point that they were virtually abandoned by traditional fishermen. As these resources recovered, new entrants did not necessarily carry with them the old traditions. With increasing mobility and regional economic integration, old traditions of local particularism and exclusivity naturally broke down.

As all this was happening, fishery biologists were gaining influence in the push for conservation, and fishery economists were beginning to be heard in their quest for economic rationality. Limited entry was transformed from a self-serving protectionist measure to a scientifically supported conservation and management tool. But fishery participants who are always looking for a new opportunity still do not like the idea of being legally excluded from a potential source of income. Most prefer to use whatever selective and traditional barriers to entry they have available rather than invoking the less discerning and predictable power of the state.

The status quo bias in fisheries management is strengthened by the inability of most fishermen to perceive the potential gains from obtaining secure harvesting rights. Risk and uncertainty may be obstacles, particularly because an individual's gain would be strongly affected by his or her initial quota allocation. Should an individual fishermen fail for some reason to obtain his due quota share, he might be worse off in a regime change though other fishermen might gain—partly at his expense. Moreover, shifting from a regime based on effort controls, which many fisherman have learned to work around, to one based on harvest controls presents distinct risks: many fishermen are quite reluctant to reveal their catch in any detail, especially to the tax collector.

Due to inexperience in the policy arena, where rent-seeking skills outweigh fishing skills, many fishermen cannot see clearly through conflicting claims by opposing parties. Most owner operators may be good fishermen but are not necessarily good managers, even of their own businesses. Most have little understanding of or interest in the broader issues of managing the entire fishery. It is the rare fisherman who can be influenced by theoretical economic arguments about rent dissipation or who cares about economic efficiency in fisheries as a management goal. It doesn't matter to an individual fisherman whether the fishery is large or small, is producing its potential, or is severely overfished, as long as he or she can make a satisfactory living. Moreover, because of controversies over past management plan adjustments to restrict fishing efforts, there is a residue of distrust between fishermen, fisheries scientists, and managers. Many fishermen believe that the fisheries managers and scientists don't know or understand the actual situation out on the water. As a result of all this, fishing interests and local community leaders typically are not swayed by predictions of potential gains. To be convinced of the desirability of a change in regime, they would have to have concrete evidence that the alternative regime works better and would work better for them individually in their own fishery.

However, if there are no examples of the alternative regime in operation for fishermen to look at, the fishery may be caught in a "social trap": without an alternative to look at, fishermen won't be convinced to change, but unless fishermen can be convinced to change, there can be no alternative regime in operation to look at. For most of recent U.S. fishing history, this catch-22 situation has been a major impediment to the adoption of secure harvesting rights. American fishermen would not regard experience in such far-flung places as New Zealand and Iceland, which have operated ITQ systems, as relevant to their own situations. And, until recently, with only three U.S. marine fisheries under ITQ management and with only a short time span of experience to evaluate, opponents have been able to point to alleged inequities in the initial quota operation to denigrate those experiments.

As William Brock's paper points out, social traps like this can be strongly reinforced if those who deviate from the prevailing view can be "punished" through social or other pressures. This reinforcement has been evident in the debates over ITQ adoption. To a considerable extent, those within a fishery constitute a community, encountering each other on the docks and in association meetings and living in or near the same fishing ports. These personal ties make social pressures possible. The relatively few advocates that ITQs have had in New England have been subject to attacks in print and in meetings by opponents attempting to discredit not only their views on the issue but their personal credibility as well. Some have been removed from leadership positions in fishing associations. As a result, far more people support ITQs than are willing to say so publicly in policy discussions. Only a small fraction of fishermen actually go to management and association meetings. Others stay away, in part because they don't want to be forced to declare their positions and in part because they are unwilling to "waste time" on endless and arcane debates. The stronger the pressures that can be brought to bear against deviations from the prevailing opinion, the longer can change be deferred, even in the face of economic losses.

In this situation, the function of a moratorium on the development or approval of new ITQ-like regimes, such as the one that opponents persuaded Congress to enact in 1996, is to prevent the emergence of new and additional concrete experience to which fishermen could relate in forming their own judgments about the desirability of change. Preventing the emergence of new evidence would preserve and prolong the social trap described above. This may explain why ITQ opponents pressed for a national moratorium, even though the adoption of such regimes must proceed on a fishery-by-fishery basis, so that those who opposed the adoption of secure harvesting rights in particular fisheries could do so within the responsible fisheries management councils. Absent a national moratorium, however, any fishery that did decide to adopt an ITQ regime would provide a new body of experience and information that might well sway the judgments and decisions of participants in other fisheries.

BLOCKING COALITIONS

Under ITQ regimes, quota holders typically benefit by capturing the increasing rents in the fishery. In many American fisheries operating under the traditional "lay" system, in which captain, crew, and owner divide the residual income from a voyage after meeting operating expenses, skippers and crew members also share in the increasing rents. Nonetheless, there will be many groups not awarded quotas that might fear that moving to an ITQ system in a particular fishery might undermine their interests. If successful in forming a coalition, these interests might succeed in blocking change, either within the Fisheries Management Council or in another venue.

Opposition to ITQs has come from a variety of economic interests: commercial fishermen in nearby fisheries who have not participated much in the past but who wish to preserve their option to participate in the future; small commercial fishermen who have been largely exempt from restrictions in the past but who fear that their operations would be limited in the future by an ITQ system; recreational fishermen's associations and charter boat captains who fear that they would not be awarded quotas and would effectively be excluded from any portion of the total allowable catch; operators using non-dominant gear types in the fishery who fear that they would not obtain a "fair" share of quota; participants in related fisheries who fear that bycatch, habitat damage, or other ecological interactions would interfere with their operations; processors who fear loss of business if a fishery is rationalized, and local community activists who fear economic decline if fishermen exit an overcrowded fishery.

Non-commercial and non-economic opposition to adoption of ITQs has also arisen. Ideological opposition to secure harvesting rights in a traditionally open-access fishery has not been limited to the fishermen themselves. Opposition to rights-based management approaches has also come from groups such as Greenpeace who oppose creating private property rights in a public resource as well as from conservatives who see such approaches as an extension of government control over a form of free enterprise and from at least one taxpayer organization that does not like the idea of "giving away" public resources. Some environmental organizations have opposed the introduction of secure harvesting rights, preferring additional stringent effort controls or closures of fishing grounds as more reliable means of conservation and having little regard for the economic costs these measures impose. These sources of opposition have been active participants in ITQ debates.

The interests of individual fishermen often conflict with the interests of fishery trade organizations and their leaders. Individually, fishermen don't care about keeping a lot of people in the fishing business. It would be in their interest to have fewer competitors. But when fishermen join together for strength in pursuing a common cause, the strength of the group and the influence of its leader are enhanced by the size of its membership. Community leaders have a similar incentive to fight for the survival of every member of the fishing industry on the mistaken perception that more boats and more fishermen are necessarily good for the local economy. Few industry or community leaders are sophisticated enough to recognize that a larger and larger portion of available fishing revenues gets sent out of town in vessel costs, such as fuel, mortgage interest, insurance, and so on when the fleet grows but revenue does not.

Fisheries scientists and fisheries managers have sometimes withheld support from adoption of ITQ regimes for a variety of possible reasons. Most fishery managers have a background in biology and consider fishery conservation issues to be biological in nature. Fisheries scientists and their colleagues who have moved into management positions typically fail to formulate the fisheries management problem as an economic issue of income maximization. Many fishery managers and others strongly object to the idea that the fishery management system should be concerned with economic outcomes at all. To the extent that they recognize the influence of economics on conservation outcomes, they tend to believe erroneously that economic considerations would argue for an increase in harvesting, not for a reduction below the maximum that would be biologically sustainable. As a result of this biological orientation and animosity toward economics as a useful science, fishery managers become embroiled in controversies over the current fish population, the maximum sustainable yield, and the effort controls that would reduce the current overfishing to an acceptable degree. Moreover, adopting secure harvesting rights and adopting income maximization as an objective in a fishery would be a controversial step and would remove scientists and managers from center stage, since exploitation rates would diminish and the pressure for additional harvesting from marginal fishermen would abate.

A striking phenomenon has been the opposition of many politicians representing coastal constituencies to the adoption of ITQ systems, even when the fisheries in their districts have been struggling. This may stem from a desire to be responsive to constituent preferences and also from a political calculus that places a lower priority on economic efficiency than on political efficiency. Politicians may value a large number of grateful fishermen voters more highly than a larger fishing income confined to a smaller number of fishermen. It is also clear that community leaders and politicians are either unaware of, or do not accept, the economists' assertion that greater efficiency and higher profits lead to overall higher employment and a higher standard of living. Rather, politicians are overly sensitive to particular jobs that are gained or lost directly because of their policy actions, relative to jobs that are created or lost due to more general economic trends that may also be policy-related but more difficult to trace. As a result, many congressmen and some senators from coastal states have been easy recruits in efforts to forestall the development of secure harvesting rights.

These diverse interests have been successful to the extent that they have been able to coalesce in opposition and thus exert a joint influence in a decision-making venue, whether that is a fisheries management council or a congressional committee. Successful coalition building has involved a considerable degree of policy entrepreneurship, often practiced by individuals from outside the fishing industry itself, since active fishermen are typically unable or unwilling to devote the necessary time to those activities.

When united in coalition, the diversity of these interests makes them formidable opponents. In arguing for an ITQ moratorium, the sight of active fishermen and environmentalists trolling the congressional corridors together for votes was politically impressive. The active participation of interests from outside the particular fisheries subject to ITQ development makes it difficult or impossible for proponents to devise negotiating strategies that would compensate opponents for real or imagined losses. The high transaction costs of reaching decision, the possibility of shifting venues, and the murky decision processes involved in making decisions about management regime changes have made it quite feasible for blocking coalitions to prevent change.

THE 1996 MORATORIUM

When the Magnuson-Stevens Act, the fundamental legislative mandate governing marine fisheries management, was being reauthorized in 1996 there were only three federal fisheries under ITQ management: the Atlantic surf clam and ocean quahog fishery, the Alaskan halibut and sablefish fishery, and the South Atlantic wreckfish fishery. The halibut FMP had only been implemented in 1995 and the wreckfish fishery was so small as to be inconsequential in the national policy debate. The surf clam plan had been in effect for five years, but it applied to a fishery that was both controversial and uncharacteristic in the degree of vertical integration in the fishery. However, several other fisheries were considering adopting ITQ-like regimes, including the crab and groundfish fisheries in Alaska, or had already developed such a system, as had the red snapper fishery in the Gulf.

Categorical opponents of secure harvesting rights thought that adopting ITQ systems in other fisheries would create unfortunate precedents and models, possibly leading down a slippery slope to a general adoption of such regimes as the dominant management approach, as had happened in Iceland and New Zealand. Consistent with the social trap model set out in William Brock's chapter in this volume, these categorical opponents sought a nationwide moratorium in order to prevent the consensus against secure harvesting rights from eroding.

These opponents supported their case with criticism of the existing halibut and surf clam systems, allying themselves with local critics. In the former, complaints came primarily from those who felt that they had been shortchanged by the initial allocation of quotas. Complaints also arose from some Alaskan fish processing companies and local communities, for reasons explained below. In the surf clam fishery, critics focused on both the initial allocation of quotas and subsequent consolidation in a fishery that even previously had had relatively few participants. The flames of criticism were fanned by allegations of wrong-doing by the National Marine Fisheries Service, which was accused of suppressing a report by a review committee somewhat critical of the ITQ system in operation in the surf clam fishery and then covering up their actions. This imbroglio gathered considerable momentum, which carried the scandal through the moratorium debates and probably influenced Congress on the need to put a moratorium on new ITQ plans.

The opposition of the processing industry in Alaska sheds an interesting light on the working of ITQ systems and alternative management approaches. Not only had the halibut harvesting sector become grossly overcapitalized with large and powerful vessels equipped to participate in intense short-term fishing derbies, the processing sector had also greatly expanded in order to handle the exaggerated "peak load" of halibut dumped on their docks at the derby's end to be packed and frozen. The replacement of these fishing derbies with more moderate harvesting stretched over a much longer period of time revealed a substantial amount of excess capacity in the processing sector. Moreover, some of the harvest was redirected to other ports, leaving less-favored processors with reduced revenues and profits. The processing sector felt that if the halibut experience were to be repeated in other important Alaskan fisheries, such as crab and pollock, many processors would be forced out of business. Their response was to adopt a strong lobbying position, both with the North Pacific Fisheries Management Council and with the Alaskan congressional delegation, of opposition to further ITQ development unless processors were awarded exclusive processing quotas to match the harvesting quotas that would be allocated to fishermen. Processors justified this "two-pie" system on the grounds that the previous management system had created the same overcapitalization problems for them as it had for fishing businesses. These arguments are very persuasive to decision makers who do not understand the distinction between the need to create secure harvesting rights and the claim to secure processing rights.

On the other side, there were relatively few and scattered advocates of the ITQ approach opposing the imposition of the moratorium. Those fisheries that had already achieved the secure harvesting rights they desired were disinclined to fight other fishermen's battles for them. A few public-interest groups, notably the Environmental Defense Fund, spoke up against the moratorium, taking a position consistent with its general advocacy of "market-friendly" solutions to resource and environmental problems. Some scattered economists and people in and around the fisheries sector who were convinced that secure harvesting rights were the best option opposed the moratorium, but this assemblage was scarcely a coalition, and with little favorable experience or satisfied beneficiaries to point to, it could not carry equal weight with those advocating a moratorium.

In addition, several more particularistic interests were important in forming an effective legislative coalition behind passage of a moratorium. Senator Ted Stevens of Alaska, senior Republican on the crucial senate authorizing committee, was responsive to the Alaskan processing industry and to local communities fearful of losing fishing sector jobs. In addition, there were vocal concerns from Alaskan fishermen that in new ITQ systems in Alaskan waters, if quota were awarded on the basis of catch history, they would be at a disadvantage to the fishing fleet from Washington State, which was longer established and had a richer harvesting history. Alaskan fishermen were not averse to a moratorium that would allow them additional years in which to catch up.

In New England, the congressional delegation lined up in support of a moratorium, led by Olympia Snowe of Maine and John Kerry of Massachusetts in the Senate, and by Barney Frank, William Delahunt, and others in the House. Since there were no ITQ systems in operation or under development by the New England Fishery Management Council and very little chance that any fishery in the Northeast would have chosen that option within the moratorium period, given the region's strong ideological opposition to entry limitations, these legislators were acting, or grandstanding, mostly in response to constituent preferences.[1] Other legislators joined the coalition in response to particular interests in their constituencies: Trent Lott of Mississippi in response to the interests of influential processors and Slade Gorton of Washington (whose family controlled Gorton's Seafoods) in response to processing interests.

With little opposition, this coalition was able to enact a four-year national moratorium, the rationale for which was to create time in which to develop a set of "safeguards" that would be enacted legislatively and would ensure that any new ITQ systems developed after the moratorium was removed would be free of any flaws or deficiencies. In association with the moratorium, a study was demanded of the National Research Council that would thoroughly review experience with ITQs in both the United States and other countries. The concrete result of the moratorium was to halt the Gulf red snapper ITQ program in its tracks and to arrest the development of ITQ-like programs in the Pacific Northwest.

EXTENDING THE MORATORIUM

Following this legislative victory, a powerful and growing alliance of organizations coalesced within the Marine Fisheries Conservation Network (MFCN) to use the time gained by the four-year moratorium to further their objectives. The MFCN had grown from a coalition of five organizations, begun in 1992. The network's core objective was to ensure the implementation of the conservation provisions included in the 1996 Sustainable Fisheries Act, as the Magnuson-Stevens reauthorization was called, especially the rebuilding of fisheries populations to the levels that would sustain maximum harvests. This was to be accomplished through significant reductions in harvesting of such overfished stocks, through reduction in bycatch and through habitat protection. In support of these objectives, the network attracted membership from many important national and regional conservation groups, including the Natural Resources Defense Council, the Sierra Club, the World Wildlife Fund, Greenpeace, Defenders of Wildlife, the National Wildlife Federation, the National Audubon Society, the Chesapeake Bay Foundation, the Conservation Law Foundation, the Alaska Marine Conservation Council, and others. The network also attracted membership from a large number and variety of fishing, fish processing, and coastal community organizations whose objectives included protection of their own perceived economic interests. Many of these organizations were opposed to the creation of any ITQ regime that did not ensure that their participation in the fishery or other interests would be safeguarded. During the period from 1996 to 2000, membership in the MFCN increased from about eighty to more than a hundred organizations.

While not opposing ITQ regimes per se, the network rejected the proposition that secure harvesting rights would be sufficient to promote sustainable fisheries and demanded that the moratorium be extended until the MFCN's somewhat lengthy list of safeguards and conditions were enacted into national legislative standards governing any future ITQ system. Foremost among these was the demand that quotas not constitute property rights that would enable holders to claim compensation for a "taking" of property in the event that quotas should be reduced or rescinded.[2] Quotas, the network demanded, should be awarded for a limited duration (preferably no more than five years) and be renewed only if the quota holder were judged to have provided additional conservation benefits, in the form of bycatch reduction, habitat conservation, and conservative gear management. Absent such good behavior, quotas should be revocable, the network maintained. In addition, ITQ regimes themselves should be subject to periodic evaluation by "public interest" panels and be continued only if contributing to sustainability and yielding additional conservation benefits. The MFCN held that catch history should not be allowed as the basis for allocation of quota, on the grounds that such a criterion would reward those fishermen most responsible for past overfishing. Instead, they argued that quota allocations should favor fishermen with a "good" record of sustainable fishing. Beyond these conservation provisions, the MFCN network demanded that any ITQ regime contain safeguards against excessive consolidation (no more than 1 percent of total quota in the hands of any holder) and safeguards to protect new entrants, small fishermen, and communities.

In a sense, the network's strategy was to hold ITQ development hostage to the acceptance of its conservation and social demands, which were supplementary to those already enacted in the 1996 Sustainable Fisheries Act. Like other participants in ITQ debates, the MFCN was engaging in a form of "rent-seeking behavior" by attempting to capture benefits important to its interests through the legislative process. Environmental groups, including some MFCN members, had successfully pursued a similar strategy in congressional negotiations over the sulfur trading provisions in the acid rain program of the 1990 Clean Air Act Amendments, obtaining a more stringent national emission reduction target in exchange for support for the permit trading system introduced in that legislation.

The growth of the MFCN illustrates an important positive feedback "bandwagon" effect that contributes to punctuated equilibrium dynamics. Building such a large and diverse coalition demanded a substantial organizational and entrepreneurial effort. Organizers attempted to prevent "agenda explosion" by limiting its goals to a core set of issues and recommendations to which members could all subscribe. This required compromises by many member organizations to modify their policy positions in order to add to and benefit from the MFCN's lobbying clout. Many organizations did compromise and sign on, illustrating a positive feedback mechanism conducive to punctuated equilibrium behavior in the policy domain: the larger and more influential the network became, the more an individual organization could gain by joining its lobbying efforts to the network's and so the greater was the incentive to compromise on policy goals. Some organizations, especially those from New England, relinquished their preferred categorical opposition to ITQs in favor of the network's conditional opposition. This experience illustrates a rational "bandwagon" effect that attracted new members to the coalition in order to improve their influence. Nonetheless, some organizations, such as the Environmental Defense Fund, one of the original five members, left the network on account of MFCN's support for continuing the moratorium.

Its organizational success and conservation agenda attracted crucial financial support from large foundations such as the Pew Charitable Trusts, the Packard Foundation, the Rockefeller Brothers Fund, and the Surdna Foundation, another illustration of the bandwagon effect. Foundations such as these, in supporting policy advocates, look for potential effectiveness and for success in building coalitions across diverse organizations. Their financial resources were essential in enabling the MFCN to build its coalition and actively represent its positions. MFCN has used a variety of lobbying tools. The MFCN members and staff have testified, developed, and submitted legislative language, worked with legislative staff, organized write-in campaigns by fishermen targeted at local and key legislators, organized media campaigns to get stories and editorials into newspapers and then referred them to legislators. They paired environmentalists with fishermen in delegations to lobby in the halls of Congress, creating a strong impression of consensus. Some member organizations, notably the Cape Cod Commercial Hook Fishermen's Association, invigorated by leadership from outside the fishermen's ranks and by foundation funding, played a particularly active role. The network was able to exert a strong influence, in both the House and the Senate, on proposed legislation creating national standards and safeguards for future ITQ systems. Bills introduced in the Senate by Kerry and Snowe and in the House of Representatives by Delahunt, Allen, and others incorporated most of the MFCN demands.

During this period the National Research Council published the review of ITQ programs commissioned in 1996 when the moratorium was imposed (National Research Council 1998). Reflecting the composition of the committee that authored it, this report offered a carefully balanced, rather equivocal assessment of ITQ programs in the United States and elsewhere. For one reason, the committee had little up-to-date data on U.S. programs on which to base its assessment. Its recommendation that the moratorium be allowed to expire was paired with recommendations for safeguards in any future ITQ program to ward off negative impacts. Despite this less-than-rousing endorsement, an important MFCN member, Greenpeace, published a rebuttal (called "Scaring the Fish") to the National Research Council's report in mid-November 1999, as the moratorium was about to expire. All in all, the comprehensive review commissioned when the moratorium was imposed did little to resolve the ITQ debates.

The "safeguards" bills before Congress in 1999 contained some provisions that were controversial, including some that were clearly designed to maintain the "social trap" preventing ITQ experiments. Legislation introduced by Senator Snowe, for example, mandated that fisheries management councils organize a referendum before any ITQ management plan could even be developed and obtain a two-thirds super-majority of all those eligible to vote in favor of developing an ITQ plan. Such an approval would not be required for the development of any alternative management option. This proposal was widely seen as a "poison pill" provision that would effectively block ITQ initiatives. People favorably disposed to ITQ regimes pointed out that very few fishermen would vote to develop an ITQ management option before knowing, at least in broad outline, what the plan would contain. Therefore, recognizing fishermen's low participation rates in management affairs, requiring such approval from two-thirds of those eligible to participate would constitute an insurmountable hurdle to ITQ plan development. Clearly, the thrust of this provision was to maintain the social trap holding fisheries within the traditional management options. In the event that the development of an ITQ plan was approved in this way, another referendum yielding a similar super-majority would be required for adoption.

In the event, as happens frequently in the closing days of a congressional session, it became clear that time would not allow a safeguards bill to clear both houses of Congress, due largely to the backlog of essential but incomplete congressional business clogging the calendars of House and Senate. Consideration of the standards bills were carried over into the lame duck session of Congress following the November 2000 national elections. Consequently, key senators, including Snowe, Stevens, Ted Kennedy, and Kerry, worked to extend the moratorium and were successful in obtaining a two-year extension, until October 2002.

THE MORATORIUM EXPIRES

Despite this success in extending the moratorium, despite the growing strength and continuing opposition of the MFCN, which by 2002 had increased its membership to more than 120 organizations, and despite the failure to pass a national ITQ safeguards bill, the moratorium on ITQ development was not extended when the two-year extension was over, and it was allowed to expire in

October 2002. What had changed during this two-year period? Why was a policy that was instituted by key legislators and supported by a powerful coalition of interests suddenly reversed after remaining firmly in place for six years? Two changes stand out as important forces for change.

First, a significant amount of "policy learning" had been taking place. Experience had been accumulating, especially in the Alaskan halibut and sablefish fisheries, demonstrating the improvements brought about by the change to an ITQ regime. In the halibut fishery, the fishing season had been extended from two one-day derbies to an eight-month harvesting period, ending the frantic race to fish and improving safety. More careful harvesting had greatly reduced losses of gear and associated harvest, saving the fleet millions of dollars per year. Overcapacity in the fleet had been reduced by a 53 percent decline in the number of active vessels, many of which had been temporarily diverted from other fisheries just to participate in the derbies. The longer harvesting season greatly increased the availability of fresh halibut at higher dockside prices and enabled fishermen to time their operations to take advantage of market conditions. Consequently, the market value of the total allowable catch increased significantly. The longer season also enabled halibut and sablefish harvesters to avoid each other's prime fishing areas and periods, reducing incidental bycatch of each species by substantial percentages. Evidence of these benefits was forcefully present in Senate testimony by the fishery arguing for the repeal of the moratorium (Alverson 2000).

Moreover, the halibut/sablefish experience provided evidence that fisheries management councils could design ITQ regimes that would not fall victim to the disadvantages predicted by their opponents. Limits on the amount of quota that could be controlled by any one holder and requirements that the quota holder be an active participant on the harvesting vessel guarded against excessive consolidation or a "takeover" of the fishery by absentee corporate interests. Limits on quota transferability outside geographic regions and vessel classes prevented unwanted community disruption. A fee structure imposed on quota holders to fund loans for new entrants into the fishery promoted openness. The fishery was also able to show that the distribution of the catch to shore-side processors and distributors had not changed radically after institution of the ITQ system, the top five landing ports remaining the same. In addition, statistics demonstrated that the ITQ regime had not led to "high grading" of the resource by discarding the young and immature fish caught; rather, the percentage of fish caught that were retained in the harvest remained constant or increased. The evidence presented from the Alaskan experiment refuted the pessimistic predictions of ITQ opponents and showed substantial advantages over the preceding management approach.

This experience was enough to persuade many people in the fishing industry around the country that ITQ systems were at least worth considering as a management option. By 2002 the chairmen of all eight of the regional fisheries management councils had taken the position that the councils needed access to the "entire toolbox" and that the moratorium should be dropped. Some specific fisheries also argued for dropping the moratorium or allowing them exemptions in order that they could pursue their desires to develop ITQ systems. These included, notably, the Gulf of Mexico red snapper and reef fisheries, which had developed an ITQ regime before 1996 and seen it rescinded by the moratorium, and the Alaskan groundfish fishery. It became more likely that even if the moratorium were extended further, it would be increasingly riddled with exemptions.

Second, the interests of some important members of the blocking coalition had shifted, reducing the value of the moratorium to them and lessening their support for it. In particular, the concerns for the Alaskan harvesting fleet and processors that had motivated Senator Stevens, whose position as chairman of the Appropriations Committee gave him a great deal of power, had abated. The catch history of the Alaskan fleet had increased during the period of the moratorium and the Washington fleet had become more integrated into the Alaskan economy with shore-side processing and other facilities. Even more significantly, the concerns of the Alaskan processing industry had largely been taken care of by the American Fisheries Act. The AFA protected processor interests in the Alaskan pollock fishery by dividing the total allowable catch among community development corporations, the fleet harvesting for inshore processors, and the offshore component. The AFA also authorized and encouraged the formation of cooperatives involving both catching vessels and processors. Such cooperatives could hold a substantial percentage of the total quota and ensure processors not only a stable supply of fish but also a share in the increasing rents of the fishery. These cooperatives could harvest their share of quota as they deemed best, creating secure harvesting rights in the pollock fishery. With the concerns of the processing industry and local communities largely taken care of and with other Alaskan fisheries asking to develop and adopt ITQ systems, the incentives for Senator Stevens and the rest of the Alaskan congressional delegation had shifted. Without their support, continued opposition to ITQs from the MFCN and most of the New England congressional delegation was not a sufficiently strong coalition to maintain the moratorium.

Now that the moratorium has been allowed to expire, it is unlikely that it will be reinstated, because it is far more difficult to take action in Congress than to prevent action. Nor has any "safeguards" bill emerged from Congress in the two years since the moratorium expired. It is likely that future advocacy for and opposition to secure harvesting rights systems will be played out in the regional fisheries management councils.

WILL THE TRAP OPEN? RECENT INITIATIVES
TOWARD THE DEVELOPMENT OF SECURE
HARVESTING RIGHTS

The social trap model predicts that increasing evidence of the benefits of secure harvesting rights should eventually create a bandwagon effect toward adoption of ITQ systems in more and more fisheries in which this management approach is appropriate. If the moratorium was effective in maintaining the social trap, then its removal should have been followed by an increase in ITQ development. Has that taken place?

Yes, to some extent that has happened. One would not necessarily expect that the pace of change would be extremely rapid because the development of any ITQ system poses difficult issues that must be resolved through arduous negotiation. For example, in fisheries in which effort controls have been the management approach, the shift to harvest controls is a major change that threatens the more productive fishermen. Moreover, allocating the catch among the many claimants, as discussed earlier, is a crucial and difficult issue to negotiate. Any settlement must also resolve concerns about excessive consolidation and market power.

Nonetheless, the Gulf of Mexico reef and red snapper fishery, whose ITQ plan was put on hold in 1996, resumed plan development by special dispensation even before the moratorium had finally expired. As of the end of 2003, the fishery had a plan to put before its members for ratification in a special referendum. By April 2004, an overwhelming majority, 92 percent, of participants had approved development of an ITQ program for the fishery.

On the Pacific coast, a committee has been established by the Pacific Fisheries Management Council to develop an ITQ plan for the Pacific groundfish fishery. The committee has traveled to British Council to learn more about the Canadian groundfish management regime there, which resembles an ITQ system.

Even in New England, where output quotas are distinctly unpopular, recent developments have favored the creation of transferable, divisible fishing rights. On December 17, 2003, the Atlantic States Marine Fisheries Commission's Lobster Management Board approved transferable trap limits for three lobster management areas under its jurisdiction. Earlier, in Amendment 13 to the groundfish management plan, the New England Fisheries Management Council adopted a provision authorizing transferability of allowable days at sea. Though these innovations do not create the conservation incentives implicit in secure harvesting rights, they move in that direction by establishing transferable fishing rights in terms of fishing effort. Moreover, in the Atlantic sea scallop fishery, limits on the number of permissible trips to harvest scallops in the groundfish closed area have been supplemented by catch limits per trip, creating de facto individual vessel quotas for scallops harvested in the restricted areas. Though those are not yet transferable, a step in the direction of secure harvesting rights has been taken. Finally in 2005, the Bush Administration embraced ITQ-like regimes as a preferred fisheries management approach.

LESSONS LEARNED

This chapter has identified the obstacles and frictions impeding institutional change, the evolution of secure harvesting rights in marine fisheries. Change has been halting, interrupted by a policy-mandated moratorium and sudden reversals. The experience has shown the applicability of the social trap model analyzed by William Brock in his contribution to this volume. Without favorable experience to look at, fisheries are reluctant to depart from traditional management approaches and are able to suppress dissenting views. At the same time, without fisheries willing and able to adopt a new approach, no new experience, favorable or unfavorable, can accumulate. The accumulation of experience with the few extant ITQ regimes, especially the one in the Alaskan halibut/sablefish sector, allowed for gradual "policy learning" through dissemination of information about the benefits of secure harvesting rights in an actual application.

Punctuated equilibrium behavior was also enhanced by the bandwagon effect generated by the Marine Fisheries Conservation Network, which was the more able to attract new adherents and funding, the larger and more inclusive it became. Its size and the diverse interests it gathered under its banner enabled it, for a time at least, to have a strong policy influence.

Changes in the payoff structure to the policy "game" also illustrate the fact that slowly changing underlying variables are capable of triggering abrupt shifts in political positions and outcomes. As the Alaskan fleet gradually accumulated "catch history" as a basis for quota allocation, and as the Washington fleet gradually integrated itself into the Alaskan economy, the economic interests prompting the Alaskan congressional delegation's opposition to ITQs diminished. Because of Senator Stevens' powerful position, the loss of his support for extending the moratorium further was a crucial change, given the uneven distribution of political power over national fisheries policy.

This case study yields several insights into mechanisms that would relax constraints on institutional evolution in the development of secure harvesting rights. These lessons might have broader applicability as well.

To the extent that the social trap was perpetuated by the lack of actual experience with ITQ systems, institutional changes that would facilitate innovation and experimentation could be expected to lead to faster emergence of new examples. Disaggregation of management responsibility and assignment of portions of the total allowable catch into smaller management units, defined either by geographic region or by gear type, would allow these multiplied management units scope to experiment with other management approaches, including ITQ systems. For example, in the NE groundfish sector, a separate catch quota has been established for hook fishermen. New England lobster management responsibilities have been decentralized to smaller subregional units. In the Atlantic sea scallop fishery, management on a unitary basis from the Gulf of Maine to the mid-Atlantic could also be disaggregated into different management units. Multiplying the management units and responsibilities creates opportunities for venturesome units to innovate and can provide more evidence of comparative performance of different approaches.

Self-management of a catch allocation by harvesting cooperatives, as authorized by the Fishery Cooperative Marketing Act of 1937, can free a fishery or subsector from the transactional costs of management decision-making by fisheries management councils. As shown in the Pacific Whiting Cooperative and the North Pacific Pollock Conservation Cooperative, such cooperatives can be formed to include traditional and commercial harvesters and processors as well. They allow rationalization of a sector and provide a clear conservation incentive while eliminating one ideological objection to ITQ-like systems, the assignment of a private transferable right to a quantity of harvest to one party, which is sometimes seen as privatizing a public resource.

Along the same lines, better information sharing and dissemination would help eliminate social traps by bringing evidence on actual performance of alternative management approaches within easy reach of fishermen who have little time or inclination to investigate experience in other fisheries or other countries. The National Fisheries Management Service, the Sea Grant program, and other credible bodies could usefully sponsor or carry out and disseminate evaluations and assessments of alternative management approaches in actual applications. Fisheries extension programs might be expanded to include fisheries management aspects as well as technical matters.

Opposition to the creation of secure harvesting rights can be reduced if in the development of such plans the concerns of actual and potential opponents are taken seriously. The potential gains from rationalization in most fisheries are so large that all participants could benefit. Plans could be developed to ensure that potential "losers" are effectively made whole. The initial allocation of quota can be carried out in such a way that particular segments of the fishery are not excluded or treated unfairly. Limits on consolidation and transferability can be built into ITQ plans to ensure against unwanted social effects, though at the cost of some potential efficiency loss. Some resource rents can be collected through quota fees to provide revenues for monitoring and enforcement, to support new entrants, or to compensate participants who can demonstrate injury because of the change in management regime.

The transaction costs of institutional change can be reduced by clear decision mechanisms. For example, if it were necessary and sufficient for approval of an ITQ plan that at least a majority of voting participants in a fishery voted for adoption in a single referendum, then venue shifting and interference by interests outside the particular fishery would be discouraged.

The case study also illustrates the possibility of creating influential advocacy coalitions by combining policy entrepreneurship with the bandwagon effects of group effectiveness. Those who built the Marine Fish Conservation Network were able to enlist many organizations, to persuade them to compromise on policy objectives, and to support them with adequate foundation funding by making use of positive feedbacks. These techniques could be used to create other advocacy coalitions as well.

NOTES

1. Senator Snowe's home state was also embroiled in a battle with the Mid-Atlantic Fishery Management Council concerning the inclusion of a small Maine fishery for ocean quahogs in the surf clam and ocean quahog ITQ system. At the time the surf clam plan was developed, the Downeast Maine fishery was ignored. When the ITQ system was implemented, however, it became illegal for Maine fishermen to continue in their fishery because they had not had federal permits and had not submitted catch reports that were re-

quired to obtain an ocean quahog quota share. This experience with ocean quahog quotas reinforced Maine's position that ITQs would be likely to disenfranchise Maine fishermen.
2. The Government of New Zealand had been forced to buy back quota from fishermen when stocks became overfished in the early versions of its ITQ management system, since quotas had been denominated in pounds of fish rather than as percentages of the total allowable catch.

Chapter 6 Behavioral Thresholds and Institutional Rigidities as Explanations of Punctuated Equilibrium Processes in Pacific Northwest Forest Policy Dynamics

Benjamin Cashore and Michael Howlett

Few policy problems have captured more attention from environmental groups, business interests, governments, and scientists than the environmental condition of forestlands in the United States Pacific Northwest. For more than a generation, natural scientists have documented significant and complex human impacts on the natural forest environment: the extensive decline in late succession (old growth) forests (Franklin 1988) and ecologically sensitive riparian areas (Independent Multidisciplinary Science Team 1999) and the increasing number of threatened and endangered species (Yafee 1994), all of which indicated considerable stress in forest ecosystems (Kohm and Franklin 1997; Franklin 1993). These problems have led to societal unrest, as environmental groups, rural communities, professional foresters, forestry scholars, and the public at large have all attempted to influence policy responses (Environmental Protection Information Center 2002).

This chapter describes how forest policy has developed in response to these pressures and answers a resulting question: why responses to these pressures have *diverged* in different governmental jurisdictions.

Forest policy on federal lands has followed a broad pattern of punctuated equilibrium (PE) development, undergoing paradigmatic change as described in Baumgartner's chapter in this volume, while forest policy regulating private forestlands has developed more incrementally (Cashore 1999). Policy changes on federal forestlands addressed an array of interrelated concerns, including streamside harvesting, clearcutting, and forest preservation, which cumulatively led in the early 1990s to a dramatic reduction in timber harvesting. Federal policy then settled into a new equilibrium. By contrast, policies affecting privately owned forestlands addressed the same concerns as those on federal land, but specific policy stipulations changed in a more limited or "incremental" pattern and harvesting levels maintained their prior level. Our comparative approach, by contrasting cases of PE with non-PE cases, recognizes that theories of policy development should recognize that the complex interplay of independent variables can produce a range of possible policy outcomes (King, Keohane, and Verba 1994).[1]

This chapter proceeds as follows: Following this introduction, a second section assesses different ways of understanding and measuring punctuated equilibrium. A third section compares the historically divergent patterns of forest policy changes in the U.S. Pacific Northwest. A fourth section assesses the applicability to this history of theories that emphasize the role of entrepreneurial and strategic environmental groups in shaping policy development. A fifth section offers an alternative "hard institutional" explanation that focuses attention on the need to specify clearly just what measure or aspect of policy is being "punctuated" (Robinson 2004; Loughlin 2004). Different aspects of policies—goals, objectives, specifications, and instruments among others—can change at different times and rates. We argue that very durable institutions with distinct self-equilibrating or thermostatic properties have produced different policy outcomes in all of the jurisdictions we examine.

CONCEPTUALIZING AND MEASURING
PUNCTUATED EQUILIBRIUM

Evidence is increasing that public policies typically change in ways that Baumgartner and Jones and others, borrowing from evolutionary biology, call punctuated equilibrium (Gersick 1991, 10–36; Eldredge and Gould 1972, 82–115; Gould and Eldredge 1977, 115–51; True, Jones, and Baumgartner 1999, 97–115; Jones, Baumgartner, and True 1998, 1–33; Jones, Sulkin, and Larsen 2003, 151–69). Typically, considerable periods of policy stability or equilibrium are interspersed with occasional dramatic changes or punctuations. This pattern of "avalanches and incrementalism," as James True has argued (True 2000, 3–18; Genschel 1997, 43–66), is useful conceptually in unifying earlier observations about the frequency of marginal change and the infrequency of paradigmatic policy change. However, it also raises several important questions that are addressed by the chapters in this volume. These include:

1. What holds policymaking in equilibrium?
2. What overloads an equilibrium and promotes paradigmatic change or "policy punctuations"?
3. Do punctuations always occur rapidly or abruptly, as suggested by the "avalanche" metaphor?
4. What exactly is being held in equilibrium or changing: policy goals, policy ideas, various types of policy specifications, or all of these together?

Some of these questions are conceptual and require clarification of key terms and assumptions made in punctuated equilibrium models of policy dynamics (Knill and Lenschow 2001, 187–215). Others are conceptually clear but require empirical answers. Like other contributions in this volume, this chapter addresses some of these issues. The very different outcomes in otherwise similar cases noted above provide an important empirical arena in which to shed light on these questions (George 1979, 43–68).

MICRO-MOTIVES AND THRESHOLDS: WHAT TRIGGERS CHANGE IN THE PUNCTUATED EQUILIBRIUM MODEL?

Punctuated equilibrium theory predicts that when a punctuation snaps a policy equilibrium, the policy system sets off on a new path or trajectory. How are these punctuations to be explained? What events or variables serve as triggers? A promising direction in the analysis of punctuations can be found in studies on the economics of micro-motives, undertaken by Thomas Schelling and others: the threshold model of policy change (Schelling 1971a, 59–98; Schelling 1971b, 143–86; Schelling 1978). This model relies on interactions in individual preferences that can cascade as small events build up over time, gradually altering the choices made by individuals until a majority move suddenly in a new direction (Bikhchandani, Hirshleifer, and Welch 1992, 992–1026). A variant of this model has also received attention from sociologists and others who have substituted the release of hidden preferences for altered ones as the main causal agent in sudden policy fluctuations (Granovetter 1978, 1420–43; Kuran 1989, 41–74; Kuran 1991, 7–48). Recently this model has been directly applied to punctuated equilibrium thinking by Wood and Doan, who focus on the reasons why policy issues and agenda-setting are prone to "tipping point" behavior (Wood and Doan 2003, 640–53).

In his contribution to this volume, Brock explicitly links threshold models to overall PE processes, emphasizing the impact of "peer effects," the same interdependency of hidden or disguised preferences found in the works of Granovetter and Kuran and others (Jones and Cullis 2003, 527–47). The work by Brock and others on threshold triggers is complemented by a second set of studies, largely undertaken by sociologists and political scientists, that focuses on the manner in which stability has been established and reestablished in many policy domains. These studies of policy equilibria emphasize the ability of existing institutional regimes to limit change and the extent to which they allow or discourage threshold effects and limit activities by individual policy actors (Goldstone 1998, 829–45; Liebowitz and Margolis 1995, 205–25; Mahoney 2000, 507–48; Pierson 2000, 251–67; Wilsford 1994, 251–84).

Understanding informal and formal institutional arrangements is a key step in determining how equilibriums are maintained and analyzing why punctuations occur or fail to occur (Deeg 2001; Lindner 2003, 912–35; Genschell 1997, 43–66). Changes in informal institutions, such as altered policy ideas and goals that come to the fore as the result of new governing coalitions, are examples of bifurcating processes that tend to be abrupt, often occurring immediately following an election and subject to reversal by subsequent electoral or partisan activity. On the other hand, some informal aspects of policymaking, such as general norms of fairness, equity, and legitimacy are much more difficult to change, often requiring prior changes in the external socioeconomic structure. Since demographic and other socioeconomic changes tend to occur slowly and cumulatively, aspects of policymaking requiring revaluation of citizens' sense of appropriate policy outcomes typically change slowly. Ideas long entrenched do not change overnight (Lieberman 2002, 697–712). However, slowly changing demographic variables, such as migration and immigration patterns, can have sudden effects on popular ideas or policy positions through cumulative effects on the relative strength of competing coalitions.

In the two following cases of Pacific Northwest forest policy, we argue that the institutional order was key in facilitating a punctuated equilibrium process on federal lands while preventing such an occurrence on private lands. We then discuss implications we think this analysis has for the study of punctuated equilibrium processes.

DESCRIBING FOREST POLICY DEVELOPMENT
IN THE U.S. PACIFIC NORTHWEST

The Pacific Northwest provides a unique setting for theoretical and empirical research on PE approaches to policy dynamics. Empirically it is important as the home to temperate rainforest ecosystems, which have aesthetic, spiritual, and biological importance to citizens in the region and across the country. Theoretically it is important because jurisdictional authority over forest management varies within the region. The federal government has regulatory authority over vast federal lands, largely through the National Forest System, while the states of Oregon and Washington regulate forestry on private lands. Because these two ownership categories include by far the most forestland within the boundaries of these two states (Figure 6.1) and because we seek to address differences between them in policy choices, we have omitted regulations on other types of forestland ownerships, such as state-owned land, from this study.

FEDERAL LANDS AND THE 1992
POLICY PUNCTUATION

After the current institutional features governing Pacific Northwest forestry on National Forestlands crystallized in 1976, both the means and ends of policy development reflected a classic incremental mode of policy development until

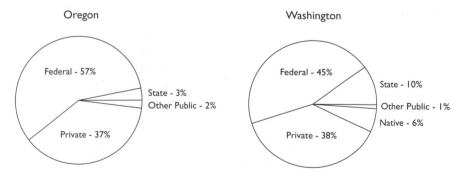

Figure 6.1. Forest land ownership by state and owner. *Sources:* Northwest Forest Industries Council; Western Forest Protection Association; U.S. Forest Service, 2001; Washington State Department of Natural Resources; Oregon Department of Forestry.

the 1990s, when policy changed dramatically. The period from 1992 to 1995 witnessed a massive change in policy specifications and their underlying paradigm. An ecosystem management approach was embraced and carried with it crucial policy changes: the allowable size of clearcuts was reduced and the allowable cut in the area's national forests was lowered from over 5 billion board feet in the late 1980s to 1.2 billion board feet by 1995. The amount of national forestland even available for harvesting declined sharply when virtually all remaining old-growth forests were excluded from any type of industrial activity. In addition, streamside riparian zones were established, including 300-foot no-harvesting buffer zones for both fish-bearing and non-fish-bearing streams (Cashore 1997a; Cashore and Auld 2003; Ellefson, Cheng, and Moulton 1997a, 195–209; Ellefson, Moulton, and Kilgore 2002, 35–41; Ellefson, Cheng, and Moulton 1995, 605–1995; Ellefson and Cheng 1994, 34–37).

By 1995 policy on federal forestlands had established a new equilibrium. Since 1995, temporary harvesting increases have been permitted, often as the result of congressional tinkering at the margins by using "rider" provisions of U.S. budgetary appropriations processes, but none of the major changes undertaken in the 1992–95 period has been altered significantly.[2] Riparian zones are now required as part of forest management plans; ecosystem management objectives must be detailed; and monitoring requirements ensure that these policy specifications stay within the bounds set by the 1992–95 policy specifications.

PRIVATE LANDS AND POLICY INCREMENTALISM

Since 1972 policy development on private lands has been incremental. Most environmental forest policies affecting private forests in Oregon and Washington have developed relatively slowly and changed more gradually than those affecting national forestlands. There are no specific policy requirements regarding annual harvest rates and, owing to private land ownership, no efforts to permanently remove private forestland from the harvesting base. However, there have been incremental approaches to endangered species preservation, including modified rules governing harvesting in riparian zones. These changed from guidelines in the mid-1970s that regulated road building near streams and encouraged owners to maintain a percentage of original shade to rules in the mid-1990s[3] regarding the number of trees that should be left after harvesting near a stream and requiring in the late 1990s relatively limited (compared to national forestlands) no-harvest zones. Similarly, clearcutting restrictions were not in existence in 1975, but relatively permissive limitations of clearcutting to 240 acres (120 in Oregon without permission) were introduced by the mid-1990s and no changes have been made since then. Species preservation requirements also have changed incrementally. By 1999, 6.5 million acres of private forestlands were covered by Habitat Conservation Plans (HCPs), which are developed to address the impacts of forest harvesting on endangered and threatened species habitat. While at first glance this may seem like significant acreage, upon closer examination we see that it reinforces existing approaches because these plans *permit* "incidental taking of endangered species"—which is *prohibited* by endangered species laws affecting national forestlands. Research on the impact of HCPs in addressing endangered and threatened species reveals substantial differences from species protection on federal lands.[4]

The cumulative impact of these different approaches is illustrated in Figure 6.2, showing that the federal harvest was dramatically reduced in the early to mid-1990s while the harvest on state-regulated private lands remained fairly steady.

Figure 6.2. Washington and Oregon timber harvest by private and federal lands, 1965–2000.

EXPLAINING POLICY DEVELOPMENT:
PLURALIST ACCOUNTS

What explains these very different patterns, one marked by incremental changes and relatively steady timber supply output, the other marked by punctuated policy changes that significantly reduced the timber supply? Most accounts of these policy developments embrace a "policy subsystem" approach that emphasizes the role of strategic environmental groups in forcing a reluctant U.S. Congress and U.S. Forest Service, through societal mobilization, to undertake these changes. They emphasize the way environmental groups conducted grassroots efforts, lobbied Congress, and used the courts, all of which eventually "tipped the scales" by taking what was a regional issue and nationalizing it. In the process the groups expanded the policy subsystem and altered the range of ideas present within it. These actor-based accounts argue that environmental groups and their brilliant manoeuvrings largely explain this punctuation and account for moving the forest management away from multiple use toward sustained yield and toward ecosystem management in a classic "tipping point" or threshold pattern as the public and policymakers gradually "came onside" with environmentalists' positions and proposals (Hoberg 2003a; Sher 1993).

Considerable empirical evidence supports the important role of environmental groups in influencing Pacific Northwest forest policy change, and indeed there is a strong correlation between the creation of environmental groups designed to protect federal lands and their ultimate protection. Likewise, the fact that very few groups even became involved in state-level private land regulation correlates with more incremental patterns noted above. However, a strong correlation does not imply complete causation. In order to shed light on what produced PE on federal lands, we point to institutionalized differences in the levels of policy development that could change and the ones that could not.

We argue that the growth and development of an array of grassroots, membership-based, professional, and litigious environmental groups were central to the story of PE but that institutions directed both the form and function of this societal mobilization and influenced the goals the groups championed and the access they sought. Ultimately, institutional differences created the mechanisms through which PE would occur on federal lands but not on private lands. The specific trigger mechanism was the thermostatic property of the U.S. institutional setting, which permitted and directed the development of litigious groups, spearheaded by the Portland and Seattle Audubon Societies and the

Sierra Club Legal Defense Fund, as important *convening agents*. But *institutions* directed environmental group activity and shaped the ultimate punctuated policy responses. Our analysis of the facts of the two cases suggests that institutional explanatory factors need to be better integrated into PE models.

INDUSTRY AND ENVIRONMENTAL GROUP PARTICIPATION IN PACIFIC NORTHWEST NATIONAL FORESTLANDS FOREST POLICY COMMUNITIES, 1960 TO 2000

A discernible difference in forest policy development within the state and federal jurisdictions is the extent of participation by environmental groups and industry associations in the policy subsystem and the role played by the institutional order in limiting or facilitating this participation. A plethora of environmental groups emerged to influence federal lands policy while the institutional structure, especially the property rights regime present at the state level, meant relatively few groups devoted their efforts to alter private land regulation.

ENVIRONMENTAL GROUPS

Since the 1960s the environmental coalition has long championed increased preservation (where harvesting should occur) and increased regulations of forest practices (how harvesting should occur). They promoted ecosystem management (Caldwell, Wilkinson, and Shannon 1994, 7–11; Kohm and Franklin 1997) and advocated maintaining and enhancing forest ecosystems biodiversity. Most environmental groups also emphasized the benefits of the traditional command-and-control approach to forest regulation found on national forestlands that gives industry limited flexibility in achieving profit-based, as opposed to ecologically based, objectives. (Hoberg 1993a 1993b, 1997, 2001, 2003b; Davis 2001; Cashore 1997a, 1997b, 1999).

The environmental coalition has historically included membership-based and professional groups. The former include the National Audubon Society, the National Wildlife Federation, the Sierra Club, and the Wilderness Society, all of which enjoyed an explosion of membership during the 1970s and again in the late 1980s. Except for the Audubon Society, all these national groups established offices in the Pacific Northwest. In addition, the National Audubon Society and the Sierra Club have numerous local chapters spread among communities in Oregon and Washington. The most important regional group is the Oregon Natural Resources Council, established in 1971 as an organization with both individual and group membership, which has developed both scientific and legal expertise.[5]

Several litigious environmental groups, including the Environmental Defence Fund (EDF) in 1967, the Natural Resources Defense Council (NRDC) in 1968, and the Sierra Club Legal Defense Fund (SCLDF) in 1971, were established expressly to enforce established laws governing environmental protection. These groups, along with Defenders of Wildlife, adopted a litigious approach to environmental advocacy and would find themselves at the heart of the forest policy struggle.

These national groups were joined by such grassroots organizations as Save Our Forests and the Western Ancient Forest Campaign (now known as the American Lands Alliance) and regionally based groups such as Headwaters in southern Oregon, which has developed a regional profile, the Northwest Ecosystem Alliance, created to monitor and enforce federal environmental policy, and Eco-trust, an environmental group with a mission to link community development goals with environmental protection.

INDUSTRY ASSOCIATIONS

Historically, industrial interests have focused on maintaining strong timber supply from the Pacific Northwest and have made long-term plans that take into account the available supply from national forests. This approach has its roots in the "German school" of forestry, which sought to enhance timber supply through wise forest management (Gregg 1989, 144–46). Industrial forestry interests, along with the dominant forestry association, the Society of American Foresters, have maintained flexible and informal arrangements with the two key land management agencies, the Forest Service and the Bureau of Land Management, and have manifested a concerted desire to limit the influence of other federal regulatory agencies, such as the U.S. Fish and Wildlife Service.

Industry groups have promoted the independence of the Forest Service, which manages most federal lands in the Pacific Northwest through the National Forest System, viewing this as a better venue in which to develop national forest management than the courts or an uniformed public.[6] Industry views long dominated policy development, but when they clashed with new formal regulatory requirements in the early 1990s, they lost any significant power in policy development. In an effort to regroup after these losses, three national associations merged at the federal level to form the American Forest and Paper Association (AF&PA), which is the largest forest industry association in the United States and includes most forest companies in the U.S. Pacific Northwest. The AF&PA was formed to give "the nation's forest and paper industries a stronger, more effective voice to address major business and public policy issues" (American Forest and Paper Association 1993). The Northwest Forestry Association (NFA) is the regional association representing those companies with interests on Pacific Northwest federal lands. The mergers were undertaken in order to have industry "speak as a central voice" on federal forest policy matters and to avoid land management agencies "playing one group off over the other."[7] After ecosystem management approaches on national forestlands were embraced, industry's policy positions have shifted slightly. Industry now emphasizes the "three pillars" of sustainable forestry and a balanced approach to national forest management.

INDUSTRY AND ENVIRONMENTAL GROUP PARTICIPATION IN PACIFIC NORTHWEST STATE-REGULATED PRIVATE FORESTLANDS FOREST POLICY COMMUNITIES, 1960 TO 2000

A very different mix of environmental group and industry organizations has emerged within state-level jurisdictions governing private forest management in Oregon and Washington.

Environmental Groups

Environmental group participation in state-level forest policy discussion is limited, in stark contrast to the many groups involved in federal lands forest policy. The group with the longest history in the Oregon forest policy community is the Oregon Environmental Council, though its interest in state forest practices policy has been minimal after its participation in 1987 rule changes. The only group to maintain an ongoing presence since the mid-1980s on private forestry issues has been Portland Audubon. The number of environmental groups active in Washington state forest policy matters is similarly small. There are only two key groups: the Washington Environmental Council (WEC) and the Washington State Audubon Society. Formed in 1967, the WEC is an organization of about 2,000 individual members and 110 loosely affiliated group members. The WEC operates solely on the state level. Owing to its diffuse and loosely integrated structure, WEC officials have had difficulty obtaining widespread support from the environmental movement when negotiating with industry, government, and tribal officials. These state-level groups have tended to promote more stringent approaches to environmental protection, but as we show below their ideas about policy ends have had only a very limited influence on forest policy development.

Industry Organizations

The main Oregon forest industry organization is the Oregon Forest Industries Council (OFIC). The OFIC strongly champions a rational scientific approach to forest management, reflecting the German model; opposes litigation and stringent rules regarding environmental preservation; and is strongly proactive in supporting legislation and state-level actions that institutionalize this approach. A similar approach is taken by the main Washington-focused organization, the Washington Forest Protection Association (WFPA), which represents most forest companies at the state level, including large private landowners.[8]

EXPLAINING POLICY DEVELOPMENT:
HARD INSTITUTIONAL LOGICS

Although these different configurations of actors in the national and state forest policy subsystems are critical to an understanding of the policy dynamics present in each, accounts of the development of these subsystems either implicitly or sometimes explicitly reveals that actor-based explanations of policy change on federal and private forestlands are incomplete. We argue that the extent to which different actors participated in these subsystems was itself determined by a larger political order that drove policy change and stability in the two cases we examined. As March and Olsen have argued, institutional orders create different "logics of appropriateness" regarding the potential for, and possible types of, policy change (March and Olsen 1989; Christensen and Rovik 1999; Sending 2002, 443–70). These different institutional orders and logics largely explain the differences that emerged in the two cases and should be taken into account in explanations of punctuated equilibrium policy development.

The different institutional structures affected not only the extent to which actors participated in policy processes but also the types of policy ideas and options that could be *formalized* within each setting. That is, preexisting institutional conditions, rather than the number of strategic efforts of environmental groups in the policy subsystem, explained where environmental groups could have influence and what kinds of influence they could have.

We develop this argument in three steps. First, we show how institutions influence different levels of policy development. Second, we trace the development of the key institutions in our cases and reveal that in both jurisdictions these institutions, despite significant societal unrest, have remained durable for over a generation. Third, we explain why one durable institution would permit a pattern of punctuated policy change while the other would not. This discussion shows how the federal arena was poised for a PE policy change, while state arenas would not permit such change, no matter how hard environmental groups might have pressed.

HARD INSTITUTIONAL LOGIC
AND THE INTERACTION OF POLICY

Just how did the institutional order lead to the punctuated changes on federal lands and incremental patterns of state regulations? Features of the federal setting required that policy specifications adjust, as a thermostat would, to outside indicators that the forest ecosystem was under stress. The institutional setting at the state level led to policy specifications designed to maintain economic development in an equilibrium or incremental mode, even in the face of ecosystem stress.

MEASURING POLICY

Policy outputs vary according to whether they involve policy ends or means and according to their degree of abstraction: from the most abstract conceptual ideas to policies governing program operations and finally to the specifics of policy implementation. Distinguishing policy ends from means and, most importantly, the three aspects of each are key to analyzing policy change and stability and assessing punctuated equilibrium policy dynamics (Daugbjerg 2000; Smith 2000, 95–114). The basic components of policy outputs are set out in Table 6.1 below.

These distinctions are crucial because these aspects of policy can exhibit very different patterns of change and development within the same sector or issue arena. It is often misleading to assert that policy development in a sector is characteristically paradigmatic because the sector will normally exhibit both incremental and paradigmatic movements in different policy components. Pure

Table 6.1. A modified taxonomy of policy measures (cells contain examples of each measure).

		Policy inputs and output		
		Conceptual ideas	Operationalized objectives	Implementation targets
Policy Focus	Ends	Overall policy goals (e.g., environmental protection, economic development)	Policy objectives (e.g., saving fish; increase harvesting)	Policy level specification (e.g., size of riparian no-harvesting zone, level of speed limit)
	Means	Overall approach to policy implementation (e.g., choice between use of coercion vs. suasion)	Policy instruments (e.g., voluntary, market-based, command-and-control-based)	Implementation level specifications (e.g., posting speed limit signs and police enforcement signs; or published written-down requirements; or guidelines regulations, inspections, fines)

paradigmatic change—that is, when all six components of a policy exhibit a paradigmatic change—is very rare. Rather than only two basic types of policy dynamics—the "normal" incremental and the "rare" paradigmatic—much more complicated patterns of policy change may exist and many more permutations of each type can occur. Instead of being atypical, some degree of paradigmatic change may be quite normal.

INSTITUTIONAL LOGICS

This more complex picture is significant because the institutional order often determines what type of policy change is likely to occur in a sector. Different institutional configurations result in different "logics of appropriateness" as to the type and range of policy change permitted in the face of differing internal and external conditions. On national forestlands, for example, massive change in policy specifications was allowable because indicators of ecosystem problems were designed to be triggers, generating instability in policy settings much the same way that a thermostat reacts to changes in temperature by shutting a furnace on or off. In such conditions, paradigmatic change in various policy components is likely. In Oregon and Washington states, on the other hand, institutional features were specifically designed to limit policy responses to changes in environmental conditions, inasmuch as economic objectives continued to play a dominating role in policymaking. Thus, paradigmatic change was less likely than a relatively limited response to increased activity by environmentalists, who were largely excluded from the policy process, and little or no change in policy objectives or instruments.

NATIONAL FORESTLANDS

The institutional features that dominate national forestland policy were developed in the 1960s and 1970s and have proven remarkably resilient since then (Hoberg 1993a; Weaver 1994; Gilmour 1990; Vogel 1993; Thelen and Steinmo 1992; Immergut 1990, 1992).[9] The two key provisions in statutes promulgated in the 1970s are found in two important laws. The first provision is found in the 1973 Endangered Species Act's (ESA) requirements stipulating what public land management agencies must do to protect threatened and endangered species on publicly owned forestland. The ESA, as we show below, contained very different provisions for requirements on private land.

The ESA is administered not by land management agencies but by the U.S. Fish and Wildlife Service (USFWS) or the National Marine Fisheries Service (NMFS) and *requires* that threatened and endangered species and their critical habitat be listed and that a plan is developed that will result in species recovery. The determination of whether a species is threatened or endangered must be based "solely on the best scientific and commercial data available" (section 4[b][1][A]) with *explicit direction that the economic effects of such a decision not be given consideration* (Davis 1995; Smith, Moote, and Schwalbe 1993, 1038– 39).[10] As a result, the law links policy specifications to ecological conditions, requiring significant policy change if evidence indicates that ecological problems are becoming acute.

A second and arguably even more important provision is found in the 1976 National Forest Management Act. Ironically, this act was promoted in Congress as a way to reduce the role of the courts in national forest planning (Humphrey 1976),[11] following a court decision that outlawed clearcutting on national forestlands.[12] While generally known for the discretion it granted to the National Forest Service (Hoberg 2003a; U.S. Office of Technology Assessment 1992), its key provision was that Forest Service land and resource management plans (LRMPs) "provide for diversity of plant and animal communities." The resulting regulations required that LRMPs maintain "viable populations of existing native and desired non-native vertebrate species," "where appropriate" and "to the degree practicable."

The above provisions were important because their mandatory requirements, enforceable by court decisions, directly tied development of policy specifications to the conditions of forest-dependent species and allowed PE processes to take place. Further provisions entrenched this logic. Rules establishing the legal standing of citizens and public organizations made it easier for environmental groups to seek redress in court when agencies whose ideas still fit with industrial interests failed to comply (Hoberg 1992). Also, the National Environmental Policy Act's requirements that key governmental projects undergo environmental assessments gave additional legal leverage to groups trying to ensure that plans for endangered species underwent a comprehensive environmental assessment. Despite repeated efforts and highly contested political battles, these provisions have remained remarkably durable.[13]

PRIVATE FORESTLANDS

The oldest and most highly durable feature of private forestland governance is the common law regarding private property rights, which requires government to compensate landlords if restrictions on their land uses amount to a "taking" of the property (Ellefson, Cheng, and Moulton 1995, 30–37).[14] These common-law institutions are extremely durable and easily trump goals of policy subsystem actors. They are reinforced by durable means: the ability of landowners to use the court system to sue regulatory agencies to obtain compensation.

The second distinct feature of private forestlands is the way institutions shape policy development in this arena. State statutes regulating private forestland were promoted by industry interests and justified as a strategy to preempt federal intrusion.[15] State laws facilitated timber extraction by creating forest practices boards that were originally dominated by industry interests, with incremental broadening of board membership over time. For the most part, these statutory regimes reduced even further the ability of state legislatures and administrative agencies to initiate changes independently.[16] Statutes are worded to avoid litigation, reduce the ability of non-resource agencies to influence the forest regulatory process, and *limit* the influence of other agencies over forest practices rules.[17]

The rules regarding species preservation on private lands were written to ensure that no triggers would link environmental protection rules directly to ecological conditions. Unlike the federal approach, Oregon's rules simply required that "consideration" be given to wildlife habitat (Cubbage and Ellefson 1980, 463, 468).[18] In Washington, statutes originally called for harvesting practices to "leave the area conducive for timber production and encourage wildlife." These statutes created a durable policy instrument in the hands of forest practices boards, reduced the ability of the legislature to have influence, and required that forest practice boards' rules be developed in a manner consistent with maintaining a healthy timber economy.

The third source of stability in the private land regime actually stems from federal environmental statutes affecting forestry management that have been crafted in a way that protects state interests. In the federal Clean Water Act, forestry is considered a non-point source of pollution and is subject to less federal regulation than are industries deemed to be point sources.[19] For non-point sources such as forestry and agriculture, the Clean Water Act requires cooperation and only voluntary action, with federal agencies supporting and encouraging state leadership.

Similarly, the requirements of the ESA with respect to private forest managers contrast strongly with those it imposes on federal land owners and federal agencies. Unlike their federal counterparts, non-federal landowners are under no obligation to recover species. Moreover, section 10 of the ESA permits non-federal landowners to escape rules forbidding endangered species habitat destruction. Section 10(a)(2) specifically permits a "non-federal landowner" to obtain an incidental take permit that allows the destruction of threatened and endangered species and habitats, provided that the landowner also prepares a Habitat Conservation Plan (HCP).

THE FORMAL INSTITUTIONAL TRIGGER ON FEDERAL LANDS

Dramatic change on federal forestlands in the Pacific Northwest was triggered by increasing evidence that forest-dependent species in the Pacific Northwest were becoming threatened and endangered. This evidence drove the subsequent activities of key change agents in environmental groups, industry, and governments. The process is best illustrated by the northern spotted owl conflict that arose in the late 1970s (Yaffee 1994, 14). Scientific research showed that the survival of the owl depended on old-growth forests that make up less than 10 percent of Pacific Northwest forests and which were in peril if harvesting practices were not altered.[20]

Yet the Forest Service, largely because of its close relationship with the forest industry and their shared ideas about forest management, did nothing to protect spotted owl habitat. So, in the early 1980s the Seattle and Portland Audubon Societies sued, arguing that land-management agencies violated the nondiscretionary requirements of the Endangered Species Act, the National Environmental Policy Act, and the National Forest Management Act. At heart, their suit attempted to force the Fish and Wildlife Service to list the northern spotted owl as threatened (Sher 1993, 41–79; Hungerford 1994, 1395–434) and eventually resulted in the listing of the northern spotted owl as endangered, requiring several agency and interagency attempts to devise a recovery plan (Thomas et al. 1990).

When it was clear that any plan to save the northern spotted owl would result in a considerable loss of timber supply in the Pacific Northwest, Congress attempted to override temporarily the endangered species requirements of federal law (Hoberg 1993a). These congressional efforts ultimately failed and the White House initiated a highly publicized "Forest Summit" in Portland, Oregon, in April of 1993, at which environmental, industry, labor, and other nongovernment organizations pleaded their cases before the president and members of his cabinet (Begley 1993). The summit resulted in the establishment of the Forest Ecosystem Management Team (FEMAT), composed mostly of government scientists, which was charged with presenting options to the Clinton administration for saving the northern spotted owl. It was also instructed to estimate each option's chances of achieving spotted owl recovery. In the end, the administration chose "Option 9," which it believed would entail the least economic impact while staying within the requirements of the law and allowing plausibly for species recovery. Option 9 contained and developed most of the changes to environmental forest policy specification reviewed above.[21]

Although many accounts emphasize the significant effects of environmental groups' litigation campaigns and their efforts to nationalize the issues (Hoberg 1997), the commitment of Clinton and Gore to the environment or indications that the Forest Service was changing its management philosophy (Davis and Davis 1988, 3–24), empirical evidence reveals the important role that institutions played in mediating this conflict and its policy outcome. Without those institutional features already in place, government actors would almost certainly have produced even more "balanced" policy responses.

While constructing counterfactuals about what would have happened in a different institutional order is challenging, evidence from events on private lands in the same region and in nearby British Columbia, where very different forest policy responses to similar environmental concerns occurred, is consistent with our argument. Notably, even the federal government was attempting to find a solution that permitted the most harvesting to occur that the laws allowed. Therefore, it seems reasonable to conclude that without the legal constraints on policy, the same punctuation would probably not have occurred. While the public's evolving ideas provided important support for environmental groups' efforts[22] and while changing norms within the Forest Service and Congress (Davis 1995, 8–11) reflected broad societal concerns for the environment, the key causal mechanism in shaping the abrupt policy changes from 1992 to 1995 was the rigid legal requirement that compelled land-management agencies to address species preservation by reducing old-growth harvests enough to restore northern spotted owl populations sufficiently to guarantee their long-term survival, without taking into account any resulting economic impacts.

Judge Dwyer, who oversaw compliance with the ESA's requirements for protection of the northern spotted owl and who had rejected previous plans that failed to ensure species recovery, ultimately upheld Option 9 in 1994 because he ruled that the plan met the legal requirements. Indeed, Judge Dwyer ruled that in order to comply with the substantive nondiscretionary requirements of the Endangered Species Act and the National Forest Management Act and "given the current condition of the forest, there is no way the agencies could comply with environmental laws without planning on an ecosystem basis."[23] As U.S. Forest Service Chief Jack Ward Thomas said: "One of the more interesting things that came out of the FEMAT/Option 9 decision was the charge that Option 9 was illegal because the law specified that these plans had to be done on a forest-by-forest and district-by-district basis. And that to use this more comprehensive process was illegal. . . . Judge Dwyer said, 'no.' . . . it was essentially mandatory: there was no way we could meet all the legal requirements without going through a more coordinated planning operation that meets ecosystem standards."[24]

Thomas argued that this ruling "may, in the end, be the most significant decision that came out of the FEMAT/spotted owl issue." The effects of the owl litigation transcend the Pacific Northwest. The spotted owl controversy in the Pacific Northwest has spurred interest in the implementation of ecosystem management, not only in the Forest Service but also in other federal land management agencies as well.

STATE-LEVEL REGULATIONS: INCREMENTALISM

Despite being located in the same forest and political region as national forest-lands,[25] policies concerning private forestlands followed an incremental approach, even as scientific evidence revealed first that the northern spotted owl and later that salmon were threatened or endangered (Washington Forest Protection Association 1999; Washington Department of Natural Resources 1998). Policy change toward private forestland was incremental[26] because institutionalized policy objectives in this sector narrowed the policy options available to regulators and restricted policy development to forest practices boards sympathetic to forest-sector interests. While courts were requiring paradigmatic changes on national forestlands, state-level agencies in Oregon and Washington continued to emphasize economic development. As a result, the Washington State Forest Practices Board as of 1996 had still not defined critical habitat for the northern spotted owl, relying instead on emergency rules that both industry and environmental organizations said were inadequate (Rowland 1994). In Oregon, the responses to owl protection initiated by the Oregon Forest Practices Board were deemed equally limited by environmental groups[27] and, ultimately, most responses came through company-initiated habitat conservation plans.

Even widespread experimentation in Washington State with multi-stakeholder processes that sidestepped the Forest Practices Board resulted in environmental groups walking away from the table and ultimately with incremental policy changes supported by industry. When scientific evidence indicated significant decline in coho salmon stocks, state efforts to address the decline in Oregon and Washington, as required by the Clean Water Act, also took smaller steps than those initiated on federal lands. Riparian "no-harvest zones" were smaller than those in national forests, and both states made use of "limited-harvesting" zones to buttress no-harvesting approaches.

CONCLUSION: PUNCTUATED EQUILIBRIUM
MODELS AND PACIFIC NORTHWEST
FOREST POLICY

The evidence from these two cases suggests that all aspects of environmental forestry policy governing private and public forests in the Pacific Northwest were influenced by the different institutions in place and the different "logics of appropriateness" they provided to policy change. The federal system allowed an open-policy subsystem, but the state subsystems were closed. Moreover, the thermostatic design of the U.S. federal institutional order, when faced with evidence about species endangerment, led to a punctuated equilibrium change in policy and established a new policy equilibrium implying much more biodiversity protection than previously existed. Policy changes continue, of course, but now more incrementally. By contrast, the three policy levels in Oregon and Washington either did not change at all or developed incrementally. While the difficulty of regulating private forestland compared to public land has always been obvious, these examples instruct students of public policy to take into account not only the interaction of different orders of policy in response to pressures for change but also the effect of sector-specific institutional features.

We have argued that in these cases the different configuration of institutions in each region resulted in a different logic as to the type and range of policy change that could occur in the face of differing external conditions. On national forestlands, massive change in policy specifications resulted from a thermostatic process at the objectives level. In the states of Oregon and Washington, institutional features were designed to limit policy responses to outside environmental indicators, since the dominant role of economic objectives was an enduring feature of policymaking. As a result, there was no change in policy objectives or instruments and relatively limited response to environmental policy problems.

Our analysis reveals the need to link punctuated equilibrium models to institutional models that channel and indeed often create societal mobilization and interest. In our cases, durable institutions determined whether and where thresholds would be permitted. Some institutional structures, such as those governing national forestlands, are designed to permit and indeed facilitate large-scale paradigmatic change at the levels of policy specifications while maintaining long-established policy objectives. Other institutional arrangements, such as those in Oregon and Washington, will not permit large variations in policy from the status quo, and in these cases institutional change would have to take place before punctuated equilibrium change could occur.

An understanding of the role of institutions cannot help us predict when punctuated equilibrium will occur. Indeed, in the U.S. federal lands setting we would expect important lag effects between the identification of an ecological change and internal policy responses since, by definition, thermostatic features of the institutional design require that scientific evidence reveal that a species is endangered or threatened and existing policy subsystem interests would be expected to scrutinize and challenge such science.[28] This would be particularly true with respect to agencies that enjoyed historically close relationships with their forest industry clientele (Culhane 1981; Foss 1960; Kaufman 1967; Alston 1984, 374; Twight 1983). However, an emphasis on the role of institutions can tell us whether punctuated equilibrium is even permitted and the mechanisms through which change can occur. Hence, understanding the structure and influence of institutions is imperative to those wishing to understand or facilitate punctuated equilibrium processes. In some cases, the institutions themselves will have to be changed and, in other cases, institutions may remain durable, but built-in thermostatic processes will have to be triggered.

Reconceptualizing the measurement and description of different types of policy outcomes and our focus on institutional rigidity as a key factor in explaining the more nuanced and complex patterns of policy choice that emerge lead us to two central conclusions: (1) that scholars must carefully distinguish between different components of policy in attempting to assess the nature of policy change; and (2) that scholars must systematically incorporate institutional elements into their analyses in order to understand the workings of punctuated equilibrium processes fully.[29]

NOTES

1. King, Keohane, and Verba (1994) have nicely documented the difficulties in explaining a phenomenon such as PE when researchers select only those cases in which the phenomenon is present, thus having no way of ascertaining whether the independent variables they identify also operate in cases where the phenomenon is not present.
2. We acknowledge that forestry is complex and that many other issues, including the use of chemicals and herbicides, exotics, and plantation management could also be considered under the term *environmental forestry*. For the purposes of this paper we have deliberately chosen those issues that appeared most prominent in forestry in the past thirty years.
3. During this phase of policy development, industrial interests circumvented the Forest Practices Board route and successfully supported a legislative change requiring that two snags per acre be left when harvesting near streams. A Portland Audubon official noted that the effect was to prevent the Board of Forestry from responding to scientific data that might indicate more than two snags were needed (pers. interview).
4. See Kareiva et al. 2000. This study by a research team from the National Center for Ecological Analysis and Synthesis and the American Institute of Biological Sciences found that 84 percent of the time, HCPs failed to provide or to use critical scientific information and analysis relevant to conservation and mitigation plans. The environmental group, the American Lands Alliance, has referred to this report to argue that "Instead of helping to restore species' habitats, most HCPs work against species' recovery. Species that are being harmed include grizzly bear, northern spotted owl, Coho salmon, red cockaded woodpecker . . . ." See also Noecker and Corn 1997.
5. The OFIC has clearly established goals from which it does not waver. Official policy is not to enter into dispute resolution processes. See Oregon Natural Resources Council 1993.

6. The Bureau of Land Management also has responsibility over a minority of federally owned lands in Oregon.
7. Personal interview, senior official, National Forestry Association.
8. The Washington Farm Forester's Association, a small landowner organization, is becoming more important as federal lands produce smaller harvests. In addition, the Northwest Forest Resources Council, an association of virtually all the state and federal forest industry organizations in the Pacific Northwest, was created in 1987 to focus exclusively on timber supply issues. Overall, the large industrial organizations tend to have the professional and organizational resources to make them effective lobbyists, whereas small landowners are less effectively organized, lacking the "financing and the technical forestry and business skills that long-term efforts require" (Leman 1988, 159).
9. Since this paper addresses policy that is consistent with a logic of appropriateness of an existing hard institutional logic, we do not detail why the features have endured so long nor do we explain why they developed. However, we do note that historical institutionalist explanations of durability and unintended effects of U.S. statutes can be traced back to key features of the U.S. macro-political system in which windows of opportunity, often created through logrolling, can lead to massive statutory change and can make change difficult once the window is closed. Hoberg, Weaver, and others have noted that the U.S. macro-institutional system, with its separation of powers and weak government, leads to logrolling, wherein some legislators support others' proposed legislation in exchange for support of their own proposals. When proposals seem to command sufficient support, interest groups and state agencies focus much of their efforts on statutory change, but after a legislative battle, attention dissipates, leaving a statutory regime in place that often shows remarkable resilience. The U.S. system can also create a "bidding up" phenomenon between the president and congressional leaders, which usually occurs when partisan differences are muted and voter preferences are clear and intense. Drawing on the work of Gilmour and Vogel, Weaver argues that this phenomenon accounts for the flurry of environmental legislation passed by the U.S. Congress in the early 1970s. See Hoberg 1993a; Weaver 1994; Gilmour 1990; Vogel 1993. For general treatment on the role of windows of opportunity, see Thelen and Steinmo 1992; Immergut 1992, 1990.
10. The important caveat to this review is that the ESA provides for the establishment of an "Endangered Species Committee," or "God Squad." This committee has the authority to decide that the "economic and social benefits of the proposed action outweigh costs to the listed species" and can therefore exempt a particular action from the requirements of the ESA (Smith, Moote, and Schwalbe 1993, 1039). This committee can only be established when no "feasible alternatives" exist and where there is "considerable" economic or social importance (ibid., 1038).
11. Senator Humphrey argued that "the fundamental issue we must face is whether forestry should be practiced in the courts, or in the woods. The next issue we face is whether Congress should write tight instructions into law, or allow the professional resource manager the flexible authority needed to apply the best scientific forestry practices in a manner that assures complete respect for the environment. In this connection, my sentiments are similar to those of a former chief of the Forest Service, who [said] in 1935,

'Forestry is a profession that will not tolerate political dominance.'" See Humphrey 1976.

12. The courts ruled that clearcutting in the Monongahela National Forest was contrary to an obscure provision in the 1876 Organic Act.

13. During the last days of the Clinton administration, a new administrative rule was proposed that would have replaced the species viability provision with even stricter language. The Bush administration revoked this proposal and proposed language that would have replaced the viability requirements with one that took a more balanced approach to economic and environmental values. Despite best efforts, these rules have not been promulgated. See Hoberg 2003a.

14. A slightly countervailing feature in the common law prohibits any forest owner from damaging other people's property through acts of "nuisance, waste or taking." See Ellefson, Cheng, and Moulton 1995.

15. The key forestry legislation governing Oregon is its 1971 Forest Practices Act, which was stimulated by U.S. congressional deliberations and eventual enactment of the Clean Water Act of 1972. The federal Clean Water Act worried the Oregon forest industry about possible unwelcome federal and/or state regulation of forest practices on private lands. The industry feared that a non-forestry agency might end up with regulatory responsibility over forest practice regulations, with uncertain and unpredictable consequences for industrial landowners. In addition, there was a widely held belief among forest industry officials that state regulation of private forest practices would be much less severe than federal regulation.

16. Washington State differs from Oregon in that court rulings regarding tribal fishing rights and a State Environmental Policy Act give it a greater degree of legalism.

17. The Department of Environmental Quality does have a role in Washington unparalleled in Oregon.

18. Slight changes made in 1987 require the Department of Forestry to collect inventories of threatened and endangered species and "ecologically and scientifically significant" sites. If, after conducting this analysis, the Forest Practices Board decides that forest harvesting may conflict with these resource sites, the board must then "consider the consequences of the conflicting uses and determine appropriate levels of protection" (ORS 527.710[3][b]). Resulting rules have usually limited harvesting during reproductive seasons or specified areas around particular sites in which no logging can occur. In Washington, any forest practices on critical habitat lands require an environmental assessment under Washington's SEPA legislation. The 1987 Wildlife Code creates a process whereby the director of the Department of Fish and Wildlife can ask the Wildlife Commission to list a species if it is "seriously threatened with extinction," though there is no timeline in the listing process. The Forest Practices Board has the power to designate critical habitat areas for individual species. See Cubbage and Ellefson 1980.

19. The Environmental Protection Agency lost a large battle three years ago to change forestry from a non–point source to a point source of pollution. If successful, this would have had serious implications for the current logic of appropriateness, but in the end, the failure to change this again demonstrated the difficulty in changing U.S. law and the narrow windows of opportunity that exist.

20. While most efforts were focused on the northern spotted owl, which became an "indicator" species, eventually not just the northern spotted owl but forest-dependent species in general would drive policy changes. We emphasize the northern spotted owl story because it has received a great deal of attention and the species' decline decidedly triggered the thermostatic process and ultimately resulted in massive policy changes.

21. Some changes, such as the clearcutting rules, were made before Option 9 was adopted, as part of initial efforts to implement ecosystem management following litigation over the northern spotted owl. Their scope was minimal and a 1992 directive limited their applicability only to circumstances "essential" for meeting forest plan objectives. See Haddock 1995 and Robertson 1992.

22. Empirical studies found that the values and ideas of Forest Service officials were slow to reflect changes that have taken place within civil society (Twight 1983; Twight and Lyden 1989).

23. It is true, as Hoberg (2003) notes, that much of Dwyer's rulings centered on the "viability" regulations under the National Forest Management Act that formed the core of his analysis, but the viability provision worked in tandem with the ESA's requirements that a management plan be developed to recover threatened or endangered species and with the National Environmental Policy Act requirement that they be published and assessed as environmental impacts statements.

24. Personal interview, June 1994.

25. It could be argued that national attention focused only on national forests and only regional attention was given to private forests. However, we urge caution against ascribing much causal influences to these differences. First, it is arguable that public sentiment both in the Pacific Northwest and nationally were responding more to the plight of national forests. Second, a clearer causal link would have to be established between the asserted differences in public values and the differences in forest policy specifications. Evidence to date apparently supports neither the differences in public values nor its asserted effects. Indeed, most data show differences in public opinion not between regional and national populations but between urban and rural communities (Pierce et al. 2000).

26. We acknowledge that on some policy issues, such as riparian zones, changes have been unidirectional. However, we treat this as only a temporary phenomenon because, as the HCPs indicate, policies have already started to reverse directions.

27. Regarding the Portland Audubon's analysis of the board's deliberations over protection of the spotted owl: "[The Board of Forestry] did adopt some rules to protect the spotted owl habitat—enough to protect the bird itself [and keep] a 'take' from occurring. But it is such a minimal amount of habitat protection it is tantamount to saying, 'We'll keep from killing the bird but we will make it so uninhabitable that the bird won't stay there'" (personal interview).

28. The existence of lag effects in no way contradicts our argument. Indeed, all interest-based accounts also acknowledge twenty-year lag effects from the time the advocacy groups were formed in the 1960s and 1970s to the noted change in the early 1990s.

29. These findings challenge not only much existing PE theory but also many existing theories of institutions that largely assume that paradigmatic change can only occur when existing institutions crumble or are replaced. On this point see Genschel 1997.

Chapter 7 The Political Economy of U.S. Greenhouse Gas Controls

Lee Lane

THE ARGUMENT IN BRIEF

This chapter assesses the prospects for implementing greenhouse gas controls in the United States. One basic fact frames the analysis: namely, controls stringent enough to stop global climate change would cost more than the damage expected from climate change. Although a modest level of emission control could yield more benefits than costs, even modest controls face formidable political challenges. The opponents of emission controls hold great organizational advantages over the proponents. To be sure, a strong surge of public sentiment might politically overwhelm all these objections and barriers but public support for emission controls is too tepid for that to be likely any time soon. Moreover, overcoming these domestic problems, could it be done, would be only the first step toward a viable international control regime, without which national controls would be futile. Because no international institution can compel cooperation of nation states, global environmental agreements are notoriously difficult to reach, to sustain, and to enforce.

Forces operating beyond the narrow arena of national and international environmental policy will also heavily influence the prospects for emission controls. Several trends suggest that these prospects are ebbing rather than rising. National security and fiscal policy challenges may well out-compete the climate issue for both public attention and economic resources. At the same time, the emerging globalization of the natural gas market will spark new conflicts between the goal of reducing greenhouse gas emissions and that of decreasing America's dependence on foreign energy.

Other factors have been cited as reasons for hoping that this unfavorable tide could be stemmed and even reversed. One of these, a possible disruption of Persian Gulf energy supplies, would—on closer investigation—have quite unfavorable implications for the prospects of U.S. emission controls. Other developments could indeed enhance the prospects for emission controls, for example, a large, favorable partisan shift, important scientific breakthroughs, or diplomatic pressure from Europe. Although these possibilities cannot be ruled out, they are too speculative to form the basis for an adequate strategy for managing climate policy.

The realistic political response is simply to admit that the current and likely future political constellation of forces is unfavorable to the implementation of all but modest emission controls and to adjust the goals of climate policy to match the political realities. Such a strategy would eliminate the benefit-cost problem because gradually slowing the growth of emissions would cost far less than Kyoto-like rapid emission reductions. Such a policy could also be shaped to achieve non-climate benefits. Concretely, linking mandatory emission controls to a plan for "tax shift" promises political and economic advantages. In addition, emission controls may actually confer useful diplomatic benefits on the United States.

DOMESTIC DIFFICULTIES OF EMISSION CONTROLS

Politically, climate change is the great white whale of environmental policy problems, a huge challenge for which definitive "solutions" seem infinitely elusive. In the United States that difficulty can be seen in the delay in formulating an effective policy response. The Clean Air Act and Clean Water Acts were already enacted by the early 1970s although air and water pollution problems had gained widespread public attention only in the late 1960s. In contrast, climate change first received wide publicity in the late 1980s; yet at this writing in 2004, no mandatory U.S. greenhouse gas emission controls are yet in place and none seem likely in the near future. The continuing failure to enact emission controls is not accidental.

THE BENEFIT-COST PROBLEM

In climate policy, the benefit-cost problem acts like a powerful gravitational field, relentlessly pulling down lofty aspirations to eliminate greenhouse gas emissions. The high cost and limited supply of non-emitting energy supplies dominates the cost side of the problem and this constraint is unlikely to disappear any time soon. Recent expert assessments suggest that the task of finding plentiful and cheap non-greenhouse-gas-emitting energy sources is likely to be slow and difficult. There are no technological "magic bullets" in evidence (Hoffert et al. 2002, 981–82; Ansolabehere and Deutsch 2003, 1).

Without such a cost breakthrough, the prospective but uncertain benefits for the world as a whole from eliminating anthropogenic greenhouse gas emissions are insufficient to justify the energy and capital replacement costs that would be entailed. Stopping anthropogenic climate change is impossible without virtually eliminating emissions. There are, of course, benefits from reducing greenhouse gas emissions but the test is how they compare with the costs. According to one study: "The problem is that the benefits appear to be relatively small for aggressive mitigation programs. Aggressive programs involve large mitigation costs that begin immediately but the benefits may be delayed by several decades or even a century. The present value of the benefits are [sic] small compared to the present value of the costs. The economic assessments of climate change thus suggest modest low-cost control programs that only slow warming slightly" (Chang, Mendelsohn, and Shaw 2003, 5–6).

As this quotation suggests, the excessive cost of aggressive emission reductions does not necessarily argue for inaction. We will later return to this point. Moreover, some scientists suggest that climate change may produce unpleasant surprises in a shorter time frame than that envisioned in the above quotation. This possibility will also be addressed later but first the pattern of current costs and future benefits merits further discussion.

The lag between costs and benefits is a key political problem in its own right. Although it is difficult to predict when continued anthropogenic greenhouse gas emissions may become economically harmful, "human-induced greenhouse warming will probably develop over many decades and may not have truly serious implications for humankind for a half century or more after the signal is first detected" (Homer-Dixon 2002, 498). In contrast, in order to stabilize atmospheric concentrations at fairly low levels, the initial costs of mitigation must be incurred soon. Technological development takes time. Replacing massive quantities of existing private and public infrastructure requires still more time.

The likely temporal pattern of costs and benefits implies that climate change mitigation is an exercise in transferring wealth from current generations to future ones. Americans, in their private affairs, often sacrifice current consumption to bequeath legacies to their children but this kind of challenge is not one that democratic political institutions handle especially well. "Taking the long-term into account requires that political decision makers be willing to ask generations living today, whether working or retired, to sacrifice a portion of their own interests for those of later generations, including those yet unborn. . . . Even if the merits of such action appear sensible in strict economic benefit-cost terms, the political costs may seem to today's politicians to be better spent addressing current needs. Yet inaction on long-term issues is itself a policy act, and one that may force more drastic action in the future, either because time has been lost in which productive investments in the future could have been made, or because the losses due to today's inaction—for example the failure to limit greenhouse gas emissions—are by their nature irreversible" (Heller 2003, 142).

INTEREST GROUP POLITICS

Beyond the handicap implied by intergenerational wealth transfers, passage of emission control legislation is further impeded by resistance from strong and well-organized energy industries and labor unions. Government policies that boost energy producers' costs would increase energy prices and reduce the demand for energy. Lower demand would degrade the values of specialized assets owned by energy suppliers and also diminish the value of their employees' specialized human capital. The managements of such firms have a fiduciary responsibility to resist the imposition of controls. Economic self-interest dictates the opposition of employees and their unions. Thus, greenhouse gas emission control policies will encounter influential and well-funded opponents.

Emission control proposals have, in fact, elicited very strong energy sector opposition. Although energy-producing industries would incur only about 10 to 15 percent of the total costs of greenhouse gas abatement, the absolute size of those costs exceeds those of previous pollution control initiatives. Some emission control proponents have speculated that granting high-emission industries a large percentage of all emission allowances might neutralize this opposition, but energy industry firms, with relatively few exceptions, have so far resisted these blandishments with apparently adamantine resolve.[1]

Producer interests not only have the motive and means for opposing emission controls, they enjoy a large organizational advantage in doing so. Economist Mancur Olson explained that coalitions composed of few entities with large per-unit stakes in the outcome can devote relatively low percentages of their resources to the task of establishing and maintaining a political organization (Olson 1965, 34–36). Hence, such coalitions have high percentages of their total resources available for achieving and using political influence. Moreover, such coalitions can organize and discourage free-riders at lower cost than large coalitions can.

Ironically, it is precisely because consumers would absorb the preponderance of the costs of carbon emission controls that producer interests have been able to appeal successfully to larger coalitions. Douglas Arnold has noted that legislators have a well-founded fear of taking actions that visibly impose costs on their constituents. Legislators anticipate the electoral problems that might result from such policy choices and seek to avoid them (Arnold 1990, 9). Government policies that increase energy prices, especially gasoline prices, are highly visible and hence politically dangerous (Nivola and Crandall 1995, 110–11). Elected officials who consider supporting policies that boost energy prices must assume that energy producers will inform the electorate of their actions and that this information will resonate ominously with many voters.

Proponents of emission controls are in a far weaker position. At best they can organize only coalitions of numerous citizens, none of whom is impelled by the prospect of significant personal economic gain or loss. Such coalitions are harder and more expensive to create and maintain. At the extreme, the costs of organizing broad, shallow coalitions may so far outweigh the expected benefits to the members that the coalition may not form at all. Unfortunately for the proponents of greenhouse gas abatement, coalitions of energy producer interests are of the inherently efficient narrow and deep pattern. Coalitions of environmentally motivated individual citizens are unavoidably of the less-efficient broad and shallow pattern.

Sometimes, of course, the American public demands action on issues, heedless of the strictures of the dismal science and the cautions of political analysts. As yet, however, that has not happened with the climate issue. U.S. public opinion on climate is muddled. Majorities of the electorate know that greenhouse warming is a scientifically established reality. They believe that anthropogenic emissions are contributing to it. They claim to believe that the problem is serious and say that they support mandatory government actions to mitigate climate change (Kempton, Boster, and Hartley 1999, 141–43).

On climate, though, the vox populi speaks in a soft, somewhat incoherent mumble. Despite the just-cited findings, the public does not regard climate with much urgency. In the latest Gallup survey, climate ranked ninth of ten environmental issues as a source of public concern (Saad 2003). Moreover, concern is waning. Over the last four years, the percentage of the public worrying about climate change "a great deal" or "a fair amount" has fallen from 72 percent to 51 percent. In the last year, the percentage fell seven points. Today, moreover, 47 percent say that they worry "only a little" or "not at all" (Saad 2003). Skepticism about climate change is widespread. In the last year, the percentage of Americans believing that the media exaggerates the importance of climate change rose from 33 percent to 38 percent. Those who think the issue is overstated now outnumber those who think that it is underestimated (Saad 2003). As to Kyoto, most polls show that majorities of Americans say that they support it. The same polls, however, say that most people do not care very much about the issue. Moreover, large majorities resoundingly reject policies that would increase energy prices. Thus, the public supports Kyoto while completely rejecting the only policies that could implement it.

This public indifference has been strong enough to withstand substantial waves of media focus on climate. Thus, the media hype surrounding the recent film *The Day After Tomorrow* entirely failed to shift U.S. public opinion on climate change. Earlier, the Turner Foundation had spent some $10 million on paid advertisements designed to raise public concerns about climate change. They had no impact.

INTERNATIONAL DIFFICULTIES OF EMISSION CONTROLS

The International Free-Rider Problem

Were some environmentally inclined sorcerer to cast a magic spell that suddenly overthrew all these political barriers, the resulting domestic controls would represent no more than a preliminary step toward the real goal of establishing an international emissions control regime. The so-called international free-rider problem makes the construction of international burden-sharing arrangements a nettlesome process. The "free-rider" problem is rooted in the fact that countries that reduce greenhouse gas emissions incur costs. But the benefits of slower climate change accrue even to countries that do not reduce emissions. Thus, all countries have an incentive to free-ride—that is, to do nothing in hopes that other countries will sacrifice for the common good.

The international free-rider problem is compounded because climate change affects countries differently. In the short run, some countries may even benefit from longer growing seasons and other favorable effects. Thus a recent study concluded that for the United States, the next century of climate change seems likely to produce a net benefit equal to about .2 percent of GDP. The same study concluded that as climate change continues, it becomes increasingly harmful (Mendelsohn and Neumann 1999, 321–23). Global impact studies have concluded that, excluding the risk of catastrophic change, the United States, Russia, and China are likely to experience little if any net damage from climate change during this century but that India and Europe may be much more vulnerable (Nordhaus and Boyer 2000, 96–98).

For international emission controls to work, those countries with the most reason to fear climate change must somehow induce those who expect to incur few early costs or even short-run benefits to bear some costs of mitigation policies. In the international arena, no supra-national power exists to coerce nation states to defer to the common good. The only alternative is agreements among states to create an international emission-control regime. The record of reaching and enforcing such agreements is distinctly mixed (Barrett 2003, 2–3).

International Power Rivalries

Both emission controls and actual climate change could have large enough and disparate enough impacts to influence the relative wealth of nations. An agreement that affects states' relative wealth will indirectly affect their relative power (Mearsheimer 1994–95, 20). If so, states would be compelled to evaluate climate proposals in light of the impact on their power positions relative to those of other states. The focus on relative gains instead of on the more permissive test of whether the state gains in absolute terms considerably complicates the task of reaching international agreement. "For sure, each state tries to maximize its absolute gains; still, it is more important for a state to make sure that it does no worse, and perhaps better, than the other state in any agreement. Cooperation is more difficult to achieve, however, when states are attuned to relative gains rather than absolute gains" (Mearsheimer 2001, 52). With the focus on relative gains, states may reject proposals in which they would score absolute gains if those proposals were more favorable to a global or regional power rival.

States seemingly differ in the degree to which their international relationships are dominated by power rivalries. The United States, Russia, and China (with India striving to join the club) are necessarily wary of relative power relationships. Interestingly, no great power has undertaken domestic emission controls. Europe, where the U.S. security umbrella has hitherto muted the importance of power rivalries, has gone furthest in adopting controls. The passage of time may eventually reveal that the intensity of a nation's international rivalries may influence its receptivity to emission-control agreements as much as its state of economic development.

Kyoto in Disarray

The disarray into which the Kyoto process has fallen illustrates the intractability of implementing international greenhouse gas emission controls. Russian ratification of Kyoto means that formally the agreement will go into force. But it is clear that reducing greenhouse gas emissions is very low on Russia's list of national priorities. And in this respect the Russians are typical. Japan and Canada seem most unlikely to meet their Kyoto targets. As one knowledgeable European observer recently noted, it is now impossible to envision the implementation of Kyoto in its initial sense, and the task of developing an alternative approach has become pressing (Müller 2003b, 3).

A serious commitment to emission reductions is very much a minority taste even in Europe. Germany and the United Kingdom, where factors other than climate policy have had a large impact on emissions, account for almost 98 percent of the emission reductions achieved so far. Ten of fifteen European Union members are not on course to meet their national targets under Kyoto (Busby and Ochs 2003, 41). Moreover, although EU majority opinion apparently supports government action on climate, European publics may be almost as ill-informed about the issue's scientific and economic realities as are their American counterparts (Kempton, Boster, and Hartley 1999, 216). If so, even in much of Europe, public support for paying the costs of emission controls may prove shallow.

Less-Developed Countries
and Climate Change Mitigation

It is particularly revealing that Kyoto seems to be foundering without even seriously confronting the hardest task of international emission controls. That task is to win the cooperation of the large, fast-growing, less-developed countries (LDCs). In order to hold atmospheric greenhouse gas concentrations below

550 ppm without constraining LDC emissions, the industrialized countries must, within thirty-five years, somehow achieve negative net emission (Yang and Jacoby 1997, 4). Thus, halting the rise of greenhouse gas concentrations is impossible without participation by the major LDCs.

Moreover, the greatest opportunities to reduce the growth in greenhouse gas emissions at relatively low cost are concentrated in the larger developing countries like China and India. In the next half-century, these countries will greatly expand their economic infrastructure. Choosing relatively low-emission technology for that expansion could significantly slow the growth rate of emissions. In contrast, the developed world has lower rates of new infrastructure investment and thus no comparable opportunities to reduce business-as-usual emission growth rates without prematurely abandoning economically productive infrastructure.

In a real sense, LDCs would benefit if they made these comparatively low-cost emission reductions. Although there are important differences among LDCs, many of them should be concerned about the long-term implications of climate change. "The bulk of the developing world has higher current temperatures, larger fractions of their economy in vulnerable sectors, more primitive technologies, and lower incomes or resources for adaptation. All of these factors would suggest that the economies of developing countries will be more vulnerable to climate change than the U.S. economy. In addition these countries could experience a suite of nonmarket effects that would not be represented in analyses of developed countries, for example disease epidemics, local famines and desertification" (Mendelsohn and Neumann 1999, 329).

The LDCs, however, do not have much latitude for responding to long-term considerations. Their urgent priority is economic development. LDCs may quite properly regard climate change mitigation, with its pattern of near-term costs to achieve long-term benefits, as an unaffordable luxury. Moreover, given the high rates of per capita economic growth occurring in some of the LDCs, the transgenerational wealth transfer of emission controls would have an unappealingly regressive effect on the intergenerational distribution of wealth over time.

Furthermore, as Thomas Schelling has pointed out, for an LDC capable of rapid economic advance, development may in fact be the best strategy for coping with climate change. Development reduces such a country's relative economic dependence on the threatened agriculture and forestry sectors. It increases the stock of resources available for investments in successful adaptation to climate change and it does not entail placing a highly uncertain bet on the prospects that international cooperation will somehow overcome the challenge of the free-rider problem (Schelling 2002, 3).

The American opponents of emission controls have successfully used the LDCs' reluctance to adopt emission controls as an objection to domestic U.S. controls. This argument was a focal point of the original U.S. Senate debate on the Kyoto Protocol. It also surfaced in more recent climate policy debates. The opponents' argument is powerful. Domestic emission controls will accomplish little unless other nations also control emissions. In fact, without LDC participation, stringent emission controls among the industrialized countries would result in the "leakage" of emissions to the LDCs. "Leakage" refers to the process in which energy-intensive industries choose to migrate rather than to incur high abatement costs. It is not likely to be a significant factor with low levels of abatement but would become worrisome with more aggressive controls.

In principle, developed countries could stop the "leakage" by paying LDCs to institute emission controls. In practice this option merely concentrates the incentives for free-riding among the developed countries. Each developed country hopes that the others will undertake the financial burden of paying the LDCs to reduce emissions and each industrialized country seeks to minimize its own share of the total burden.

Paying LDCs to reduce emissions would improve the cost effectiveness of emission controls. It was possible to work out such an agreement in the case of ozone depletion, but with climate change, the improvement in cost effectiveness, although large, has so far still been insufficient to overcome the nemesis of aggressive emission control proposals, the excess of costs over benefits (Barrett 2003, 378–80).

Emerging Trends and U.S. Climate Politics

The world now seems further from solving these problems than it did in 1997, when the Kyoto Protocol was agreed to, and the future trends are inauspicious.

NATIONAL SECURITY CONCERNS

First, the coming decades are likely to thrust important and persistent national security challenges onto the United States, as the brutal realities of the global terrorist jihad have made obvious. More generally, in the mid-1990s Huntington wrote: "Islam and China embody great cultural traditions very different from and in their eyes infinitely superior to that of the West. The power and assertiveness of both in relation to the West are increasing, and the conflicts be-

[handwritten margin note:] US. says no to kyoto because of LDCs "leakage" may be a problem - Some thought pay LDCs but this would amount to free riding (who will pay?)

tween their values and interests and those of the West are multiplying and becoming more intense" (Huntington 1996, 185).

Today the part of Huntington's threat analysis that pertains to China remains more speculative than that pertaining to Islam. Other analysts, using frameworks entirely different from Huntington's, come to similar conclusions about the likelihood of escalating Sino-American tensions. For example, John J. Mearsheimer has recently argued that China and Russia remain great powers. Mearsheimer predicts that in both Europe and northeast Asia the existing highly favorable power structure is unlikely to survive for long (Mearsheimer 2001, 385–86). He is particularly concerned that the dynamics of the international state system seem likely to push China toward security competition with the United States: "A wealthy China would not be a status quo power but an aggressive state determined to achieve regional hegemony. This is not because a rich China would have wicked motives, but because the best way for any state to maximize its prospects for survival is to be the hegemon of its region of the world. Although it is certainly in China's interest to be the hegemon of Northeast Asia, it is clearly not in America's interest to have that happen" (Mearsheimer 2001, 402).

Mearsheimer and Huntington are not alone in their assessments of rising tensions ahead. Yet a third international relations theory, "power transition" theory, also points to possible rising international tensions. Power transition theory focuses on changes in the relative power and status of nations as a source of conflict. "Should Russia recover and begin to develop rapidly again, it might well reemerge as a potential challenger. More likely the current and near-future challenger to American dominance is the People's Republic of China. With nearly one billion people and some of the fastest economic growth on record, China looks certain to achieve parity with the United States early in . . . [the twenty-first century]. Should China evaluate the status quo negatively (a strong possibility given the differences between China's and America's domestic political and economic systems) power transition [theory] anticipates war between them" (Kugler and Lemke 2003, 146).

Even these theories, which seem well corroborated by historical experience, do not prove that future armed conflict is inevitable, but they do show that several sets of forces, each of which has been associated with past international conflict, all militate for Sino-American conflict. The future seems noticeably more ominous than in the 1990s, America's "holiday from history." Hence, from the standpoint of contemporary climate policy, the 1990s may appear in retrospect as a now-vanished golden age just because they were also, from a broader national perspective, an era of illusions.

FISCAL PROBLEMS

Domestically, fiscal problems may occasion a somewhat similar darkening of the political scene. Fiscal problems may complicate the security challenge as well as pose a serious political dilemma in their own right (Ferguson and Kotlikoff 2003, 22). Because the U.S. population is aging, a relatively slowly growing work force will have to economically support a rapidly growing elderly population. At the same time, each retiree is becoming ever more costly to support because of the long-running increase in the cost of medical care. These economic facts portend fiscal consequences. A recent estimate found that the combination of these factors implied that the current commitments of the U.S. Social Security and Medicare programs exceeded the federal government's projected revenue by a present discounted value of $44.2 trillion (Gokale and Smetters 2003, 2).

Fiscal problems imply the obvious "solution" of increasing taxes, but tax increases imply a sacrifice in economic growth because the higher tax rates discourage labor participation and investment (Heller 2003, 8–9). Indeed, many economists believe that as a tax rate rises, the deadweight loss that it imposes on the economy rises by a larger percentage than will the tax revenue. Thus the fiscal "solution" of higher taxes is itself an economic problem. At the same time continuing fiscal imbalances imply the risk of higher interest rates, depreciation of the dollar, and inflation—none of which is good for the economy.

A GLOBAL LNG MARKET

The third important trend is occurring within the energy sector and is of direct relevance to the climate issue: the market for natural gas is probably evolving from the continental scale to a global scale. Yergin has referred to this transformation as the "next prize" in the evolution of energy markets (Yergin and Stoppard 2003, 103–14). Hitherto, most natural gas markets have been dominated by pipelines and therefore have been continental in scale. Now, the rising global demand for natural gas, combined with the lower costs of liquefied natural gas (LNG) tanker operations, is fostering the growth of international maritime transportation of large volumes of natural gas.

"This 'liquefied natural gas' (LNG) will be carried in tankers that can change direction on the high seas to respond to sudden shifts in demand or prices. Thanks to this emerging global commodity market, lights, air conditioning and factories in the United States will run on electricity that is sometimes generated with natural gas from Indonesia, the Algerian desert, the seas of Trinidad or Nigeria, the island of Sakhalin in the easternmost part of Russia, the frigid northern waters of Norway, or the foothills of the Andes" (Yergin and Stoppard 2003, 103).

This development will transform the debate about energy security. Some years ago David Montgomery wrote, "Energy security is largely an oil issue, although if there were substantial world trade in natural gas, similar concerns would pertain to it as well" (Montgomery 1992, 621). Today, Montgomery's hypothesis seems poised to become fact.

IMPLICATIONS FOR CLIMATE POLITICS

The combination of these trends may have profound implications for the climate issue. If U.S./Chinese relations become highly competitive, the task of forging a cooperative international system of emission controls will become considerably harder. The absence of any Chinese commitment to emission controls is already an important source of strength for U.S. emission control opponents. A more contentious relationship between the two countries would certainly redouble the political salience of ensuring that China undertakes emission reductions in parallel with those of the United States, while simultaneously diminishing the credibility of solutions entailing U.S. side payments to China.

Heightened security concerns could also harm the climate issue by simply crowding it off the domestic and international agendas. Human beings are "attention misers" (Jones 2001, 101). Political science research has long noted that only a comparatively few issues can be prominent at any one time: "There is a limit on the capacity of the system to process a multitude of agenda items. . . . A real perceived problem has a solution available, and there is no political barrier to action. But these subjects queue up for the available decision-making time, and pressing items crowd the less pressing ones down in the queue" (Kingdon 1995, 184).

Security threats are likely to trump climate in any direct competition for the limited supply of public and governmental attention. This effect was demonstrated by the abrupt disappearance of the controversy over the U.S. withdrawal from Kyoto in the aftermath of the 9/11 attacks.

Similarly, the economic stakes of the issues associated with the aging of the U.S. population are larger than those of climate change and at this time far more tangible. The industries and interest groups involved in those issues are larger and better funded than are the proponents of greenhouse gas emission controls and the institutions of government budget cycles, and the bond markets will force the age-wave issues onto the public agenda in ways for which there is no climate policy analogue. In sum, if climate competes with the entitlement problem, climate will lose.

That prediction extends easily from the competition for attention to that for dollars. In the next several decades, the nation's unfunded liabilities will apparently require government to impose economic sacrifices on the electorate. Experience suggests that the process of exacting sacrifices often engenders tax fatigue and political backlash. As demands on public sector economic resources rise, the competition for scarce dollars is likely to become increasingly Darwinian. Such conditions would seem unpropitious for demanding additional sacrifices in the name of climate change mitigation.

The rise of a global LNG market will change the relationship between climate policy and the touted goal of national energy independence. What had been a basically synergistic relationship between these goals will become an ambiguous one at best. Hitherto, reducing petroleum imports from abroad seemed to serve both the goal of restoring U.S. energy autarky and the goal of reducing greenhouse gas emissions. The appearance of a global LNG market seems likely to end this approximate congruence of policy goals. From the standpoint of reducing carbon emissions, natural gas is almost the only available large-scale substitute for coal. This substitution caused no real energy security concerns so long as Canada was the major source of additional gas supplies for the U.S. market. However, as the U.S. finds itself increasingly in a global market in which suppliers are the Persian Gulf, the Caspian Basin, and West Africa, the process of substituting gas for coal becomes more problematic. "One of the more haunting aspects of this new global gas business is its reminder of the transformational years of the late 1960s and early 1970s, when the United States became integrated with the world oil market. In a few short years, the United States went from being a minor petroleum importer to a major one. The surge in demand from the world markets, pulled by the engine of the American economy, helped set the scene for the oil crises of the 1970s and created dependencies with which the world still wrestles" (Yergin and Stoppard 2003, 103–4).

The question here is, what will be the implications for the future politics of greenhouse gas emission controls? It is a question that deserves further exploration.

CLIMATE POLICY AND ENERGY SECURITY

Thinking of the past in which oil was America's "problem" energy import, one might be tempted to conclude that a new energy supply crisis would boost the cause of domestic greenhouse gas controls. One would be wrong.

PETROLEUM DEPENDENCY
AND CLIMATE POLICY

The two oil price shocks of the 1970s illustrated the world economy's vulnerability to oil supply disruption. Recently, documents became public suggesting that the United States seriously considered militarily seizing Persian Gulf oil fields during the 1973–74 oil embargo (Frankel 2004, 22). This revelation highlights the great geo-strategic importance of Persian Gulf oil, an importance further reconfirmed by more recent events.

Much of the national discourse on energy policy assumes that energy independence is desirable and possible. Perhaps because the goal is so widely accepted, the actual objective is seldom spelled out. In fact three quite different ideas are involved. First, the economy's vulnerability to macroeconomic disruption from oil price shocks constitutes an external cost of petroleum use. "A number of analysts have called attention to the significant and apparently negative relation between oil price volatility and macroeconomic performance" (Portney et al. 2003, 206). Incorporating this external cost of additional macroeconomic risk into the price of petroleum products could correct the economy's tendency to consume more oil than is appropriate.

Second, government intervention in the market for petroleum products might diminish the monopoly rents being captured by the OPEC cartel of oil producers. While no individual oil user can affect OPEC prices, the U.S. government has some capacity to do so. It can influence the behavior of enough purchasers of petroleum to have what economists call "monopsony power." "Some observers have suggested that this power could be used to neutralize or minimize the anti-competitive behavior of OPEC and reduce the world price of oil" (Portney et al. 2003, 207). (One might consider, in passing, that the goal of a lower world oil price is not entirely consistent with the goals of climate policy.)

Third, some commentators have asserted that there is a national security or defense externality associated with oil consumption (Portney et al. 2003, 207). If oil dependence can require U.S. military expeditions to the Gulf, so the speculation goes, perhaps the United States should discourage oil consumption in order to reduce its defense costs. Considered from the viewpoint of climate policy, this conventional wisdom would suggest that at least part of the policy to lower greenhouse gas emission could then be "sold" as enhancing national security.

At the current time the combined effects of the first two justifications for market intervention are of quite modest significance. A 2002 National Research Council investigation found that the combined market shock and monopsony power considerations justified an increase of about $5 per barrel of oil. This amount would translate into about 12 cents per gallon of gasoline.

Thus, the combined effects of oil-related macroeconomic risk and the opportunity for monopsony pricing imply that United States should be consuming only slightly less oil than it currently is. For example, a recent study of the Congressional Budget Office (CBO) found that achieving an eventual 10 percent reduction in U.S. gasoline consumption would require a 46-cent-per-gallon fuel tax increase (Congressional Budget Office 2003). Hence, the price increase needed to decrease consumption by ten percent would be nearly four times higher than that indicated by the actual (non-climate) under-pricing of oil. It seems likely that, at least in the case of gasoline, adjusting prices by the mere twelve cents a gallon that is actually justified would diminish consumption by only a small fraction of the 10 percent benchmark target assumed by CBO.

The trends that affect the importance of these factors are mixed. On the one hand, OPEC has discovered that oil price stability confers significant advantages for cartel management and national budgeting (Bohi and Quandt 1984, 18). This development certainly has seemed to dampen the Gulf States' temptation to produce price shocks and may indicate that future price shocks are less likely than the experience of the 1970s would suggest. On the other hand, Gulf market share is destined to rise. World demand for oil, propelled largely by the Asian LDCs, is rising rapidly. According to the National Intelligence Council assessment of global trends to 2015, "Total oil demand will increase from roughly 75 million barrels per day in 2000 to more than 100 million barrels in

2015, an increase almost as large as OPEC's current production" (National Intelligence Council 2000, 28). In the long run, the fact that the Gulf States have a larger share of reserves than of production implies an inevitable rise in Gulf market share (barring a competitive breakthrough for non-conventional oil) (Müller 2003, 5).

OIL CONSERVATION, NATIONAL SECURITY, AND POLITICAL OPPORTUNITY

Based on these facts and trends, U.S. oil prices may currently be about $5 per barrel too low, even before consideration of climate change. But, perhaps noting that the implied oil price adjustments are really quite modest, some proponents of domestic emission controls assert that a third factor, national security costs, justifies additional restrictions on domestic U.S. oil consumption. Presumably they do so in hopes of arguing that greenhouse gas controls applied to oil would produce added co-benefits.

For the asserted link between domestic oil consumption and national security costs to be valid, two conditions would have to be met. First, it would have to be possible to identify military forces and costs that could be avoided were it not for the need to protect oil flows from the Persian Gulf and elsewhere. Second, it would be necessary to show that reduction of domestic oil consumption would materially diminish the U.S. need to protect world oil flows. Neither condition is true.

It is not possible convincingly to identify military expenditures that could be avoided were U.S. interest in securing world oil flows to dissipate. A recent panel of the National Academy of Science reached this conclusion after having investigated the matter. They found no credible evidence linking levels of domestic petroleum consumption to the national security expenditure of the United States (National Research Council 2002, note 6). The lack of a connection is unsurprising. It is the very nature of the United States military's expeditionary capabilities that they assist in coping with multiple threats. Forces protecting Persian Gulf oil flows simultaneously offer capabilities to suppress terrorism, project power into the Levant, supply coercive force to regional nonproliferation objectives, and implicitly threaten the oil supplies of America's potential great power rivals. With forces deterring and dissuading such a multiplicity of threats, the search for the marginal costs of the oil flow protection mission becomes an exercise of nearly metaphysical insubstantiality.

Further, the connection between domestic consumption and the need to protect and control oil flows is itself extremely weak. Regardless of domestic consumption levels, the United States is and will remain inexorably dependent on oil flows from the Persian Gulf: "[The] simple fact is that the United States is vitally dependent on the health of an integrated world economy. Instability in oil supplies has a rapid impact on the world economy and thus on that of the United States. In addition it is an established interest of the United States to prevent weapons of mass destruction by regimes that may threaten that oil supply" (Rathmell et al. 2003, 4).

The quotation suggests that a substantial part of the macroeconomic costs of an oil price shock may strike the U.S. indirectly through the impact on the economies of U.S. trading partners. To this degree, the damage cannot be deflected by domestic energy conservation.

Indeed, viewed at all realistically, the potential impact of domestic oil conservation on world markets is too small and too ambiguous to produce significant benefits: "The largest conceivable reduction in petroleum imports would still leave the United States linked to world oil markets and exposed to risks of volatile oil prices. Policies to reduce petroleum imports might even increase the instability of world oil markets. With significant reductions in demand the high-cost suppliers (who also tend to be secure sources of supply) would be shut in first, and the Middle Eastern OPEC countries with low production cost could end up with a larger rather than a smaller market share. In this situation, petroleum conservation might lead to less, rather than more energy security" (Montgomery 1992, 625). It follows that domestic oil conservation cannot affect America's need for the capacity to project military force into the Gulf region.

OIL SUPPLY DISRUPTION
AND CLIMATE POLICY?

Although the prospect of a new supply disruption does not seem to justify nearly enough petroleum conservation to suit the advocates of strong greenhouse gas emission controls, there is no disputing that were a disruption to occur, it would have consequences for the politics of greenhouse gas controls. Despite their scant national security merits, conservation policies might result from a supply disruption, as they did from earlier "oil shocks," but domestic conservation is only one possible political response. Others include renewed emphasis on domestic hydrocarbon production and intensification of efforts to bring non-OPEC and non–Persian Gulf supply sources into the market. Like

like domestic conservation measures, these efforts will not fundamentally alter the world's dependence on Persian Gulf oil, although they are certainly no less reasonable as responses to a supply disruption.

The point is that a supply disruption would offer an opportunity for both proponents of supply-oriented policies and advocates of energy conservation. If the disruption were severe and long enough, the likely outcome would be a jumbled collection of self-contradictory supply and conservation policies. The net implications of the contest between supply and conservation policies would largely depend on which side more successfully framed the issue. In this contest, the supply proponents would enjoy a major advantage. Namely, the public associates conservation with the actual sacrifice of energy services and, therefore, intuitively rejects it (Kempton, Boster, and Hartley 1999, 136–41).

A second, still more powerful reason for doubting that a supply disruption would redound to the net advantage of the greenhouse gas emission control proponents is the potential political impact on future LNG imports, discussed above. The Gulf States account for about 35 percent of the world's natural gas reserves (Energy Information Administration 2002, 45, Table 14). If oil supply disruption produces a knee-jerk public demand for energy autarky, greenhouse gas emission control strategy in the all-important utility market could be crippled. Coal and railroad interests could seize on an oil supply disruption as a pretext for restraints on LNG imports.

WILL OTHER EVENTS RESCUE EMISSION CONTROLS?

Even though an oil price shock does not seem likely to benefit the cause of greenhouse gas emission controls, more generally it remains true that events can often suddenly and discontinuously divert the course of politics. The proponents of controls have long hoped that fortuitous developments might suddenly allow them to overrun or to evade political defenses that currently seem impregnable. Political science confirms that such transforming events do sometimes occur.

PUNCTUATED EQUILIBRIUM

Two prominent political scientists, Baumgartner and Jones, have recently described a framework for issue image management that they refer to as a theory of "punctuated equilibrium." Issues, they note, remain dormant or subject to only incremental change for long periods and, then, rather quickly become fluid (Baumgartner and Jones 1993, 25–30). The discussion in the previous section suggests that an oil price shock is an example of the kind of event that would indeed "unfreeze" the politics of emission controls, albeit probably to the advantage of opponents of controls rather than their advocates.

Baumgartner and Jones believe that issues can suddenly become fluid when a number of positive feedback loops within the political system are activated by the course of events. In some instances the resulting periods of intense activity may lead to institutional changes that persist and influence political outcomes after the focus of activity has moved on to other issues. The Baumgartner and Jones theory is similar to and reinforces an earlier discussion of what political economist John Kingdon referred to as "policy windows." In Kingdon's discussion, too, policy windows might open quite suddenly (Kingdon 1995, 166–68). He suggested that the opening occurs when the political circumstances, the definition and perception of a problem, and a policy solution all exist at the same moment. Both theories would suggest that the previous lack of political success for emission control proposals does not necessarily imply future failure. It might be that a period of fluidity or a policy window is just about to open. Hence, assessing the future prospects of emission controls requires exploring possible events that might align the climate problem with solutions and politics or to unleash the various positive feedback described by Baumgartner and Jones.

Political scientist Anthony Downs has explained that attention to problems is often cyclical. For a while, a problem gathers a great deal of attention; then attention wanes. Downs argues that attention may dissipate when the difficulty of a solution finally becomes apparent. Baumgartner and Jones agree that this pattern does sometimes occur but point out that a key question is whether important institutional change occurs before the waning of attention. In that case, they argue, the cyclical pattern of attention is not necessarily a sign of futility (Baumgartner and Jones 1993, 86–88).

Climate policy, though, has so far corresponded quite well to the pattern described by Downs. The issue has gone through surges of media coverage (Michaels 2003). Such surges occurred around the times of the Rio Conference, the Kyoto agreement, and President George W. Bush's rejection of Kyoto. Presumably each of these surges in attention has been associated with the positive feedback loops described by Baumgartner and Jones. The spate of media coverage following the recent release of a DOD study of a worst-case climate change scenario was a mini-version of the same phenomenon. None of these attention surges, however, resulted in institutional change in the form of mandatory emission controls.

The pattern indicates that, in the United States, political forces have precluded enactment of mandatory emission controls. Future events will certainly again stimulate surges in media coverage but future surges in public attention are likely to be as sterile as those that have preceded them, unless those future events change the membership of the opposing coalitions or change the relative power of the groups in those coalitions.

POSSIBLE POLICY WINDOWS FOR CLIMATE

A large pro-Democratic shift in the partisan balance of political power would improve the political prospects of emission controls. To matter, though, the partisan shift would have to be big. A new book highlights the unique power of the political right in America. The authors, Micklethwait and Wooldridge, explain that American conservatism encompasses a powerful populist alliance of businessmen, property rights advocates, gun owners, and philosophical libertarians. New communications media including the Internet, talk radio, and cable television have emerged to serve this movement. At the same time, conservative intellectuals dominate much of elite political discourse. Micklethwait and Wooldridge explain how the perceived success of President Reagan's policies shifted America's political center of gravity and set conservatism as the default value for America's governing philosophy (Micklethwait and Wooldridge 2004, 176–97).

The resulting conservative consensus limits U.S. climate policy. Nationalism and rejection of big government are among American conservatism's long-dominant leitmotiv. Emission controls would greatly extend government's economic role. Kyoto would have slowed economic growth. And it would have transferred American wealth abroad for no environmental gain. Unsurprisingly, conservative legislators resist these proposals. These legislators, moreover, exercise a collective veto. In the U.S. Senate, as few as forty votes can stop legislation. The combination of conservative and hydrocarbon interests can easily muster this number. It follows that, for Congress to accept emission controls, at least some philosophically conservative legislators will have to vote for them.

The normal fluctuations in the partisan power balance seem most unlikely to break this potential veto power. Even Bill Clinton's electoral prowess fostered only marginally more liberal policies. And despite many current political handicaps, conservatives' legislative veto power appears safe in the impending national elections.

Even with a much-strengthened Democratic party, emission controls might prove elusive. Although environmentalists are a core constituency of the Democratic party, they are far from the most important one. Typically less than 5 percent of voters choose candidates primarily on environmental issues, and the vast majority of voters highly motivated by environmental issues are partisan Democrats (Ladd and Bowman 1995, 44–45). Given this fact, Democratic office holders may be reluctant to advance policies that would raise energy prices. Such policies are enormously unpopular with the general public. They are, therefore, likely to alienate constituencies that are larger and more politically contestable than are the greens. The Clinton administration's tentative handling of domestic emission control proposals is entirely consistent with the ambiguous implications of climate for Democratic office holders.

Conversely, the Bush administration would greatly enhance the prospects for emission controls by dropping its opposition to them. But hitherto, Mr. Bush has steadfastly opposed mandatory controls. The initial public and media controversy over the administration's stance evaporated after the terrorist attack in 2001.

The electoral realities may also limit what European leaders can do to change the U.S. climate policy. At least the U.K. government has been reputed in the media to be encouraging the Bush administration to adopt more ambitious climate policies. Prime Minister Tony Blair has suffered from acerbic criticism for being excessively deferential to American interests. He would presumably benefit domestically were he able to claim political credit for moving the Bush administration on climate and he would seem to be uniquely well situated to do so, should he choose to use his political credits with Mr. Bush on the climate issue.

A scientific breakthrough that proves there is a threat of near-term catastrophic climate change damage in the United States could, of course, transform the political dynamic without producing a realigning election. Many issue realignments take place without electoral realignments (Baumgartner and Jones 1993, 22). New, highly credible scientific evidence implying near-term catastrophic harm to American society would certainly almost guarantee the implementation of emission controls.

Proof of large irreversible changes, even if only modestly threatening to America, would at least noticeably heighten the prospects for mandatory controls. Regardless of the immediate implications for the United States, conclusive proof that anthropogenic emissions were causing the shutdown of the thermohaline circulation or disruption of important hydrological patterns like the monsoon would also transform the domestic politics of emission controls. Once it were clear that large anthropogenic climate change was occurring, fear of future unknown consequences would weigh more heavily. The expected benefits of controls would rise.

④   A breakthrough on emission-free energy might have an almost equally dramatic impact by shrinking the expected costs of emission controls. The proponents of emission controls have typically assumed that controls would be necessary to induce private-sector technological innovations that would then allow for lower emission levels. An alternative model proposed by the Bush administration, among others, is that lower-cost, emission-free energy sources may be a political prerequisite of stringent emission controls. In this case the success of government-funded energy R&D might be viewed as a prerequisite for emission controls rather than a product of the controls.

The fact that these various political, scientific, and technological shifts are possible does not make them a good basis for political strategy. In contrast to the regularities of classical drama, in politics the appearance of the deus ex machina is uncertain. The timing is unknown and it is unclear in whose favor the divine intervention will occur. Republicans could win a realigning election. Climate science could discover that feedback loops will delay and dampen the harmful effects of climate change. Technological progress could extend the cost advantages of fossil fuels rather than curtail them.

Some emission control proponents are not, however, waiting for divine intervention in the form of political events, scientific discoveries, or technological breakthroughs. On the contrary, in a strategy discussed by Baumgartner and Jones, they are seeking to move the locus of political action to the state ⑤ level. As a result, there are now a number of new state-level emission control proposals, especially in the electric power sector.

The economic disadvantages of a state-level approach are manifest. State-5.a level controls could easily lead to costly leakage of energy production from states with controls to those without them. Indeed, with a unified electricity grid, imposing controls only in states supplied by power generators with below average emission rates could produce perverse results. If the cap-and-trade system is designed to block this option, energy-intensive businesses may simply move to states without carbon controls (Keeler 2004, 6).

The proponents of state-level emission controls realize that the global problem of greenhouse gas emissions is ill suited to state-by-state action, but their meager federal prospects have, they feel, foreclosed the more direct route. Moreover, from a political standpoint, they hope that state-level action may 5b. break the federal political impasse. Because some regions are more environmentally conscious than others, measures that are politically unacceptable in the country as a whole may be acceptable in a few states. If so, state legislation might spark a new competitive dynamic within the electric power sector. Some power generators may seek nationwide controls to escape the competitive disadvantage created by unequal and burdensome controls imposed by the states in which they operate.

The incentives created by state-level controls are, however, a distinctly double-edged sword. The fact that state controls place some power producers at a competitive disadvantage implies that the controls create an equal and opposite competitive advantage for other power producers. State-level action will strengthen the incentives to resist controls for all those power producers located in the less environmentally sensitive regions. Such producers would gain competitively from the more environmentally conscious regions' adoption of emission controls. Moreover, with time, power producers will make investments necessary to serve markets in the environmentally constrained states. Once these investments are made, substituting national for state-by-state controls risks transforming these investments into devalued stranded assets, a development likely to redouble their owners' political resistance to nationwide controls (Keeler 2004, 6).

The political net effect on industry politics is uncertain. The prospect of state controls does encourage some power producers to support a national system. Others will find new and stronger reasons to oppose federal controls. In the end, if state emission controls are perceived as competitively harming local industries, the results would seem as likely to discredit the concept of emission controls as to encourage their extension to the remainder of the country.

Moreover, state-level controls may pose hard problems for the design of later nationwide emission control proposals. For one thing, state cap-and-trade programs will create property rights in the form of emission allowances. They will also call forth capital investments that will be at considerable risk of becoming stranded assets as the result of the imposition of a national program. The more states enact disparate programs and the longer these programs persist, the harder the task of fashioning a federal system is likely to become.

Some emission control proponents hope that recent California legislation imposing greenhouse gas emission controls on automobiles might force auto companies to back federal preemption. Federal-level emission controls would almost certainly be part of the political price for such preemption. This scheme suffers from defects that parallel those of the electricity sector proposals. It is not clear that the California legislation will survive legal challenge. If it does, Congress may still resist auto-industry pleas for preemption. And if preemption were to occur, it is more likely to entail federal fuel economy limits rather than the far more cost-effective, economy-wide cap-and-trade controls. A recent study by the Congressional Budget Office documented, yet again, the high cost of fuel economy standards relative to the putative external costs of automobile fuel consumption (Congressional Budget Office 2003). Thus, even if the California legislation were to succeed politically, any emission reductions would be expensive. Combined with society's limited willingness to pay, such a cost-ineffective system would seem to offer only trivial impacts on climate change.

INNOVATIVE POLICY MANAGEMENT: A FABIAN ALTERNATIVE

The future will reveal whether the shift of activity to the states was a brilliant example of political indirect strategy or a costly blunder. But, as the above discussion suggests, in the end the issue of emission controls must return to the federal level. When it does, the need to define a politically and economically realistic policy objective will also return. Whatever happens in the states, barring political realignment or transforming new discoveries, political and economic conditions are generally unfavorable to aggressive emission control proposals. The best course for climate policy would be to accept this reality and aim for a more "Fabian" goal of modestly slowing the OECD countries' rate of emission growth.

SUCCESS REDEFINED

The analysis so far has taken pains to dispel what the author believes to be hype and over-optimism about emission controls. This section argues, however, that a more modest Fabian emission control strategy is worth the costs. There are five reasons for favoring a Fabian emission limitation plan while eschewing more draconian alternatives:

- If the emission reduction targets are kept low, their costs are likely to fall below the expected benefits from slowing the rate of climate change.
- Modest emission controls are very unlikely to increase self-defeating emission leakage and the resulting political complication for the problem of future LDC emission controls.
- The imposition of OECD emission controls is probably a political prerequi-

site for encouraging LDCs to implement emission reduction strategies, which may be a more fruitful approach to slowing the rate of emissions growth than anything that can be accomplished within OECD.

- Even modest emission controls would increase incentives for private sector technological development, thus possibly enhancing the cost effectiveness of future emission controls.
- Greenhouse gas emission controls produce co-benefits in the form of reducing local air pollution problems, especially in the cases of methane and black carbon but also in the case of carbon dioxide emissions resulting from the combustion of coal (Hansen 2004, 18).

WOULD PROPONENTS ACCEPT MODERATE GOALS?

Slowly emission control proponents have seemed to be lowering their political aspirations. Some progress in that direction has already been made in the recent decision to scale back the emission reduction targets contained in the legislation introduced by Senators John McCain and Joseph Lieberman. Observed political behavior suggests that, while success leads to escalating demands, "unambiguous failure of a group to achieve a political objective is followed by a lowering of the aspiration level" (Edelman 1985, 157).

Although the failure of the strategies of the 1990s is for some proponents not yet "unambiguous," it seems likely to become so over time. For a few more years, proponents may continue to hope that harder work or a craftier strategy will finally produce success. At some point, however, even the most intransigent proponent of the Kyoto strategy will be compelled to reexamine the realism of that approach.

Hitherto, emission control proponents have disparaged the application of benefit-cost analysis to climate. They feared that it would impose a ceiling on abatement costs. That ceiling would be incompatible with the goal of stabilizing atmospheric concentration of greenhouse gases at some relatively low level. Although benefit-cost analysis appears to impose an unwelcome lid on costs, it could also establish a floor for defining prudent emission control policy. From this viewpoint, many economists have concluded that a moderate carbon tax would be justified, given the risks of climate change. Although these prescriptions fall far short of the goals of the more enthusiastic emission control proponents, they provide, nevertheless, a rationale for moving beyond the status quo. The unfavorable political constellation of forces that dominates climate policy and the likelihood of further unfavorable changes suggest that the floor offered by benefit-cost analysis would be politically more relevant than the ceiling that it might someday impose.

Moderating emission control objectives would reduce the present discounted cost of abatement. Presumably, at least some of the interests threatened by controls would moderate their opposition. More moderate goals do not, however, solve the more basic problem of the weakness of the political demand for action on climate. Harnessing emission controls to other national policy objectives, especially high-priority objectives, might address this more fundamental difficulty. The national security issue, we have argued, does not provide a profitable link-up. However, it would be worthwhile to try to create a linkage between emission controls and the very fiscal and foreign policy challenges that would otherwise be likely to out-compete climate for public concern and attention. At best, climate would ride in the slipstream of these issues rather than be supplanted by them. For such a link-up strategy to work, proponents of climate change would have to move beyond the narrow world of environmental policy and see their issue in a larger context of national priorities. The next section will discuss some of the considerations that could emerge from such innovative management approaches.

CLIMATE AS A FISCAL FIX 6 A

The German Model

Despite the differences in political systems, the German experience may suggest an opportunity that could arise in the United States. When Chancellor Helmut Kohl was first considering adopting an aggressive greenhouse gas emission reduction target for Germany, the Ministry of Finance reportedly enthusiastically supported the idea. Climate policy seemed to offer the prospect of increasing government revenue. Eventually, the promise of increased revenue was fulfilled with the German Ecological Tax. Although the tax is quite unpopular with the electorate, it has survived and been repeatedly increased (Interwies et al. 2002, 22–23). It has survived and grown partly because it is a source of revenue for an increasingly cash-short German government.

The initial enactment of the Ecological Tax was especially interesting to American observers because it was an example of what economists sometimes call "tax shift." In tax shift, pollution is subject to a tax, and the tax revenues are used to reduce the taxes on economically productive activities like saving and employment. (An emission rights limitation plan can also be used as a revenue source, as long as the government auctions at least part of the emission allowances rather than giving them away gratis.)

ADVANTAGES OF TAX SHIFT

For proponents of climate change mitigation, the tax-shift approach offers clear advantages. The most obvious is the prospect of an extra source of economic benefits from emission controls. Lower taxes on saving and labor would increase those activities. And the added economic output would boost society's total economic well-being. "Revenues from an auction of allowances or externality tax could be used to offset distortionary taxes and achieve some mitigation of the overall cost of the regulation at a macroeconomic level" (Smith, Ross, and Montgomery 2002, 4). The increased growth from lowering taxes on productive activity is an additional macroeconomic benefit over and above the initial gains from reducing harmful emissions.

Although estimates vary, the gains per dollar of tax avoided can be large. For example, a recent analysis found that using allowance revenues to reduce personal income tax rates could reduce the total cost of an emission control program by more than 40 percent, compared with simply grandfathering the allowances (Smith and Ross 2002, 22, Table 3). MIT's EPPA model indicates that using carbon emission allowance revenues to reduce the personal income tax rate could cut program costs by about 25 percent (Babiker, Metcalf, and Reilly 2000, 13,Table 11). Other studies find that each dollar reduction in income taxes yields an economic benefit of $0.20 to $0.50 (Parry 2002b, 5).[2]

At $10 to $30 per metric ton, a tradable emission allowance system would generate an annual revenue stream of approximately $15 billion to $45 billion. (For comparison, the federal gasoline tax raises about $25 billion annually.) However, there are many competing demands on the revenue stream that would flow from emission limitations. Perhaps 9 to 21 percent of total carbon tax revenue (or emission rights auction revenues) would be needed to compensate the energy sector and related businesses for the asset value losses implied by emission controls (Smith, Ross, and Montgomery 2002, 6). Approximately another 30 percent would be needed to offset the loss of government revenue that would result from the slower economic growth occasioned by the emission controls (Smith, Ross, and Montgomery 2002, 16, Figure 1). Thus, only about half of the revenue would actually be available to reduce other taxes. Assuming that only about half of the total revenue were available for tax shift would produce a net revenue estimate of approximately $7.5 to $22.5 billion. Given the uncertainty about the per-dollar benefits of tax reduction, a tax shift of this magnitude would generate an initial annual benefit of $1.5 to $11.3 billion. This figure would of course grow as annual emission levels increased.

By boosting the apparent economic net benefits of emission controls, a tax shift approach would presumably also confer a political advantage on the concept of emission controls. There are other potential political benefits. For instance, in terms of the competition for public and governmental attention, making climate a source of revenue would transform it into a partial solution to fiscal concerns. In the process, it would also inject emission controls into a political arena where future legislative activity will be much greater than in environmental policy. And positioning emission controls as an alternative to otherwise unavoidable conventional tax increases might cause some Republicans to reconsider their stance on climate.

It may be possible to improve the odds of achieving a tax shift by steering emission control revenue into privately held savings accounts of some type. Such proposals are a common feature of many entitlement reform plans. Plans based on substituting private savings for future entitlement benefits usually entail explicit recognition of fairly substantial transition costs. And revenue is needed—especially early on—to avoid the problem of creating many privately held accounts that are too small to be managed efficiently. In sum, entitlement reform is likely to absorb a significant amount of government revenue. There is no particular reason that some of that revenue could not come from charges on greenhouse gas emissions.

Using emission controls as a revenue source would be consistent with the goal of modestly slowing emission growth. If the tax per ton is moderate, revenue can continue to grow, albeit at a rate slower than that of the economy as a whole. While proponents of steeper emission reductions might find this outcome disappointing, it is more appealing than no emission controls whatsoever.

IS TAX SHIFT FEASIBLE?

A tax-shift emission control plan is, therefore, attractive for several reasons, but is it feasible? The answer is unclear. Even when future fiscal troubles do become more clear and pressing—as they will—there will still be important barriers to tax shift. The institutional structure of Congress militates against mixing issues in a way that crosscuts committee jurisdictions, as tax shift clearly would do.

Also, unlike committees with traditional environment jurisdiction, the tax committees are less likely to contain members with high degrees of environmental interests. Emission control proponents might therefore resist mixing taxes and emission controls. Indeed, the strategy of tax shift requires a strange-bedfellow ideological coalition that would be uncomfortable for both sides.

Most importantly, tax shift is only attractive if the resulting tax reductions are permanent. To put the issue in context, the need to cover unfunded liabilities offers an opportunity to practice tax shift by substituting emission controls for part of tax increases that would otherwise have occurred. However, what assures that the emission controls are not merely additional increases used to avoid benefit reductions and other spending cuts? In that case, carbon emission charges are merely a net tax increase, not the substitution of one revenue source for another.

AN ALTERNATIVE REVENUE-BASED STRATEGY

It is clear that tax shift is a strategy for the future rather than for the present. It is likely to become more appealing as the need for revenue becomes more acute. Ferguson and Kotlikoff argue that government's large unfunded liabilities are likely to affect financial markets suddenly rather than gradually (Ferguson and Kotikoff 2003, 26). But Heller suggests that the impact may not occur until those liabilities begin to affect the security of the specific bonds being offered (Heller 2003, 116). Because most government bonds are short term, the markets may anticipate future fiscal troubles by quite short lead times.

In the interim, emission control proponents could still find political benefits by focusing on revenue issues. Using carbon taxes or tradable emission allowance revenues for R&D may be the most politically attractive option with a claim to enhance the cost effectiveness of controls. After all, there is already some government-funded R&D on emission-free technologies, so government support for such work is undoubtedly a politically viable concept, at least under current fiscal conditions. The connection between the problem of emissions and the solution of increased R&D spending on non-emitting energy sources is relatively transparent. Indeed, the logic of increased R&D spending may be more understandable than that of emission control incentives. However, some political scientists have speculated that the public has difficulty understanding the linkage between emissions and R&D spending (Arnold 1990, 24–25). Some German opinion research seems to suggest a similar conclusion (Interwies et al. 2002, 28–29).

THE ECONOMICS OF GOVERNMENT
RESEARCH AND DEVELOPMENT

In theory, such government-funded research could also enhance the cost effectiveness of the emission control program as a whole. Economic theory suggests that markets typically underinvest in R&D. "The economics literature makes a convincing case that increasing R&D beyond the amount that the private sector is willing to support has large potential benefits" (Cohen and Noll 1991, 22). Carbon taxes or tradable emission allowance schemes would not address this market failure. Such policies would create incentives to reduce emissions. And they would create some incentive for R&D aimed at this goal. But they cannot more than modestly remedy the tendency of for-profit enterprises to underinvest in R&D as a strategy for reducing emissions. Hence, even with an economically efficient greenhouse gas emission allowance price, the market would produce less than optimal amounts of R&D on climate solutions.

Despite its theoretical strengths, the concept of using emission control revenues for energy R&D has problems in practice. Two concerns merit consideration. First, the theoretical justification cited in the previous section applies only to increases in R&D, not to spending that merely substitutes government climate-related R&D spending for private spending that would occur with an emission control regime or for non-climate related R&D. So the question of the alternative employment of climate R&D dollars is of considerable significance in assessing this use of resources. In general, "the extent to which federal R&D substitutes for, or actually encourages, privately sponsored R&D is a matter of considerable dispute, but the most recent work indicates a reasonably high level of substitution" (Cohen and Noll 1991, 48–49). If government climate-related R&D does substitute for other R&D, it could fail a cost-benefit test even while producing benefits in excess of the government expenditures. Currently, an additional dollar in R&D expenditure produces $4 in benefits (measured in present value). To be cost-beneficial, therefore, each dollar spent on climate research instead of other research would also have to produce $4 in benefits (Nordhaus 2002, 267).

Second, the political incentives affecting government-funded R&D may make high returns hard to achieve. For example, government R&D has sometimes proven to be shortsighted because "legislators are prone to pay too much attention to distributive benefits from near-commercial pork barrel projects relative to more fundamental R&D activities" (Cohen and Noll 1991, 382). At other times, government R&D can be captured by organized interests, as happened, for example, when government R&D was committed to making synthetic fuel from high-sulfur eastern coal, even though it was clear that the prospects for success were better in the case of western coal (Cohen and Noll 1991, 368). It may of course be possible to devise novel institutional arrangements that could ensure that government's climate R&D expenditures were reasonably cost effective. The investment process could be insulated in various ways from congressional temptations toward pork barrel spending, but the prospects of success are uncertain. In the long run, a program that is too well insulated from pork barrel tendencies may be poorly positioned to survive fiscal hard times.

In conclusion, in the period before the fiscal stringency becomes more visible and salient, the use of emission controls to generate R&D revenue would probably enhance the controls' political appeal. It could enhance their cost effectiveness. It will, however, only produce additional net benefits if government succeeds in advancing the development of valuable new energy sources, a possibility but by no means a certainty. If and when entitlement funding problems become manifest and begin to dominate the political landscape, tax shift will become a more appealing destination for emission control revenue. In any case, the ability to apply revenue to a popular cause would give a political boost to an emission control regime. Emission control proponents would probably be prudent to begin with an emphasis on the R&D option but be prepared to shift focus as fiscal problems emerge.

CLIMATE POLICY AND INTERNATIONAL DIPLOMACY

Even if one dismissed the climate policy and fiscal reasons for adopting a moderate U.S. emission control policy, controls would have a strong justification from the standpoint of international alliance policy. That task will not be easy. In a widely discussed analysis, Robert Kagan has pointed out that widespread European attitudes toward multilateralism and the international use of force will engender periodic outbursts of hostility to the United States (Kagan 2002, 6, 9–10). With the Russian threat in long-term remission and as the United States responds forcefully to threats from beyond Europe, European opponents of U.S. policy are likely to grow stronger and more vocal. Yet America cannot however afford to simply write off the European alliance: "There is no doubt that the United States and Europe have different attitudes toward power, military force, and sovereignty or even that the divide is growing. The question, however, is whether these differences are now so fundamental that the United States can or should dismiss its alliance with Europe as irrelevant, concluding either that it does not need allies or that it might find better ones elsewhere. And the answer is no" (Gordon 2003, 74).

Accepting the transatlantic alliance's importance to the United States does not entail the embrace of some international relations theory of neo-liberal institutionalism or constructivism. On the contrary, it is perfectly consistent with a fully realistic response to the manifest reality of the threat posed by violent Islamic fundamentalism and the possibility of a new Chinese *Machtpolitik*. The alliance remains worth the considerable trouble that is likely to be needed to maintain it, just because the current and future security threats to the United States are real and serious. Although U.S. and European interests are not perfectly congruent on these problems, they appear to be more consistent than they are conflicting.

Realistically, though, maintaining the transatlantic alliance is likely to remain a trying exercise. France, in particular, seems likely to persist in seeking to build a French-led power block designed to constrain U.S. freedom of action (Davis 2003, 193–215). Hostility to the United States is deeply ingrained in French culture and shared across the political spectrum (Mead 2003, 140–42). In acting as they have, "the French are doing precisely what the Americans are doing; namely, developing policies that accord with their interests, based on a realpolitik assessment of emerging power trends, global challenges, threats, and alignments in the international system" (Davis 2003, 193). The very fact that French motives are interest based indicates that they are unlikely to change no matter how the U.S. responds to them or no matter what it does on climate policy.

Nevertheless, a more forthcoming U.S. climate policy could help in coping with the difficulties of alliance maintenance. Specifically, a U.S. emission control policy would narrow rifts in U.S./German and U.S./U.K. relations, rifts from which unfavorable diplomatic combinations might otherwise emerge. The keystone of the French strategy is the French/German alliance, without which France would have no prospect of dominating the EU (Dale 2003, 5–6). And in Germany, the United Kingdom, and in some of the smaller northern European nations, the climate issue is politically of some importance; so U.S. refusal to implement emission controls may contribute non-trivially to anti-U.S. sentiments.

The problem is likely to worsen with time. Some claimed that the German floods of 2002 were caused by climate change. Similar charges are likely to be repeated about other weather-related natural disasters and the international re-lations damage may escalate sharply with particularly unfavorable circum-stances: "If the United States is perceived abroad as the lone outlaw causing global warming, then intense storms, coastal flooding, and crop losses in des-perately poor countries—whether or not actually caused by global warming—may become flashpoints for anti-American backlashes" (Stewart and Wiener 2003, 45).

Conversely, a more affirmative U.S. climate policy may well contribute to achieving U.S. objectives in policy areas judged by some to be much more im-portant than that of climate: "Indeed, the United States may find benefit in pursuing a negotiating strategy of issue linkage that trades sensible U.S. coop-eration of climate policy for others' cooperation on issues of greater interest to the United States. In effect the United States could receive in-kind side pay-ments on other strategic issues in return for agreeing to act on climate" (Stew-art and Wiener 2003, 51). In this manner, the earlier U.S. decision to withdraw from Kyoto could be vindicated and perhaps turned to national advantage.

FINAL THOUGHTS

Structurally flawed international and domestic emission control proposals have made it difficult to focus debate on more attractive policy options. Currently, future political trends, as far as we can descry them, seem likely to reduce the at-tention accorded to the climate issue. One of the tasks of this chapter has been to explore whether, in light of the best available theories of political science, it might still be possible to enact domestic emissions controls despite these unfa-vorable factors. And the best answer would seem to be that—absent com-pelling evidence of dire, imminent threat from climate change—the success of even modest emissions controls is uncertain. Aggressive controls are most likely unachievable.

Shifting from political feasibility to a wider national-interest point of view raises a more acute question: why should the United States enact emission con-trols at all, even modest ones? The chapter has also addressed this question and found that some of the putative answers are clearly invalid. U.S. domestic emis-sion controls would have only the most marginal direct impact on global emis-sions, which will continue to rise regardless of what the United States does or does not do. A change in U.S. domestic policy seems unlikely to rescue the Ky-oto process from the shambles into which it has fallen. Nor are there significant energy security co-benefits from a U.S. domestic climate policy.

Nonetheless, there are three valid grounds for implementing modest domestic emission controls. First, domestic controls would eliminate one barrier to adoption of emission reduction policies in China, India, and other LDCs where, in principle, policy changes could noticeably lower the global emissions growth trajectory. Second, emission controls could raise revenue for energy R&D or eventually for dampening the size of the tax increases otherwise required to cover the nation's unfunded entitlement liabilities. Third, domestic U.S. controls would ameliorate U.S. image problems and enhance important international relationships in Europe and, potentially, in the global South.

Opponents of emission controls will correctly object that these benefits are modest, but modest benefits are acceptable when the costs are also modest. Meanwhile, emission control enthusiasts will doubtless protest that achieving such modest goals would not stop climate change. Yet a policy exceeding the public's willingness to pay and the value of the apparent benefits is neither politically viable nor economically desirable. Perhaps instead of viewing climate policy in isolation, emission control proponents should shape their proposals to more affirmatively contribute to the larger security and economic imperatives of the nation.

NOTES

1. For industry, advocating emission controls in hopes of winning a favorable allocation of emission allowances would be a high-risk, high-stakes gamble. *Ex ante,* no firm could know that it would receive enough allowances to offset the losses from emission controls. In the legislative deal-making, a firm might simply be outmaneuvered by its rivals. Conversely, too much success might result in political scandal—a troubling risk for highly regulated, high-public-profile firms in the energy sector. Finally, grandfathered allowances provide firms with only modest protection against future escalation of government demands for tighter emission controls. Moreover, advocating emission controls would alienate some of industry's best friends in Congress, never a step to be taken lightly.
2. Some economists speculate that the macroeconomic benefits of tax shift might even exceed the costs independently of environmental gains (Parry 2002a, 33–34). This view, though, is now much less widely held than it once was (Smith, Ross, and Montgomery 2002, 3).

Chapter 8 Automobile Fuel Efficiency Policy:

Beyond the CAFE Controversy

James A. Dunn, Jr.

Since 1975 the Corporate Average Fuel Economy (CAFE) standards have been the centerpiece of the federal government's efforts to improve the energy efficiency of passenger motor vehicles. CAFE's supporters maintain that it has been the nation's single most successful policy effort to save petroleum (Greene, Sperling, and McNutt 1998, 216). They argue that the fuel efficiency requirements should be increased substantially and that imperfections like the "SUV loophole" should be eliminated. CAFE's opponents denounce it as largely ineffective, a costly burden on the auto industry, an interference with consumers' freedom of choice, and a safety threat to automobile drivers and passengers. Many not only oppose strengthening the miles per gallon (mpg) standards, they call for CAFE's outright abolition (Nivola and Crandall 1995).

It's no surprise, therefore, that policymaking about passenger vehicle fuel economy has been at an impasse for nearly twenty-five years. This chapter will outline the political dimensions of the deadlock over CAFE. It will summarize the defects in the CAFE regulatory regime that each side claims make the current policy unsatisfactory. It will show how the political conditions surrounding the "policy window" that opened in the mid-1970s resulted in regulations that were crafted in a way that resulted in a deadlock-cum-policy monopoly once the original window closed. It will examine the main policy options under discussion for constructing a different approach and examine the political weaknesses that have prevented them from being adopted. Finally, it will describe the political dynamics that must underlie any reframing of the issue in a way that would undermine the policy monopoly and enable policy development to move beyond the CAFE controversy and to launch a new drive for energy-efficient technology in the nation's fleet of passenger vehicles.

This chapter will not examine in detail the arguments why public policy should attempt to reduce automobile fuel consumption in the first place. That case has been made so often in so many places, from scholarly journals to newspaper editorials and senatorial speeches, that it has been established as the conventional wisdom. The present chapter assumes that enhancing automobile fuel efficiency is a worthwhile policy goal if done in a reasonably (not necessarily optimally) cost-effective way. The goal here is to explore how the punctuated equilibrium approach can be useful in identifying a politically feasible way to resume progress toward improved automotive fuel efficiency.

DIMENSIONS OF DEADLOCK: FROM PROGRESS TO POLITICAL IMPASSE

In 1975 Congress passed the Energy Policy and Conservation Act in the aftermath of the Arab oil embargo and the onset of the "energy crisis." One section of the law, "Improving Automotive Fuel Efficiency" added Title V to the Motor Vehicle and Cost Savings Act, which created the system of sales-weighted Corporate Average Fuel Economy standards for automobiles (United States Code). The act established 18 miles per gallon (mpg) as the CAFE standard for cars in 1978, 19 mpg in 1979, 20 mpg in 1980, and 27.5 mpg in 1985. For 1981–84, the act directed the Secretary of Transportation, through the National Highway Transportation Safety Administration (NHTSA), to establish the annual mpg increases in the standard. The secretary via NHTSA was also given authority to set mpg standards for light trucks and post-1985 mpg standards for both cars and trucks. The Secretary was also authorized to lower the 27.5 mpg standard by as much as 1.5 mpg if it was not technologically feasible or economically practicable to achieve it.

The automakers' initial response to CAFE was to "downsize" their models, especially their largest and heaviest ones. They also began to make more use of certain proven technologies—front wheel drive, radial tires, better aerodynamics, etc. In 1979–80, gasoline prices again skyrocketed in the wake of the Iranian revolution. President Jimmy Carter made energy conservation the centerpiece of his domestic policy agenda. The schedule of annual increases in CAFE standards took effect in 1978 at 18 mpg and increased in each successive year. Sales of fuel-efficient Japanese imports rose steadily, increasing from 5.7 percent of the market in 1971 to 21.2 percent in 1980 (American Automobile Manufacturers Association, 1997). All this sent a strong and consistent message to American automakers that major improvements in fuel economy were inevitable and that the companies had better make the best of it in their product planning and marketing decisions. Detroit seemed to be getting the message. In July 1980, General Motors president E. M. "Pete" Estes announced that GM's projected fleet fuel economy average in 1985 would be 31 miles per gallon (Sorge 1980). This was the high point of Detroit's acceptance of CAFE.

Table 8.1 highlights the events and actions that reflect the impasse over CAFE. Without covering these events in detail, this section will simply identify political factors that have been associated with the impasse. As soon as Ronald Reagan was elected president, Detroit saw a much more sympathetic administration and a Congress more concerned with auto workers' jobs than with tougher fuel economy regulations. Detroit's planning for fuel efficiency in its

Table 8.1. Milestones in the policy impasse, 1981–2004.

1981: Reagan cancels NHTSA's Proposed Rule Making on CAFE increase
1985: Reagan rollback of CAFE to 26 mph for model years 1986–89
1986: Inflation adjusted price of gasoline plummets below 1978 levels
1989: Bush I sets CAFE for cars at 27.5 mpg for model year 1990
1991: Bryan bill to increase CAFE dies in Senate energy deal
1993: Clinton and Gore announce PNGV; do not push for higher CAFE
1995: House attaches CAFÉ—freeze rider to DOT budget
2001: CAFE freeze rider removed at request of Bush II administration
2002: National Academies assert higher CAFE possible with existing technology
2002: Bush II cancels PNGV, announces FreedomCAR and Hydrogen initiatives
2002: McCain-Kerry amendment for major increase in CAFE defeated 38 to 62 in Senate
2003: Bush II increases light truck CAFE standard to 22.2 mpg in 2007
2003: Durbin amendment to increase CAFE defeated in Senate 32 to 65
2003: NHTSA proposes "reformulation" (not increase) of CAFE
2005: Durbin amendment to increase CAFE defeated in Senate 28 to 67

products lost priority. The problem of Japanese imports was handled by a "voluntary" restraint on exports of Japanese vehicles to the United States that the Reagan administration negotiated with Tokyo. At the same time, the new Republican administration announced thirty-four deregulation actions to help the auto industry recover (Kahn 1981). One of these was cancellation of the Notice of Proposed Rule Making on an increase in post-1985 CAFE standards, which NHTSA had issued in the waning days of the Carter administration. This 1981 cancellation marks the beginning of the political impasse over CAFE standards for passenger cars that has lasted to this day.

Since 1981, no president, Republican or Democrat, has made a serious effort to increase CAFE beyond the initial 27.5 mpg level. Reagan was openly hostile to CAFE. At the request of the auto manufacturers, his transportation secretary rolled the standard back 1.5 mpg, the maximum permitted by law, for model years 1986–89. Both President Bushes approved minor upward adjustments of 1.5 mpg while resisting congressional efforts to require much larger changes. President Clinton decided not to spend any political capital on a CAFE increase. In 1993 he opted instead for the Partnership for a New Generation of Vehicles (PNGV), a joint government-industry research effort aimed at producing a family sedan that could get 80 mpg by 2003. The PNGV did do some interesting R&D work, but its fatal flaw was that it lacked any requirement that the auto companies actually build and sell 80 mpg family sedans (Sperling 2001). Some observers saw PNGV as aimed more at providing political cover for President Clinton and Vice President Gore than at actually improving the fuel economy of American vehicles.

When the Republicans won majority control of Congress in the 1994 elections, CAFE's prospects dimmed even further. In November 1995 the House of Representatives added a provision to the Department of Transportation's FY 1996 budget appropriation forbidding NHTSA to spend any money "to prepare, propose, or promulgate any regulations . . . prescribing corporate average fuel economy standards for automobiles" that were higher than the existing standards (Public Law 140–50, Section 330). The same proviso was added to the DOT's budget appropriations for the next four years, through FY 2001. President George W. Bush's administration terminated PNGV in 2002, replacing it with the Freedom Cooperative Automotive Research (FreedomCAR) program and a Hydrogen Fuel Initiative, long-term research partnerships that also include no requirement for actually building or selling vehicles with any new technology. Proposals to toughen CAFE standards generated much publicity between 2002 and 2005, but legislative efforts were defeated in the Senate by large margins and did not even come to a vote in the House. The only increase in CAFE since the Bush I administration approved the reinstatement of the 27.5 mpg standard for cars for model year 1990 was the Bush II administration's 2003 announcement of a modest increase in the CAFE standard for light trucks from 20.7 mpg to 22.2 mpg in model year 2007.

WHAT'S WRONG WITH CAFE?
CRITIQUES FROM BOTH SIDES

The anti-CAFE groups argue that it threatens jobs, safety, and customer choice.[1] Their primary arguments are:

- Increasing the mileage standards, especially for light trucks, will require auto makers to make expensive changes in their vehicles, shift the mix of vehicles they sell to emphasize smaller and less profitable models, shut down plants assembling popular SUVs and large cars, lay off tens of thousands of workers, and impoverish their communities.
- American auto makers will be put at a disadvantage. U.S. companies derive much of their manufacturing profits from large "American"-style cars and light trucks. Foreign automakers can undersell their U.S. competitors in the small, fuel-efficient vehicle market segments.
- Detroit auto companies are contractually obligated to pay very heavy pension and health insurance costs for their retired UAW workers. This "legacy cost" amounted to over $1,200 per vehicle sold in 2002. Ironically, if a large number of customers followed Jesus' presumed example and bought small economy cars, the result could be that thousands of retired auto workers might lose their pensions and health insurance.
- To meet higher mileage standards, automakers would have to sell many more lighter vehicles, which are inherently more dangerous in crashes than heavy vehicles. Respected scholars have estimated that CAFE has already cost thousands of lives. Higher standards would cost thousands more.
- Fuel savings from higher standards are exaggerated. Reducing the amount of fuel burned per mile driven makes it cheaper to drive. This will encourage people to drive more, reducing the total amount of fuel saved. Moreover, cars conforming to a higher CAFE standard will be more expensive to buy. This may encourage people to keep their old gas guzzlers on the road longer, reducing promised fuel savings still further.
- In any case, the higher standards will only apply to new cars, which only make

up about 7 percent of the total fleet in a given year. It will take well over a decade before the goal of significant energy savings will be approached.

- An increase in gasoline taxes is a far better tool to promote automotive energy savings: it takes effect immediately; it will slow growth in vehicle miles traveled; and it will lead some customers to choose more fuel-efficient vehicles than they might otherwise have purchased.
- CAFE inevitably distorts the automobile market and limits customers' freedom of choice. American consumers have historically and for valid reasons preferred larger, heavier, and more powerful vehicles than Japanese or European auto buyers. Individuals are the best judges of what their automotive needs are—not politicians, bureaucrats, or social engineers.

The pro-CAFE groups argue that action is needed both to close loopholes in the regulations and to raise the mileage standards significantly. Their primary points are:

- The lower mileage standard for light trucks is CAFE's biggest flaw. NHTSA first established light-truck CAFE standards in 1979 at 17.2 mpg for two-wheel-drive trucks and 15.8 mpg for those with four-wheel drive. This represented 90.5 percent and 83.2 percent, respectively, of the automobile CAFE standard for 1979, which was 19 mpg. Separate two- and four-wheel-drive standards were finally abolished in 1992. Today's combined standard for light trucks is 20.7 mpg, making it only 75.3 percent of the 27.5 mpg standard for automobiles. Detroit has literally driven millions of pickups, vans, and SUVs through this loophole. With light trucks now making up close to 60 percent of all new vehicles produced in the United States, the total fleet efficiency of new vehicles is actually declining.
- The lower light-truck standard does not even apply to the heaviest pickups and SUVs. Vehicles like the Hummer and Navigator that weigh more than 8,500 lbs. are not counted toward any CAFE list.
- Auto companies manipulate classification of vehicles between categories. Chrysler got its small PT Cruiser counted as a light truck, enabling it to sell more of its Dodge Durangos while still meeting the CAFE standard.
- Manufacturers get automatic credits for building "dual fuel" vehicles that can run on either gasoline or other fuels such as E85, a mixture of 85 percent gasoline and 15 percent ethanol. Few buyers of such vehicles actually use E85, since only a tiny minority of service stations sell it, but the credits count nonetheless.

- Current lab testing procedures to determine fuel efficiency overstate a vehicle's miles per gallon by approximately 15 percent, compared to real-world driving conditions.
- The heaviest SUVs get large income tax credits for their buyers, ostensibly aimed at small businesses, but increasingly available to customers who use them mainly for personal transport.
- CAFE standards are applied only to new vehicles. Manufacturers can ship excess SUVs to Canada, where entrepreneurs buy them at a discount and bring them back to the United States to be sold as used cars. When Canada adopted U.S. emissions standards in 1997, imports of such "used" vehicles increased by 1,200 percent in the next two years.
- For years, light trucks were allowed to meet lower emissions standards than cars, making them not only less fuel efficient but also more polluting.
- Most importantly, the mileage standards for the whole vehicle fleet should be significantly strengthened. The standard for SUVs should be raised to 27.5 miles per gallon immediately and should eventually be made the same as the car standard. Over a ten- to fifteen-year period, the whole fleet should have to meet a standard in the 35 to 40 mpg range. This can be done with existing (but underused) technology and without sacrificing safety or convenience.

These are the political and intellectual dimensions of the deadlock that has blocked forward movement on CAFE standards since the early 1980s. For the auto companies, operating within the policy deadlock has by now become a position tantamount to a policy monopoly. The manufacturers themselves do not put any serious effort into lobbying for CAFE's outright abolition. They have learned to live comfortably with "the devil we know" and to exploit all the loopholes and advantages of the current system. They can comply with the 27.5 mpg standard for cars and will probably meet the model year 2007 standard of 22.2 mpg for light trucks without much difficulty.

For liberal Democrats, maverick Republicans, and environmental and energy activists who support higher CAFE standards, the Senate debates—and defeats—from 2002 to 2005 may have seemed more like a ritual than a real opportunity to change policy. They have not been able to take advantage of terrorism, wars in Afghanistan and Iraq, publicity about rising dependence on oil imports, or growing concern about global climate change to shake the status quo. The deadlock is more than just political stalemate between two antagonistic lobbies that offset each other's political strengths like wrestlers in an unbreakable hold. It appears to be a genuine intellectual and policy analytic dead end as well—a classic case of "paralysis by analysis." As evidence of this analytic dead end, consider the recent article on "The Economics of Fuel Economy Standards," by four noted policy analysts, in the *Journal of Economic Perspectives* (Portney et al. 2003a). The authors are Paul Portney, who chaired the committee that produced the 2002 National Research Council report on the effectiveness and impact of CAFE; Howard K. Gruenspecht, who is now deputy administrator of the Energy Information Administration; and Ian Parry and Winston Harrington, a fellow and senior fellow, respectively, at Resources for the Future, a well-known Washington, D.C., environmental "think tank." These scholars review the range of information available on CAFE, assess the most frequently mentioned policy options, and reach the following conclusion: the two most economically efficient tools for reducing oil consumption and CO_2 emissions—gasoline taxes and tradable carbon emissions allowances—face especially stiff opposition in the current political climate and are unlikely to be adopted. Thus, they conclude, "if the only choice before us were tightening CAFE standards as they now exist or doing nothing at all, the authors of this paper could not reach agreement on a recommendation."

PUNCTUATED EQUILIBRIUM: FROM NON-REGULATION OF THE AUTO INDUSTRY TO ADVERSARIAL TECHNOLOGY FORCING

With the pro- and anti-CAFE lobbies deadlocked and even with sophisticated energy analysts unable to agree on whether increasing CAFE is better than doing nothing, one has to wonder if the initial choice of the CAFE path was not virtually preordained to end up in a dead end. CAFE's regulatory approach belongs to the era (1965–75) when public policy shifted abruptly from a hands-off approach to Detroit to one of highly political confrontation. A brief sketch of how auto regulatory policy emerged in those years will help us understand how and why activists' influence has diminished over time, particularly in the fuel efficiency area.

Before 1965 the U.S. automobile industry was essentially unregulated. Auto companies could design and manufacture virtually any kind of vehicle they could sell with no interference from the government (Rae 1984). After that date this privileged status changed rapidly and dramatically. The lightning rod that directed pent-up public discontent at Detroit was Ralph Nader and his crusade for auto safety. General Motors was exposed as having hired private investigators to discredit its main critic without addressing his criticism. Nader, the outside activist and policy entrepreneur, quickly found such insider allies as Senator Abraham Ribbicoff, chair of a Senate subcommittee about to hold hearings on auto safety, to help attack the traditional "no-regulation regime" for automobiles (Mashaw and Harfst 1990). It was then seen that automobile regulatory policy was essentially a power vacuum. In addition to safety, there now appeared to be many other auto-related problems that could be addressed by federal regulation. Soon, all of the positive feedback processes associated with the punctuated equilibrium model (bandwagon effect, media mimicry, social contagion/social learning, and the creation of new policy subsystems and public interest groups) rushed in to fill the new policy-political space created by the destruction of the no-regulation policy monopoly.

James Q. Wilson, a leading scholar of regulatory politics, noted that the confrontation between Nader and the auto industry exemplified a classic type of regulatory situation in which a small but powerful group is strongly motivated to resist a policy that narrowly focuses costs on itself, while the great majority of citizens is relatively indifferent to the policy because its benefits will be spread widely but thinly over the entire population. "It may seem astonishing that regulatory legislation of this sort is ever passed. It is . . . but it requires the efforts of a skilled entrepreneur who can mobilize latent public sentiment . . . put opponents on the defensive . . . and associate the legislation with widely shared values" (Wilson 1980, 370).

This "big bang" punctuation of the auto industry's policy monopoly unleashed three successive waves of adversarial regulation on the auto industry, focusing first on vehicle safety, then on reducing exhaust emissions, and finally on reducing automobile energy consumption. The general approach to auto regulation that was adopted in this period has been labeled "technology forcing"— mandating that auto makers incorporate equipment into their vehicles that most consumers would not purchase if it were optional, extra-cost equipment. Seat belts, air bags, and catalytic converters are obvious examples. The strategy was to put the direct costs of regulation onto the auto manufacturer, not on individuals. Consumers ended up paying somewhat higher prices but they also received real benefits in the form of safer, less polluting cars. As long as the price increase was not too steep or the mandated device too intrusive (for example, the ignition interlock device aimed at drunk drivers), consumers accepted the added costs and auto companies eventually learned to live with the new regulation.

CAFE'S UNIQUE POLICY WINDOW:
THE ENERGY CRISIS OF THE 1970S

The "exogenous disturbance" of the oil shock brought about by the Arab Oil Embargo of 1973–74 put energy policy at the top of the U.S. political agenda. It brought home the fact that America had become dangerously dependent on imported oil to power its economy, heat its homes, and move its people and goods. Pressure mounted on policy makers to do something in response to the crisis. President Nixon announced that the energy crisis would be overcome in "Project Independence" from oil imports. Congress agreed about energy independence but added that energy policy also had to protect the American people from price gouging by the OPEC oil cartel and windfall profits by multinational oil companies.

The Energy Policy and Conservation Act (EPCA) of 1975 was the first major legislative response to what appeared to be a different world of scarce and expensive energy. Many economists faulted EPCA for avoiding the hard decisions they believed were necessary to address the long-term problems (Staubaugh and Yergin 1983). The legislation failed to deregulate oil prices, which had been government-controlled since President Nixon's New Economic Policy of 1971. It failed to raise taxes on gasoline as a way to conserve energy, despite a push by Representative Al Ullman, chair of the House Ways and Means committee, to legislate a twenty-five-cent increase over three to five years. It failed to enact stiff "gas guzzler" taxes on automobiles with very low fuel economy (Nivola 1986). Standing out from the act's half-measures and pork barrel subsidies was the section labeled "Improving Automotive Fuel Efficiency," which created the CAFE standards and was offered as both a politically acceptable alternative to a gasoline tax increase and as a tool that would produce long-term energy savings.

In view of how strongly the auto industry attacked CAFE in subsequent years, it might seem surprising that the auto companies were not able to prevent the legislation from being enacted in the first place, but in the mid-1970s a combination of economic and political circumstances arose that is very rare in American politics. In the first place, Detroit was still on the defensive politically. Its objections to safety and emissions regulations had recently been overridden. Its image as an arrogant industry abusing its power was still prevalent in public opinion and the halls of Congress. Second, everyone knew that there was a lot of room for improvement in the fuel efficiency of American-made cars. The auto companies themselves had promised to make a voluntary 40 percent improvement in fuel efficiency in return for a delay in enforcing clean air standards, and President Ford had recommended accepting their proposal in his 1975 State of the Union address (Congressional Quarterly 1975, 140–43). Third, the president—a former congressman from Michigan and quite sympathetic to Detroit—was in a weak position to sell Detroit's quid pro quo offer to Congress. He was the first "unelected" president the country had ever had. He had not been on the Republican ticket in 1972, but was nominated in 1973 by President Nixon (and confirmed by Congress) to succeed Spiro Agnew, who resigned as vice president amid a bribery scandal. In August 1974, Ford succeeded (then controversially pardoned) President Nixon when Nixon had to resign because of the Watergate scandal. Fourth, in the November 1974 congressional elections unusually large "post-Watergate" Democratic majorities were returned to the Congress, particularly in the House of Representatives. Democratic control of the lower chamber jumped from a lead of 239 to 192 to a margin of 291 to 144. Congressional Democrats were eager to take back policy leadership from the executive branch and to reduce the power of what they were calling the "imperial presidency."

There were also industry-specific factors that made CAFE-style regulations the energy policy of choice. In 1975 the United Auto Workers Union supported establishing fuel economy standards—as long as there were separate lists for domestic and imported autos. In later years, the UAW would join the companies in opposing significant increases in the standards, but at the inception of CAFE, the union's overriding concern was to prevent American companies from meeting the standards by bringing in fuel-efficient "captive imports" from their overseas plants (Reuther 2001). Imports of fuel-efficient Japanese cars were beginning to surge into the United States. From a market share of only 5.7 percent in 1971, they reached 9.4 percent in 1975 and 21.2 percent by 1980 (American Automobile Manufacturers Association 1997). Finally, a key reason why CAFE survived the legislative elimination process while so many other measures failed was that, as Nivola noted, "The mileage regulations . . . were regarded by the United Auto Workers . . . [and] the auto companies, as well as by most politicians, as a fairly painless way of subduing gasoline demand" (Nivola 1986, 225). It was believed that the extra cost of making cars more fuel efficient would be recouped by money saved in lower fuel consumption over the life of the vehicle. The more the price of gasoline rose, the more money consumers would save with their new fuel-efficient cars. For customers who actually needed to drive larger vehicles like pickup trucks or work vans, the CAFE standards law permitted their vehicles to meet lower fuel economy standards. So, rather than making consumers pay more to drive or change the type of light truck they needed for their business, CAFE would actually help them pay less for fuel and keep the kind of large vehicle they needed.

What is the lesson to be learned from the politics surrounding the adoption of the CAFE standards? It is that the Congress, even when dominated by an extraordinarily large and liberal Democratic majority, had no stomach for imposing large automotive fuel tax increases on their constituents. Despite the widespread perception of energy crisis and rising danger from dependence on oil imports, Congress preferred to continue the technology-forcing strategy of requiring the auto companies to redesign their products to address the problem. No political changes in or outside Congress since 1975 provide any evidence that this clear preference for technology forcing over taxes has changed. What has changed in the intervening years are, first, expectations about energy price and availability; and second, the growth of new profit opportunities in the market for larger, less fuel-efficient vehicles. Unfortunately, from the perspective of the pro-CAFE environmental and energy groups, these market developments have made it much more difficult for auto interests and their supporters in Congress and the executive branch to accept any significant increase in CAFE beyond that agreed to in 1975. These market trends and their impact on the prospect for CAFE increases are summarized in the next section.

DECLINING GAS PRICES OPEN A PROFITABLE NEW MARKET NICHE

In the mid- and late 1970s, it was assumed that the price of gasoline would continue to increase at a rate above that of inflation. This did not happen. By 1986 gasoline prices had declined very sharply, reaching an inflation-adjusted level below their 1978 level, a benchmark preceding the decade's second oil shock (U.S. Department of Energy 2003a). Consumers began to pay less and less attention to fuel economy when purchasing new vehicles. Recently, the Energy Information Administration calculated that in 2002, the average retail price of gasoline was $1.44 per gallon. In unadjusted dollars this was more than twice the 65 cents per gallon motorists paid in 1978. But adjusted for inflation, motorists in 2002 were paying the equivalent of 62.4 cents per gallon—4 percent less than they paid in 1978 (U.S. Department of Energy, 2003a).

This decline in real energy prices helped produce the second key economic change. Sales of larger, more powerful passenger cars rebounded in the mid-1980s. Even more important, sales of light trucks also began to rise steadily.

Table 8.2. Light trucks as a percentage of total U.S. vehicle production, 1975–2002.

Year	Total U.S. vehicle production (millions)	Light truck production (millions)	Light trucks as % of total
1975	8,986	2,269	25.2
1980	8,010	1,634	20.3
1985	11,653	3,468	29.7
1990	9,783	3,706	37.8
1995	11,985	5,635	47.0
2000	12,773	7,231	56.6
2002	12,091	7,064	58.4

Source: Ward's Motor Vehicle Facts and Figures 2003, p. 3.

Light trucks had been exempted from the 27.5 mpg standard that applied to passenger cars and also from the stricter emissions standards that cars had to meet. At first light truck sales were mainly pickups and panel trucks, but to exploit the fuel and emissions loopholes, Detroit's designers over time created several entirely new classes of vehicle that fell under the light truck classification: the family minivan, the 4x4, the sport utility vehicle (SUV), and the upscale pickup truck. Table 8.2 shows that light truck production amounted to only 25 percent of total domestic vehicle production in 1975. By 1990 their share had risen to 37.8 percent, and by 2002 it stood at 58.4 percent of domestic vehicle production.

What had started as a relatively small exception designed to help farmers and small businesses has turned into the most profitable segment of the auto companies' product line. A fully loaded Lincoln Navigator is said to have earned as much as $15,000 profit per vehicle in 2000.[2] This, say auto industry analysts, is not simply unconscionable price gouging. Profits from pickup trucks and SUVs have become vital to the survival of the American auto companies. One single factory, Ford's Michigan truck plant where Expeditions and Navigators are assembled, made $2.4 billion in after tax profits in 1998, one-third of the company's entire profits that year (Bradsher 2002, 89).

It is well known that the former "Big Three" (or the "Detroit Three" as some have suggested they now should be called) have been steadily losing market share in the passenger car segment to the imports and transplants of Asian and European manufacturers. In 2003 Detroit's share of the passenger car market

Table 8.3. Light truck sales and market share, by weight and manufacturer, 2002.

Manufacturer	Total sales (thousands)	3, 100 lbs. to 4, 000 lbs.		Over 4, 000 lbs.	
		Sales	Share	Sales	Share
GM	2, 412	486	18.5	1,926	36.0
Ford	2, 060	568	21.7	1,492	27.9
DCX	1,772	541	20.6	1, 231	23.0
Toyota	747	493	18.8	254	4.7
Honda	336	138	5.3	198	3.7
Nissan	287	161	6.1	126	2.3
Isuzu	79	53	2.0	26	0.5
Hyundai	83	83	3.1	0	0.0
Suzuki	51	51	1.9	0	0.0
Kia	97	47	1.8	50	0.9
BMW	39	0	0.0	39	0.7
VW	11	0	0.0	11	0.2
TOTAL	7, 974	2, 621	99.8*	5, 353	99.9*

Source: U.S. Department of Transportation, National Highway Traffic Safety Administration. 2003. Reforming the Automobile Fuel Economy Standards Program. 49 CFR Part 533 [Docket No. 2003-16128] RIN 2127-AJ17, Table 1, p. 14. Weight classes collapsed and market shares recalculated by author.
*Does not add up to 100.0 due to rounding error.

was only 44.9 percent (Teahan 2004). The profit margins on many of the smaller and medium-sized cars that American auto companies produce have been falling, and in some cases, disappearing. The Ford Escort was profitable in the 1980s but became a money loser in the 1990s. The Ford Taurus was once the best-selling model in the country. By the late 1990s Ford had to sell half the Tauruses it produced to rental car companies at steep discounts just to keep its two Taurus plants open, since its contract with the UAW forbade it to close any major plant (Bradsher 2002, 92).

Light truck sales and profits have become indispensable to the Big Three but are now being threatened by international competition. Table 8.3 offers a snapshot of the penetration of the light truck market by Asian manufacturers. It shows that by 2002 they had already reached 39 percent of total sales of light trucks weighing between 3,100 lbs. and 4,000 lbs., leaving Detroit with 60.8 percent. In the market for the heaviest and most profitable light trucks—those over 4,000 lbs.—Detroit was still dominant, capturing 86.9 percent of sales in 2002. The days of Detroit's dominance are numbered, however. The main Japanese automakers are determined to break into this profitable bastion of American strength. In 2003, Toyota launched its large Tundra double-cab pickup model. At the 2004 auto show, it unveiled an even larger model, dubbed the FTC, with production scheduled to begin at a new plant in Texas for the 2006 model year (Jensen 2004). Nissan also began offering a new large pickup, the Titan, which comes equipped with a 305-horsepower V-8 engine, 5-speed automatic transmission, and two- or four-wheel drive (Knoll 2004). The Titan comes with either a crew cab with a roomy backseat or a king cab passenger compartment, which, it advertises, "blurs the line between truck and living room" (Nissan advertisement, *Newsweek,* March 1, 2004). The Titan is assembled at a new plant in Mississippi with a capacity of over 100,000 vehicles per year.

Profits and employment at American auto manufacturers are more dependent on sales of light trucks than any time in history. Anything that threatens profit margins in the light truck category is a direct threat to the financial solvency of Ford Motor Company—and GM and the Chrysler division of Daimler Chrysler would not be far behind. "SUVs and pickups account for a highly disproportionate share of Ford's earnings. Moreover, these product segments are experiencing ongoing intensification of competition from a proliferation of new products," stated a Standard and Poor's analyst, explaining a 2003 downgrade in Ford's credit status to the lowest investment grade (Hakim 2003b; Gilpin 2003). A recent analysis of the "carbon intensity of profits" sponsored by the World Resources Institute and Sustainable Asset Management estimated that 80 percent of Ford and Chrysler's profits and 70 percent of GM's profits were derived from vehicles that got less than 20.5 mpg (Austin et al. 2003). Detroit is out on a limb labeled "light trucks," which it fears could be sawed off at any time by a major CAFE hike or continued foreign penetration of its last remaining highly profitable market niche (Maynard 2003).

How much longer can this go on? Can policymakers end the impasse without risking bankruptcy of several major companies? Can they punctuate this deadlocked policy equilibrium by creatively reframing the issue in a way that preserves vital jobs and profits but moves the country toward an automobile fleet that lowers the risks of oil import dependence and global climate change? Clearly there is not yet a new consensus on how this can or should be accomplished. The next section examines the main contenders for punctuating the deadlocked policy equilibrium, and assesses their political strengths and weaknesses.

PUNCTUATION SCENARIOS:
SOMETHING OLD, SOMETHING NEW

Back to the Future: Another Crisis
Pushes Up Fuel Economy

The past twenty-five years provide little evidence that supporters of a substantial CAFE increase can win their perennial lobbying battle in Congress. Since 1980, the CAFE deadlock has persisted through recession and prosperity, Republican and Democratic control of the presidency and Congress, war and peace in the Persian Gulf, and declining and rising dependence on oil imports. Several of the factors that can sometimes undermine a policy monopoly have made an appearance but have not had much impact. For example, new scientific and technological information on the feasibility of improved fuel efficiency was widely publicized in a congressionally mandated report by a special committee of the National Research Council in 2002, which is often referred to as the National Academies study (National Research Council 2002). Republican Senator John McCain and Democratic Senator John Kerry tried their hands as tandem policy entrepreneurs sponsoring a CAFE hike bill and failed. Religious and environmental organizations attempted to change perceptions of vehicular ethics with their anti-SUV campaign asking, "What Would Jesus Drive?" Yet in 2003, an attempt sponsored by Senator Richard Durbin to increase CAFE standards to 40 mpg was rejected by the Senate by a vote of 65 to 32 (Behr 2003). One must conclude that only a very serious crisis in the price or availability of petroleum can create conditions conducive to a major legislative increase in CAFE standards (defined as an increase in the combined car and light truck fleet average to the 35–40 mpg level).

Indeed, it is a commonplace "inside the beltway" that only a crisis can produce progress on energy policy. For example, Steven M. Nadel, executive director of the American Council for an Energy Efficient Economy, told the *New York Times*, "If we truly have an energy squeeze like we did in the 1970s, then it's possible to get a decent energy policy." He went on to say that without a crisis, "no one wants to sacrifice their SUVs or tax breaks . . . and most votes will tend to be on parochial interests rather than the big picture" (Revkin 2003). But to break the deadlock over CAFE, any new oil crisis would have to be perceived by policymakers and public alike as a long-term structural change, not just a temporary price spike like the price surge followed by decline that proved to be the case in the 1970s. Oil prices have indeed risen substantially since 2002, due to uncertainties surrounding terrorism and the war in Iraq. And some analysts believe that world oil production is approaching "Hubbert's Peak," and will soon inevitably begin to decline, which will drive the price to stratospheric heights and could lead to economic depression, resource wars, and even mass starvation in many parts of the world (Dreffeyes 2003; Goodstein 2004; Heinberg 2004; Roberts 2004). Faced with a major new oil price crisis, Congress would vote differently on auto fuel economy standards—but not simply because the members suddenly would become public-spirited statesmen acting on the "big picture." With gasoline selling at five, six, or even ten dollars a gallon, the market for gas-guzzling SUVs would shrink drastically—and so would the auto companies' motive for lobbying against higher CAFE standards. The market and public policy would be sending the same message they sent in the 1975–80 policy window: improved fuel efficiency is the surest way to return to profitability.

As in the crisis of the late 1970s, some or all of the American auto companies would need financial assistance to survive, since it would surely send their sales and profits plunging. Recall that the oil shock following the Iranian revolution of 1979 led to the federal loan guarantee to Chrysler and then to the indirect but important subsidies to all U.S. auto companies in the form of limits on Japanese auto imports. With dramatically higher gas prices pushing customers into fuel-efficient vehicles and federal financial assistance as a quid pro quo, a major strengthening of the fuel economy standards could certainly emerge. The auto sector would still lobby hard on details of the higher standards. They would want them to be no higher than their own estimates of market acceptability. They would want rules that did not give some firms "unfair" advantage. There would still be disputes about whether to have standards based on a percentage improvement in each company's fleet average, whether to have separate weight categories, whether to maintain separate lists for domestic and imported vehicles, and the like. As long as the price of motor fuel remained high, the manufacturers would have little choice but to meet the double demand for fuel economy from consumers and from regulators. But the motivating crisis would impose a high price in lower economic growth, lost wages, and economic disruption, both in the United States and around the world.

TAKING OUR MEDICINE: HIGHER GAS TAXES AND SMART GROWTH

Clearly, most people would prefer not to have to wait for a costly oil crisis to break the impasse over CAFE. Why not get to the same level of fuel efficiency improvement and energy savings using alternative policy measures while in a period of relative prosperity and stability? American taxes on motor fuel are among the lowest in the world and only encourage drivers to over-consume gasoline (Parry 2002a). Economists are virtually unanimous in saying that a significant increase in motor fuel taxes could equal or surpass the effect of an increase in CAFE standards (Porter 1999; Nivola and Crandall 1995). The gasoline tax increase could be phased in over a period of several years but from the beginning would be sending the message to car buyers and car makers alike that fuel efficiency will be an increasingly important aspect of marketing cars in the future. The revenue from the increased taxes could be used to reduce the deficit, if that were a priority, or it could be rebated to motorists as a tax credit or a direct payment if equity and economic stimulus concerns were paramount. This policy option has the added political benefit that, at one time or another, all of the American auto companies have said they would prefer higher fuel taxes to an increase in CAFE (Dunn 1998).

A closely related policy option is to increase federal spending for smart growth, perhaps using some of the revenue from the gas tax increases. Many environmental and community development groups have been calling for stepped-up public investments in urban transit systems, transit villages, urban growth boundaries, location-efficient mortgages, car sharing and car pooling, and the like. Smart growth, it is said, could slow the increase in vehicle miles traveled by single-occupant vehicles and make a long-term contribution to lowering oil consumption and carbon dioxide emissions (Newman and Kenworthy 1999; Calthorpe 1993). The spending aspects of smart growth will attract political support. Federal grants are always popular with mayors, governors, and other elected officials. Whether more light rail lines and transit villages would actually save much energy is problematic, however. At the very least, it would take decades for enough people to change their residences and travel options for even modest overall savings to appear (Giuliano 1999).

More importantly, the political prospects are very poor for a gasoline tax increase large enough to achieve the same level of energy savings as 35 or 40 mpg CAFE standards. How much would the gas tax have to be raised to be a CAFE equivalent? No one can say with absolute certainty. In op-ed pieces, one often sees suggestions for a dollar per gallon tax increase (Friedman 2004). It's impossible to imagine Congress voting for such a tax. Two Brookings Institution scholars, Pietro Nivola and Robert Crandall, developed an equation that estimated that a tax as low as 25 cents per gallon, if it had been imposed in 1986, would have saved 3.3 percent more gasoline than CAFE did by 1992. Interestingly, the new car fleet average in miles per gallon in Nivola and Crandall's increased gas tax scenario was 24.7 mpg. That was actually lower than the 27.7 mpg that was achieved in reality (Nivola and Crandall 1995, 49). The extra fuel saved in their tax increase scenario came from suppressing vehicle miles traveled—not a result likely to be appealing to many motorists, let alone the hotel, restaurant, and tourism sector.

A more recent study by the Congressional Budget Office compared a higher gasoline tax to increased CAFE standards. Its analysis was based on achieving a "benchmark" of a 10 percent reduction in gasoline consumption to a fleet average of about 31.3 mpg for cars and 24.5 mpg for light trucks. It concluded that a gasoline tax increase of 46 cents per gallon would be needed to reach that goal. Its econometric model found that the increased tax would impose lower total costs on the economy than the CAFE standards—3 percent lower than a CAFE hike coupled with the option of credit trading among manufacturers, and 19 percent lower than the CAFE increase without credit trading (Congressional Budget Office 2003).

The problem is that Nivola and Crandall's twenty-five-cent increase would be five times larger and the CBO's forty-six-cent increase nine times larger than the largest federal gas tax increase in history. That record-holding gas tax hike, a nickel per gallon, was passed in 1982 under the Reagan administration. But the widely accepted purpose of that tax increase was to fund more highway and transit construction, not to suppress auto travel or to save gasoline (Dunn 1998). Economists, especially academic economists, are far more enthusiastic supporters of large tax increases than are politicians who have to face reelection. Reframing the issue from increasing CAFE standards to increasing gasoline taxes is not the way to move forward on auto fuel economy policy.

CALIFORNIA DREAMING? CHANGING VENUES FOR PUNCTUATION

Because it experienced more severe automobile air pollution problems than most states, California began issuing its own regulations before major policies were enacted at the federal level. Its lead in air pollution control was recognized when the Clean Air Act of 1970 explicitly authorized California to set its own auto pollution emissions standards as long as they were at least as strict as the federal rules. In 1990 the California Air Resources Board (ARB) issued its "Zero Emission Vehicle (ZEV) mandate," a technology-forcing regulation requiring that 2 percent of an auto company's sales be ZEVs by the year 1998.

The ZEV sales quota then rose to 5 percent in 2001 and 10 percent in 2003. (California Environmental Protection Agency 2004d). At the time the mandate was issued, it was generally agreed that only electric vehicles could meet a zero tailpipe emissions standard (Shnayerson 1996; Grant 1995).

The auto manufacturers were aghast. They complained loudly that the mandate's schedule could not be met, that electric battery technology was not yet ready for widespread introduction, and that compliance would force them to sell electric cars far below their cost. The Air Resources Board modified the mandate by removing the "ramp up" quota requirements for 1998 and 2001. But it left the 2003 quota of 10 percent of sales in place. The auto companies then sued the ARB, arguing that some of the revised mandate's provisions amounted to an attempt to regulate automobile fuel economy, a power reserved exclusively to the federal government by the Energy Policy and Conservation Act of 1975, the law that created the CAFE standards. In the case of *Central Valley Chrysler-Plymouth v. Witherspoon,* the federal district court in Fresno issued a preliminary injunction prohibiting the ARB from enforcing the sales quotas in 2003 or 2004 because the ZEV mandate was an effort to regulate fuel economy and was preempted by EPCA. This litigation was settled in 2003, when the ARB modified the terms of the mandate and the companies agreed to drop their lawsuit (California Environmental Protection Agency 2003a, 2003b).

Automakers can now get credits toward their ZEV quota for various kinds of partial zero emission vehicles (PZEVs). A PZEV is defined as a vehicle that has 90 percent lower tailpipe emissions than the average 2003 new car, has zero evaporative emissions, and has a fifteen-year or 150,000 mile warranty on its emissions reduction technology. Manufacturers can also choose an alternate compliance path in which they produce fuel cell vehicles to meet their corporate sales–weighted share of a gradually rising statewide quota of fuel cell ZEVs. The current schedule calls for sales of 250 fuel cell vehicles in the state by 2008, with quotas gradually rising to 50,000 fuel cell vehicles sold between 2015 and 2017 (California Environmental Protection Agency 2003a).

An even more ambitious step toward regulating auto emissions was taken in 2002, when the California legislature passed and Governor Gray Davis signed Assembly Bill A.B. 1493, the so-called Pavley bill. This law directed the Air Resources Board to develop regulations reducing the emission of greenhouse gases emitted by passenger cars and light trucks. Carbon dioxide is specifically listed as among the greenhouse gases to be regulated. The law required the ARB to develop and issue the regulations by January 1, 2005. The regulations will apply to vehicles sold beginning in model year 2009 and thereafter. Technology forcing is even more central to this effort, since the law explicitly prohibits the ARB regulators from relying on other policy measures to achieve greenhouse gas reductions. For example, they cannot raise taxes on vehicles, fuel, or miles traveled. They cannot ban the sale of a particular category of vehicle, such as SUVs. Nor can they reduce the speed limit, limit the weight of vehicles, or limit the number of vehicle miles traveled. (California state legislative information, 2002.) In 2003, California's new governor, Arnold Schwarzenegger, announced that he supported the Pavley bill, and he retained Gray Davis's appointee, Alan Lloyd, as chairman of the ARB, symbolizing the bipartisan nature of California's drive to reduce greenhouse gas emissions from automobiles.

In September 2004, the ARB's board of directors approved a detailed set of regulations to implement the Pavley bill (California Environmental Protection Agency 2004b). The ARB staff had assessed a whole range of "near-term, or off-the-shelf technologies" in order to identify possible packages that could achieve the "maximum feasible and cost-effective" reductions in greenhouse gas emissions. These included "discrete variable valve lift, dual cam phasing, turbocharging with engine downsizing, automated manual transmissions, and camless valve actuation," among many others. It then proposed an ambitious schedule for phasing in the standards year by year from 2009 to 2016. Since the standards are ostensibly aimed at reducing greenhouse gas emissions, they are officially stated in terms of grams of CO_2 per mile. But two independent researchers have published a table giving the standards in miles per gallon for easy comparison with their CAFE equivalents (An and Sauer 2004, 8). Table 8.4 below gives the standards in miles per gallon.

The regulations group vehicles into two categories. The first category includes all passenger cars as well as all light duty trucks weighing up to 3,750 lbs. The second includes light duty trucks weighing between 3,751 lbs. and 8,500 lbs., as well as vehicles between 8,500 lbs. and 10,000 lbs. that are designated as medium-duty passenger vehicles, for example, most of the heaviest SUVs. The amount of improvement being required by these standards is very ambitious. Consider that increasing the fuel efficiency of the vehicles in the first category from 27.6 mpg to 43.4 mpg in eight years requires a greater improvement than the original CAFE standards schedule, which only required a move from 18.0 mpg in 1978 to 27.5 mpg by 1985. The ARB staff projects that the new regulations will reduce greenhouse gas emissions from new vehicles in California by up to 22 percent in 2012 and between 25 and 30 percent in 2016. It estimated the costs for installing the new technology as being around $325 per vehicle in

Table 8.4. California ARB-approved greenhouse gas emission standards, 2012–16 (in CAFE-equivalent miles per gallon).

Year	Passenger cars and light-duty trucks 1	Light-duty trucks 2
2009	27.6	20.3
2010	29.6	21.2
2011	33.3	22.8
2012	38.2	24.7
2013	39.2	25.1
2014	40.1	25.4
2015	41.8	26.1
2016	43.4	26.8

Source: An and Sauer 2004, p. 8.

2012 and $1,050 in 2016. It calculated that the extra costs should be more than offset by lower operating expenses, mainly less gasoline consumption (California Environmental Protection Agency 2004a, 2004b).

The Pavley bill provides for a one year period, January 1 to December 31, 2005, during which the state legislature can review the ARB's proposal, receive comments and public input, and decide whether to require any modifications in the regulations. The auto manufacturers are predictably hostile to the new regulations, and immediately began making their objections known to the legislature and the public. They believe the ARB staff has seriously underestimated the costs of meeting the new regulatory standards. Their estimate of the costs of the standards is $3,000 per vehicle. At that price, there are no real benefits in it for Californians, they say, since the gasoline savings over the life of the vehicle would be less than the up-front cost (Alliance of Automobile Manufacturers 2004a). Even the greenest of the auto companies, Honda, has doubts. John German, Honda's corporate manager for environment and energy, said, "We don't know how to do it right now. It means using unknown, unproven technology" (Hakim 2004).

More significantly, the auto companies are going back to court. On December 7, 2004, the industry's lobbying arm, the Alliance of Automobile Manufacturers, joined with a group of automobile dealers in California's Central Valley in another suit filed in the federal district court in Fresno to challenge the ARB regulations. Their position appears to be based on the same grounds as the suit they settled in 2003 after the ARB modified its ZEV mandate—namely, that federal law gives the federal government exclusive authority to set automotive fuel economy standards, preempting any state attempts (Alliance of Automobile Manufacturers 2004b). What are the prospects for this new industry suit against ARB regulation? Of course, one can never be sure in advance how a court, whether district, appellate, or ultimately the U.S. Supreme Court, will rule on an issue until it has to decide a specific case. But in a recent preemption case in 2004, *Engine Manufacturers Assn. v. South Coast Air Quality Management District,* the U.S. Supreme Court held that a California effort to mandate fleet operators to purchase low emission and alternative fuel vehicles that met strict ARB emissions standards was preempted by the federal Clean Air Act (Duke Law, Supreme Court Online 2004). The Bush administration had filed an amicus brief supporting the engine manufacturers precisely on federal preemption grounds. In her detailed study of preemption issues relating to California air quality regulations, UCLA Law School professor Ann Carlson has noted the Rehnquist court "has frequently sided with parties seeking federal preemption of state statutes and regulations." On the specific issue of how the Supreme Court would decide a challenge to the AB 1493 regulations, she notes that "California appears to have the stronger doctrinal arguments . . . but the trend in the Supreme Court and within the Bush Administration may well tip the balance to the challengers" (Carlson 2004, 306, 309).

There is still another legal/constitutional barrier to California's proposed greenhouse gas emissions regulations. The Bush administration has already taken the position that the Clean Air Act does not give the federal Environmental Protection Agency the authority to regulate carbon dioxide as an air pollutant (Carlson 2003, Baltimore 2003). It will be very difficult for California to argue that it can regulate CO_2 emissions as air pollutants if the federal government can not. California will have to challenge the Bush administration in court over this question (Swope 2003). If the U.S. Supreme Court ultimately agrees with the Bush administration's position, that too could put an end to the Pavley bill approach. Thus the key to California's hope of taking the lead in reducing greenhouse gas emissions from automobiles by technology-forcing regulations is in the hands of the courts. As the editor of a special symposium on the legal issues surrounding AB 1493 wrote, "whether California's approach to automobile emissions foreshadows a coming wave of sister state environmental regulation or is merely an aberration from a land of tree-hugging extremists remains to be seen" (Special Edition 2002).

Are we to dismiss all of California's efforts to reduce greenhouse gas emissions from autos since 1990 as "California dreaming"? Only about two hundred electric vehicles were sold or leased in California in 2002 and the number fell to near zero in 2003 (Orski 2003). Nor can it be said that the ARB's efforts have slowed sales of Hummers, Excursions, and Escalades appreciably. Trying to force manufacturers to design and market vehicles they do not believe will be profitable has proved much more difficult than the ARB and clean air activists imagined in 1990. But in another sense it can be argued that California has indeed taken the lead in auto fuel economy policy development. Its 1990 ZEV mandate and its 2002 greenhouse gas reduction bill have pushed policy-level research and discussion of new automotive emissions and propulsion technology considerably further than if the debate had been limited exclusively to the federal level (Swope 2003). Actual implementation of the new technology has obviously lagged. But California's clear commitment to reducing automotive emissions across the board has fostered growth of an impressive new pool of human and organizational resources in the fields of analysis, research, development, and public relations supporting its emissions reduction goals. One analyst has argued that this kind of sustained public support can create "agglomeration economies"—economies of scale external to the firm when many companies are located in close geographic proximity (Gilson 1998). Another has noted that the state has become a "magnet for the clean vehicle community," with at least seventy-five advanced auto technology centers, and a growing number of private firms and university research labs focusing on the development of hydrogen vehicle and fuel issues (Carlson 2003). This is what ARB chair Alan Lloyd was driving at when he said that although he believes AB 1493 will be upheld in court, "if we lose in the legal arena we're going to win in the court of public opinion" (Hakim 2003a). He expects that the pressures (from public opinion and the growing clean car community) to respond to global warming will continue. If the courts rule out the kind of unfunded mandates inherent in technology-forcing regulation, California policymakers will have to find other tools to advance the goals of emissions reduction and fuel economy. We will return to consider how this might be done in California (and elsewhere) in the concluding section of this chapter.

HOPE OR HYPE? THE HYDROGEN CAR

A truly pathbreaking new technology that moves beyond petroleum internal combustion engines has been a staple vision of the automotive future for several decades. In the early 1990s it was assumed that the electric vehicle was the wave of the future. The Earth Day 1990 announcement by GM chairman Roger Smith of GM's Impact electric vehicle is said to have inspired the zero emission vehicle mandate in California (Shnayerson 1996). Since the turn of the millennium, the hype has shifted to hydrogen. The auto manufacturers are working to develop hydrogen fuel cells and new vehicle platforms for them. The Bush administration's FreedomCAR and Hydrogen Fuel Initiatives lend some credibility to the vision of a commercially viable hydrogen-driven vehicle fleet emerging sometime between 2015 and 2040. The U.S. Department of Energy proposed a timeline showing a four-phase development process for the "hydrogen economy." The research and development phase lasts until 2015; transition to the market begins at 2010 and lasts until 2025; expansion of markets and infrastructure starts around 2015 and lasts until 2035; full realization of the hydrogen economy culminates around 2050 (Gross 2003). In his 2003 State of the Union address, President Bush himself said that a child born in 2003 might drive a hydrogen vehicle as his or her first car. Since most states permit young people to drive at age sixteen or seventeen, that would imply fairly widespread commercial availability of hydrogen cars by 2020.

Not all energy experts agree with this timetable. MIT's Laboratory for Energy and the Environment issued a report in March 2003 that stated that even with aggressive research, 2020 is too early for the hydrogen fuel cell vehicle to be superior to hybrids, diesels, and improved gasoline engines in terms of fuels savings and CO_2 emissions reductions (MIT Laboratory for Energy and the Environment 2003). The MIT scientists called for continued research but put the time frame for the hydrogen transition somewhere between thirty and fifty years away. In February 2004, a report by the National Academy of Sciences called the Bush Energy Department's plans and timetable "unrealistically aggressive." Over the next twenty-five years, the impact of hydrogen fuel cell cars on oil imports and greenhouse gas emissions is "likely to be minor" (National Academies 2004; Wald 2004).

The timing of future scientific progress is inherently difficult to predict. In part, the speed of progress will depend on the resources devoted to research and development. Combining funding for the hydrogen initiative and FreedomCAR research funds, the president is asking Congress to invest $1.7 billion in new vehicle propulsion technology over the five years FY 2004–08 (U.S. Department of Energy 2003c). This amount over five years seems a very modest sum to launch such an ambitious undertaking. There are major scientific and engineering problems that must be solved: how to produce hydrogen cheaply and cleanly enough on the massive industrial scale that will be necessary, how to store it, and how to distribute it safely and conveniently enough to offset gasoline's current advantages as a transportation fuel. The administration hopes that once R&D is complete, the transition process will be self-sustaining, funded by private investors and state and local governments. This is almost certainly a serious underestimate of the amount of public funds required to ensure the advent of the hydrogen vehicle, let alone the hydrogen economy (Sperling 2003; Hoffman and Rose 2003). Once the process moves into the infrastructure creation and commercialization stages it is likely that greatly increased public investments would be needed. Financial incentives will be needed for automakers to put new propulsion systems into vehicles. A stream of public funds would have to support major investments in new hydrogen fueling and storage infrastructure facilities. Incentives would be needed to bring other major economic and political players on board, including oil companies and electric utility companies. Where would the funds for such a long-term, pathbreaking program come from? Unless this question is answered, the hydrogen transition could stall before it really starts.

Convincing the Congress and the people to fund the whole program of hydrogen fuel cell research and development, and construction of new infrastructure for the production, distribution, and storage of hydrogen, will require bold and shrewd leadership from the president. Whether it takes the form of Eisenhower's "hidden hand" in creating the interstate program or Johnson's arm twisting on Medicare will depend on the temperament of the leader and the temper of the times. Such leadership is always a rare commodity. Without more direct and high-profile leadership from George W. Bush (or his successor), the odds are that the FreedomCAR and Hydrogen Initiatives will produce an outcome more like Clinton's PNGV (that is, an underfunded, temporizing, research-only program that puts little new technology in actual vehicles) than the sparkling, futuristic visions in glossy press brochures from DOE.

IT'S THE CARBON, STUPID: A BROAD-BASED
CAP-AND-TRADE SYSTEM FOR CLIMATE

This scenario shifts the policy goal from reducing dependence on imported petroleum to reducing emissions of greenhouse gases, particularly carbon dioxide. It shifts the policy focus from the auto industry to the entire energy production sector. And it shifts the policy tool from command-and-control regulation to a market-like cap-and-trade system for carbon dioxide emissions and other greenhouse gases. It would be generally modeled on the emissions trading system for sulfur dioxide (SO_2) created by the 1990 Clean Air Act Amendments, which is recognized as a successful and cost-efficient program to reduce smokestack emissions causing acid rain.

The Climate Stewardship Act (S. 139), known also as the McCain-Lieberman bill, introduced early in 2003, sought to create a cap-and-trade mechanism for carbon dioxide and five other greenhouse gasses (Lieberman 2003). Electric utilities, oil refineries, and large industrial corporations that emit at least 10,000 tons of greenhouse gasses annually would be required to report and reduce their emissions, ultimately down to 1990 levels by 2016. These emitters would receive some emission allowances for free. They would have to purchase the rest initially from a nonprofit climate change credit corporation, which would use the revenue to promote new energy technologies and to aid dislocated workers and impacted communities.

Supporters of this approach claim that it can save up to one million barrels of oil per day by 2013. After that date, net savings begin to accrue to consumers, reaching $48 billion annually by 2020 (Tellus Institute 2003). The Energy Information Administration analyzed the bill and found that the cap-and-trade system would increase retail gasoline prices by 19 cents per gallon in 2010 and by 40 cents per gallon in 2025. The system's impact on petroleum demand is estimated to decrease consumption by 0.3 million barrels per day in 2010 and by 2.7 million barrels per day in 2025. This would reduce projected oil import dependence in 2025 from 67.7 percent to 64.7 percent of total U.S. consumption. But the EIA model estimates that over the years to 2025 there would be a net loss of $106 billion in GDP. This would amount to about $47 less per capita income per person per year over the life of the program (Department of Energy 2003b). Again, we see that dueling computer models of the total economic impact of policies that have yet to be enacted are not a very effective way of moving forward.

In 2003, Senators McCain and Lieberman were able to get a floor debate and a recorded vote on their Climate Stewardship bill. It was defeated 55 to 43. Some saw this as encouraging, since it was a narrower margin of defeat than the 62 to 38 Senate rejection of the McCain-Kerry effort to toughen CAFE standards in 2002. "The vote shows that the U.S. Senate is catching up with the scientific consensus," said the president of the Union of Concerned Scientists (Ris 2003). Opponents of the McCain-Lieberman bill downplayed the significance of the 43 positive votes, however; they claimed that many senators knew that the bill would never pass in the House, and felt they could get some political credit for a pro-environment vote without having to pay a political price for it.

But Senator McCain said that the long fight for the bill had just begun: "We will be back on this issue just like we were back on the issue of campaign finance" (Lee and Revkin 2003).

Senator McCain has shown he can be a determined policy entrepreneur for ideas he believes in. The McCain-Feingold campaign finance reform bill took over six years to pass. Winning approval for any greenhouse gas cap-and-trade system would probably take longer, since it would affect such a very broad range of interests. At this point, there is disagreement among policy analysts about how much such a system would cost the economy and individual consumers. There is even disagreement among analysts about whether it would be better to include a special quasi-CAFE component just for automobiles or to abolish CAFE and rely on the broader system (Smith 2003). Clearly, opposition from auto interests would be greatly muted if CAFE were abolished as part of the deal. But some environmental groups would resist abolishing CAFE. They see it as a floor below which vehicle fuel economy will not be allowed to decline and they point out that a carbon cap-and-trade system would not directly address the issue of oil imports (Friedman 2003). Finally, an emissions trading system that would raise gasoline prices by nineteen to forty cents per gallon would look suspiciously like a tax increase to many motorists.

CONCLUSIONS: THE PROSPECTS FOR PUNCTUATION

It is safe to say that none of the scenarios sketched out above will occur in pure form and be the single determining influence on policy change. Even the crisis scenario could just as easily give rise to shortsighted responses aimed more at protecting motorists and our auto-dependent economy (gas rationing, opening the strategic petroleum reserve, rolling back environmental regulations on refineries, and so on) than at generating new long-term fuel efficiency regulations. Nevertheless, the scenarios do cover most of the major elements that make up the "policy primeval soup" from which any new serving of automobile fuel economy policy is likely to be ladled up (Kingdon 1995). Legislation, like soup making, involves blending a variety of disparate ingredients into something that is reasonably palatable to different groups of voters, interests, administrators, and the courts. This concluding section will relate the basic political dynamics of automobile regulatory policy we have observed over the past forty years to the elements of threat and opportunity that we identified in the scenarios. It will suggest a possible strategic synthesis that might be likely to punctuate the current stalled policy equilibrium, if not with a bang at least with a slow leak.

Automobile Policy Dynamics

The results of the 2004 elections confirm that the macro-political conditions of 1965–75, the period of dramatic breakthroughs in federal auto regulatory policy, are not going to return any time soon. For George W. Bush, in his second term, to "turn" on his allies in the petroleum and automotive industries by proposing challenging new CAFE standards would be an about-face more startling than Nixon going to China. A Republican-dominated congress will not challenge a Republican president on this issue. Even if the Democrats win control of one or both houses in 2006 or 2008, how much would it change the political prospects for increased CAFE mileage standards? In the first place, Democrats are very unlikely to win the large and liberal-leaning majorities like they had in the Great Society years and the post-Watergate period. This is especially true in the House, given the way pro-incumbent redistricting has shrunk the number of competitive swing districts. And, of course, there are a fair number of Democrats like Senators Levin of Michigan and Bayh of Indiana who represent states with major auto production facilities and who are reluctant to vote for CAFE hikes. In fact, nineteen Democratic senators voted against the Durbin amendment to increase CAFE standards in 2005. (U.S. Senate. Legislation and Records, 2005) So the prospects for an "adversarial" punctuation of the kind engineered by Ralph Nader and his congressional allies must be rated quite slim.

What about the prospects for a bipartisan coalition acting in an innovative and non-adversarial way to achieve the long-term public interest? The answer here is more complex. One of the most difficult challenges for democratically elected politicians is to enact a policy that imposes concrete costs on constituents in the present in order to obtain possible collective benefits in the distant future. The proponents of reducing the amount of petroleum consumed by the auto sector argue for goals that are future, collective, and contingent. They say that less gasoline consumption now will allow the whole nation to enjoy the benefits of reduced dependence on imported oil and enable the whole planet to lower the risk of global warming. Worthy as these goals may be, they are clearly rather far in the future since their full benefits can not be obtained for a decade or more. They are collective, since it is difficult to exclude individuals who have not paid their share of the costs of the policies from enjoying the benefits of the policy's success—hence the free-riding temptation. And they are contingent upon other factors, especially the dubious prospect that China, India, and other developing nations would not continue rapidly increasing their combustion of coal and oil (Business Daily Update 2003). Rallying cries for widespread personal sacrifice have not been notably successful in American peacetime politics. Four decades of auto regulatory policy have shown that elected policymakers decisively prefer technology solutions aimed at auto companies over policy measures that would make individual automobile travel more expensive (large tax increases) or less convenient (ride-sharing mandates).

But technology-forcing regulations directly target auto manufacturers, workers, suppliers, and dealers, who are convinced that the costs of the policy will be concentrated heavily on them. They are thus strongly motivated to resist. This had made the auto interests the key political bottleneck to progress toward greater fuel efficiency. The fact is that only they can design, manufacture, and market cars. They must also make a profit. Regulations that threaten to lower their profits are anathema. Therefore, any proposal to reframe the issue of auto fuel efficiency has a much better chance of being adopted if it is designed so that the auto makers will see it not as a threat, but as an opportunity—a profitable opportunity.

Two successive presidents, Bill Clinton and George W. Bush, attempted to reframe the auto fuel economy issue by moving away from a posture of adversarial confrontation with the auto industry to a "partnership" with it. PNGV and FreedomCAR were indeed perceived more as an opportunity than a threat by Detroit. However, the opportunity that the industry perceived was one of profiting from the delay in setting higher fuel efficiency goals to exploit the very profitable new market niche in light trucks. Both Clinton and Bush only went halfway toward a successful reframing. They avoided conflict between the government and the industry but they did not effectively "move the market" toward high fuel economy vehicles. The next step toward a truly effective policy partnership is to have public policy assume an appropriate share of the costs and risks of introducing new fuel efficiency technology into the new vehicle fleet. *Simply put, to achieve the future collective goods of lower oil imports and lower CO_2 emissions, it will be necessary to pay the auto companies to put more fuel-efficient technology in their vehicles.*

Reframing Auto Fuel Economy Policy Strategy

A new approach must be acceptable to American motorists and auto makers. Motorists are both consumers and voters. They do not want policies that require them to drive less or to buy smaller, less comfortable, or less safe vehicles. Their preferences set the boundaries of what is feasible. Manufacturers, workers, and dealers do not want policies that reduce their profits, threaten their jobs, or reduce their sales. Their lobbying power and legal challenges have created the deadlock. A new approach should be designed to remove, or at least dramatically reduce, auto industry political opposition. It should, of course, continue to foster cooperation in research and development. But it must also have strong incentives to actually manufacture and market more fuel-efficient vehicles. Punitive, unfunded mandates requiring auto companies to meet rising fleet average mpg goals are not acceptable to the large majority of auto manufacturers. A more politically attractive framework will eschew unfunded regulatory mandates in favor of publicly funded promotion of more fuel-efficient vehicles. There is no obvious legal barrier to a program that publicly establishes fuel economy goals as long as it does not punish companies that do not achieve the goals, but only rewards companies that do. This would be the opposite of an unfunded mandate. It would be a fully funded opportunity.

The new incentive-based strategy should focus both on long-term breakthroughs and on taking maximum advantage of existing fuel efficiency technologies that are underutilized in current vehicles. A breakthrough to the hydrogen vehicle and the "hydrogen highway" is a goal that should be generously funded over the next fifteen years. But there will be 225 million vehicles sold in the United States over that period. If half of them are SUVs getting less than 20 miles per gallon, it will signal the continued impasse of energy policy making. So there must also be incentives to "jump start" a steady increase in the market share of hybrid-electric, battery-electric, clean diesel, advanced gasoline engines, and other efficiency-enhancing propulsion technologies.

The fuel efficiency goals of the program could be expressed in CAFE-like terms (sales-weighted mpg fleet averages) or stated in terms of the number or percentage of specific new technology vehicles a company needs to sell, or some combination of the two. The incentives would need to be high enough to be attractive to the companies and to consumers, yet reasonable enough not to be a pure giveaway. This means they should be based on measurable criteria such as the industry's average cost per vehicle to achieve a certain mpg or to reach a stipulated level of new technology vehicles in a company's fleet. The incentives could take the form of direct cash payments to automakers for meeting the goals, cash rebates to consumers for buying specific models of vehicles, tax deductions or tax credits to either producers or consumers. More detailed research and policy development in consultation with the industry will clearly be needed to clarify and reach agreement on many important details about the level of payments needed and the form(s) they should take.

Would this incentive-based approach work best strictly at the federal level, like CAFE? Could it come in the form of a federal-state partnership, like the highway program and transit programs? Or could it be put in place by one or more states without federal participation? There is no a priori answer to this question. It will depend on political circumstances. One can imagine a situation in which the bottom falls out of the auto market, with multiple bankruptcies and massive job losses looming, and the federal government might have to pull off a "Chrysler bailout"–style rescue. It could legitimize its subsidies by linking federal payments to improvements in energy efficiency. On the other hand, it might simply do the bailout without any quid pro quo, like the Reagan administration's "voluntary" export restraints with Japan in the early 1980s.

In the current political environment, it is also possible to imagine a state-level initiative launching an incentive-based program for improving auto fuel economy. If California were to lose its case for greenhouse gas regulatory authority in the U.S. Supreme Court, but the public still wanted to do something against global warming, then the state might very well decide to proceed with a program of subsidies and incentives that could pass legal muster. As noted above, California has developed its own technical capabilities to stand toe-to-toe with the industry in discussing the engineering and economic details of fuel efficiency programs. If the seven other states (and Canada) that have indicated they would adopt California's greenhouse gas emission standards were to follow its lead in adopting an incentive-based approach, it would be a powerful reason for the industry to go along, since they would represent one-third of the North American auto market (Hakim 2004).

Regardless of the level of government, any incentive strategy must deal with the issues of the form they should take and where to find the resources to pay for the program. Tax breaks are a very tempting choice for elected politicians, since they offer benefits in the present and defer the costs to the future. Federal tax law began to offer deductions for purchase of hybrids in 2002, although the breaks are scheduled to be phased out by 2006. The Energy Future Coalition, a foundation-funded effort that includes both Democrats and Republicans, sponsored a national-level proposal calling for an "aggressive set of tax incentives [that] would jump-start acceptance of hybrid vehicles by consumers" (Wirth, Gray, and Podesta 2003). Direct cash payments have the benefit of being able to provide public funds to companies in periods when business is bad. Corporations with no taxable profits have little use for tax breaks. In a financial crisis, a properly designed system of cash incentives could accelerate progress toward fuel efficiency even more, thus achieving an important general public goal in addition to simply preserving jobs and restoring profits.

In the current deficit-driven budgetary environment of government at both federal and state levels, a "pay as you go" policy that raises the revenues at the same time as it offers public incentives is clearly preferable in principle. Where might the revenues to assure a stable source of funding for these incentives come from? Senator John Kerry suggested that the royalties paid by the energy companies for the right to drill for oil and gas on public land could be used to "help fund the manufacture of more fuel efficient cars and trucks" (Kerry 2004). There is an even more broad-based and more flexible source of funding: gasoline taxes. While it is true that op-ed page proposals for large gasoline tax increases are inevitably ignored, it is also true that the federal and state governments periodically make modest increases in their gas taxes to meet their highway and public transit investment needs. All our experience with the politics of gasoline tax increases demonstrates that the key to winning political approval for gas tax hikes is to dedicate the revenues to trust funds supporting transportation-related expenditures. The interstate highway system is a monument to the power of dedicated trust fund financing. But even before the federal highway trust fund was created in 1956, over forty states had created their own highway trust funds to receive revenues from their state gasoline taxes and other automobile-related levies. They were the institutionalization of a social compact between motorists and the authorities. Drivers would pay the taxes as long as the governments promised to use the revenues to make public infrastructure investments that enabled them to get more benefits from their automobiles (Dunn 1998).

The creation of "Energy Independence and Climate Stabilization Trust Funds" could be the financial/political mechanism to take automotive technology "from here to hydrogen." As noted, such funds could be introduced at either the state or federal level or both. Currently, one cent per gallon of federal gasoline tax yields over $1.5 billion dollars in annual revenues nationally. One cent per gallon of California's gas tax yields approximately $175 million. In the early years of the trust fund–based spending program, when most activity would likely be research and pilot-incentive programs, a tax increase of a few cents per gallon would be all that was needed. As the program moved toward higher mpg/more innovative technologies and, perhaps, major hydrogen infrastructure investments, additional pennies or nickels per gallon would be added, just as was done over the years to finance the interstate system.

Political support for such a fund would be broadened if some of its benefits were extended beyond the auto manufacturing industry. First, the fund's political flanks would have to be secured by assuring the highway and transit lobbies, the principal beneficiaries of existing gas taxes, that their flow of funds would not be threatened in any way. Then, invitations might be issued to the energy industry, the research community, the universities, and probably the electric utilities to show how they could participate in the program. Other interests might well have to be brought into the coalition to prevent them from opposing the taxes and the fund. For example, farmers and agribusiness might need to be held harmless as ethanol was supplanted by hydrogen.

Once such a well-funded program of technology "risk sharing" (not unfunded technology "forcing") were launched, the classic distributive pressures built into the American political system would work to ensure its growth. Auto companies would lobby for higher cost reimbursements instead of lobbying against CAFE hikes. Oil companies and electric utilities would push for incentives for investment in hydrogen infrastructure or clean electric power for the batteries of "city cars." Republican and Democratic legislators would unite to make sure their states and districts got their fair share of federal spending on the program. By making a dedicated source of funding the key driver of auto fuel economy policy—instead of CAFE's fines or California's unfunded mandates—the politics would turn from a zero-sum knife fight into a popular process of logrolling and pork barrel.

Beyond CAFE

Undermining a policy monopoly and punctuating a policy equilibrium requires a correct analysis of the underlying political dynamics. Good intentions are not enough, nor are economic analyses of the total societal costs and benefits of different policy alternatives. Perceptions of the distribution of concrete costs and benefits are more important than the abstract societal total. To succeed politically, the new policy must spread present costs as thinly as possible (a few cents per gallon paid by all drivers), and concentrate present benefits on those groups (auto interests) that have been most responsible for blocking further progress in the current CAFE system.

Americans want to keep their cars, their pickups, and their SUVs. They want them as safe, as powerful, and as luxurious as they can afford. Americans also want clean air, less dependence on oil imports, and less risk of global warming. Making auto propulsion technology cleaner and more efficient in ways that do not threaten auto sector profits and jobs is the most politically acceptable way of reconciling these desires. American motorists are realistic about paying gaso-line taxes. These per-gallon user fees have long been linked to transportation investments that enable motorists to enjoy improving mobility. It is not too much of a stretch to suggest that the same powerful mechanism of user taxes dedicated to a trust fund could also be applied to the task of developing and de-ploying advanced automotive fuel efficiency technology. Thus two classic American strengths—dedicated user fees and technological progress—would be combined in a way that reconciles our long-standing passion for "automo-bility" with our growing desire to protect the environment and to preserve the world's resources and protect its climate for our children. The key to moving beyond the CAFE controversy is to develop a policy framework that does not unite the community of auto interests in opposition to it. Carrots are always more acceptable than sticks in American politics. When auto manufacturers see profit in advanced technology, fuel-efficient vehicles, they will build them.

NOTES

1. Rather than clutter the text with references for each argument, I will cite only a small sam-ple of the voluminous literature on the CAFE controversy, both pro and con. On the anti-CAFE side, Robert Crandall, the Brookings economist, has been one of its most persis-tent independent critics. See Crandall et al. 1986; Crandall and Graham 1989; Nivola and Crandall 1995, and Crandall et al. 2002. See also the book by James Johnston, former GM vice-president for industry-government relations (Johnston 1997). For the pro-CAFE side of the argument see Bradsher 2002; Doyle 2000; Greene, Sperling, and Mc-Nutt 1998; and National Research Council 2002.

2. Auto manufacturers decline to publish profits broken down by individual model or as-sembly plant. They do give special briefings to Wall Street analysts, however. Reputable journalists like Keith Bradsher of the *New York Times* often get their information about profit margins on particular models confidentially from these analysts and sometimes can get them confirmed in general terms by auto executives. See Bradsher 2002, 445, note 4.

Chapter 9 The Politics of Grazing on Federal Lands: A Policy Change Perspective

Charles Davis

Analyzing change in public land programs that have historically been dominated by sub-governments offers a challenging task for students of American public policy. Sub-governments (also known as subsystems, policy whirlpools, or iron triangles) tend to limit participation in policy decisions to public agency administrators, legislators, and interest group representatives with shared programmatic concerns, a low degree of visibility within the media and the general public, and a high degree of stability over time (Griffith 1939; Maas 1949; Freeman 1965; Cater 1964). Such governance systems exemplify distributive policymaking, in which benefits are provided for a relatively small number of individuals or firms while program costs are borne by all U.S. taxpayers (Lowi 1964).

Over the past two decades, the assumption that sub-governmental policymaking arrangements were stable over time and either impermeable to or immune from external political forces has received considerable scrutiny. Several writers have explored policy change within the context of substantive program areas like pesticides (Bosso 1987), agriculture (Browne 1988), energy (Jones and Strahan 1985; Jenkins-

Smith 1991), water resources (McCool 1987; Lowry 2003), and nuclear power (Temples 1980; Duffy 1997). Others have focused on external factors contributing to change. These include, among others, the enactment of crosscutting policies that subsequently escalate distributive programs to a regulatory mode of governance (Thurber 1991); the willingness of such formerly quiescent policy actors as the federal courts and the Office of Management and Budget (OMB) to question politics as usual (Ingram 1990; Melnick 1985); and the greater use by chief executives of managerial tools to disrupt established patterns of interaction, such as administrative reorganization or reliance on bloc grants (Ripley and Franklin 1987; McCool 1990).

Change in programs dominated by sub-governments has been attributed in part to moves made by established institutional actors, but attention has also been directed toward organizational interests and individuals with strong programmatic concerns. Research has increasingly focused on issue or policy networks consisting of a larger array of participants within a policy community (Heclo 1978), including policy actors whose involvement may be transitory over an extended period of time (Jenkins-Smith, St. Claire, and Woods 1991). Moreover, program decisions are often influenced by the activities of highly motivated policy entrepreneurs within government who maintain a strong interest in particular issues (Kingdon 1984; Mintrom 1997).

Nonetheless, some policies, such as the federal land subsidy programs, have been notoriously resistant to change over time because their policy networks are quite adept at playing defense. My research objective in this chapter is to analyze policy change affecting one of these programs; that is, the grazing policies administered by the U.S. Forest Service and the U.S. Department of the Interior from the 1960s to the present.

My analysis of federal grazing policy shifts follows the punctuated equilibrium approach advanced by Baumgartner and Jones (1991, 1993). In their work, such information sources as content analyses of legislative hearings or the press, regulatory activities, and court decisions are used to track efforts by would-be reformers to break through systems of limited participation. Of particular importance is the attempt to alter the prevailing policy image from a positive or benign governmental program to a more negative portrayal of programmatic worth and to increase public awareness of these shortcomings through media campaigns. Next, change advocates seek out alternative policy-making venues such as the courts, administrative agencies, or institutions within a differing level of government where policy shifts would be viewed more positively. Over time, the interaction between an increasingly negative policy image and the active consideration of new or amended policy proposals on differing institutional agendas may result in significant change.

THE RANGE POLICY SUBSYSTEM

Livestock grazing on federal lands has been regulated since the early 1900s, largely because of initiatives undertaken by Gifford Pinchot, the first chief of the newly established U.S. Forest Service and a close confidant of President Theodore Roosevelt. Early efforts to cut back on livestock use and to levy grazing fees to enhance conservation objectives were controversial but ultimately successful because of the ability of field rangers to contain disputes at the local level (Graf 1990). Pinchot's political skills, coupled with agency success in projecting an image of professionalism in the application of scientific forestry to management on the ground, allowed the Forest Service to acquire and retain considerable autonomy and enabled it to operate with relatively little interference from elected officials (Klyza 1996). Forest Service regulation was largely confined to land within forested and mountainous terrain, however, while the larger area of public rangelands within western states remained substantially unregulated until 1934. Congressional enactment of the Taylor Grazing Act provided livestock operators with access to lands administered by the Grazing Service (later renamed the Bureau of Land Management, or BLM) within the U.S. Interior Department. The law called for the issuance of permits to ranchers, allowing them to graze a certain number of cattle, horses, or sheep on a given parcel of land over a period of time (up to ten years) depending on existing rangeland conditions (the actual number was not supposed to exceed the "carrying capacity" of the land, which was determined by estimating the amount of forage). Each permittee was also assessed a grazing fee for each animal unit month (AUM).

This law's original goal was to enhance economic stability for western ranchers by creating a new agency to manage and distribute livestock more efficiently on hardscrabble lands that had been decimated by overgrazing and extreme drought. Ranchers were appeased by statutory requirements aimed at keeping grazing fees low, by assurances that existing users would receive greater priority in the allocation of permits, and by the delegation of substantial management authority to local grazing advisory boards staffed mostly with ranchers (Culhane 1981; Klyza 1996). An unarticulated goal of the ranching industry was also realized through the TGA: namely, to impede efforts by Forest Service officials to assume control over grazing activities on all public lands. Ranchers had complained about earlier Forest Service measures to revitalize depleted land parcels by reducing stocking levels and it was widely assumed that permittees would receive considerably less oversight by Interior Department range managers than by their Forest Service counterparts (Rowley 1985).

These decisions illustrate quite vividly how Congress and agency administrators were able to create the building blocks of a dominant sub-government. Ranchers were able to exercise disproportionate influence over decisions because of ranchers' mandated influence over grazing advisory boards, close political ties between stock-growers associations and the Interior Committees of the U.S. Congress (later renamed the House Natural Resources Committee and the Senate Energy and Natural Resources Committee) and a tradition of managerial decentralization within DOI's Grazing Service and the Forest Service (Voigt 1976; McConnell 1966). From the 1930s through the 1950s, livestock operators and their allies on the advisory boards took advantage of risk-averse agency managers, successfully resisting efforts to reduce livestock numbers on overgrazed rangelands and to raise grazing fees to levels that more closely approximated the economic value of the resource (Foss 1960).

FEDERAL RANGE POLICY AND THE ENVIRONMENTAL ERA

By the early 1960s, members of the range policy subsystem were clearly dominating grazing policy. For example, participants in congressional hearings over grazing fees in 1963 consisted overwhelmingly of ranchers, with only token representation of conservation groups (Davis and Ellison 1996). Nonetheless, things were about to change. The first major challenge to the range policy subsystem's political dominance was raised by the growth of the environmental movement during the 1960s and 1970s, coupled with the enactment of numerous federal statutes affecting both pollution controls and natural resource conservation. Laws that directly affected land-use decisions made by the Department of the Interior and the Forest Service included the Wilderness Act of 1964, the National Environmental Policy Act (NEPA) of 1969, and the Forest and Rangeland Renewable Resources Planning Act (RPA) of 1974. This last enactment called for a major increase in agency planning, opportunities for public participation, and other procedural requirements, as well as increased sensitivity to environmental policy goals in making land-use decisions (Hirt

1994). Other environmental policies that would eventually complicate the implementation of traditional range policy objectives included the Clean Water Act (CWA) and the Endangered Species Act (ESA).

A second factor affecting range management decisions was the increasing activism of Interior Department secretaries as major participants in federal policy debates over the grazing program and related policy goals. President Kennedy's appointment of Stewart Udall as Interior Secretary was a direct response to public concerns about federal land-use issues. These concerns included increasing demands for recreation, the desire for a wilderness policy that would result in the withdrawal and preservation of large tracts of scenic land and an end to the presumption that miners, ranchers, and loggers had a superior claim to resource use as extractive industries. Secretary Udall successfully pushed for the enactment of the Classification and Multiple Use Act (CMU) in 1964, a policy that gave BLM temporary authority to manage rangeland resources under multiple-use management principles. This statute was particularly important to BLM administrators who had sought the same type of decision-making autonomy based on range science that the Forest Service had attained for many years (Fairfax 1984) and to environmental groups who were beginning to appreciate the ecological significance of rangeland reform.

Third, public rangeland policies began to receive more attention from such federal staff agencies as the Office of Management and Budget (OMB) and the General Accounting Office (GAO), and from groups favoring major reforms in grazing policy (environmentalists, some fiscal conservatives) or maintaining the status quo (livestock associations, range management professionals within western land grant universities). Thus, decisions formerly made by Forest Service or BLM administrators with minimal interference from others and with little media coverage were now subjected to greater scrutiny. A prime example was the emergence of livestock grazing fees as an increasingly important policy issue. In 1964, the U.S. Bureau of the Budget (later renamed OMB) issued a report dealing with natural resource user charges, concluding that the sale or lease of federally owned resources should follow pricing or fee-setting guidelines that approximate fair market value. Ideally fees would be established through appraisal or competitive bidding, taking comparable fees charged by state government or the private sector into account. This foreshadowed a major theme that would emerge in the arguments of range reform advocates—that grazing permits on BLM lands were underpriced and that fees ought to be raised to ensure that the government received a fair rate of return.

Meanwhile, a task force consisting of analysts from the U.S. Departments of Agriculture and Interior (USDA/DI) undertook a major research project to provide information about the costs of ranching operations on public and private lands. The results of this project, titled the *1966 Western Livestock Grazing Survey,* were used in the preparation of a new grazing fee formula that was unveiled by both departments in November 1968. Proposed fee levels eschewed prior approaches based on the price of livestock in favor of the principle that average total costs incurred by ranchers operating on public lands should equal those of private sector ranchers. Since the subsequent increase in charges per AUM to meet this new standard was quite pronounced, USDA/DI officials proposed that the ensuing financial burden on permittees be eased somewhat by phasing in the fee increases gradually over a ten-year period (Backiel and Rogge 1985).

CONGRESSIONAL BACKLASH

The political fallout from the proposed fee increase was immediate and predictable. Both the House and Senate Interior Committees scheduled hearings in early 1969 to allow feedback from affected constituents. Testimony from western legislators, livestock associations, and individual ranchers was overwhelmingly negative. A frequent claim was that many small ranchers would be unable to afford fee increases and would be forced off the land, creating negative ripple effects on the economies of nearby communities. Another point of contention was the interpretation of "reasonable" compensation for public land use found in the language of the Taylor Grazing Act. An increase of this magnitude was surely incompatible with the statutory goal of a stable livestock industry; hence, policy moves in the direction of fair market value were not only ill conceived but illegal as well. A smaller coalition of groups including BLM and Forest Service spokesmen and representatives from wildlife and environmental organizations argued in favor of the proposed fee hike, citing the unfairness of existing fee structures.

Under pressure from Congress, USDA/DI officials imposed a moratorium on fee increases in 1970 (the first of four delays initiated during the 1970s) citing difficult economic times in the cattle industry and drought conditions in the West. On a related front, several range policy bills requiring BLM to give greater weight to environmental criteria in land management decisions were defeated in the early 1970s because of opposition from livestock associations and western legislators. Members of the pro-grazing coalition were beginning to recognize the importance of competing groups within the range policy arena but were not intimidated by the initiation of policy reform proposals.

THE COURTS AS A CATALYST
FOR POLICY REFORM

Discouraged by unfavorable policy outcomes emanating from the executive and legislative branches, environmentalists—led by the Natural Resources Defense Council (NRDC)—turned to the courts to regain political momentum and in 1974 they succeeded. In *Natural Resources Defense Council v. Morton,* environmental lawyers made strategic use of NEPA to force BLM to change its administrative procedures. After the agency filed a draft environmental impact statement (EIS) covering its entire grazing program in the western United States, NRDC attorneys filed suit arguing that BLM could not thereby adequately address local impacts arising from overgrazing or other poor management practices. Their main argument revolved around the need for a site-specific EIS to provide necessary information for land-use decisions. Federal District Judge Thomas Flannery agreed with this position. He and other parties recognized that the decision had important implications for BLM, which stood to gain additional funding and manpower to implement the edict (which eventually called for the preparation of 144 EISs by 1988) as well as additional political leverage that could be used by field administrators to negotiate livestock reductions or other contentious issues with ranchers (Nelson 1985).

Having received a temporary boost from the *NRDC v. Morton* decision, environmentalists and other range reform advocates turned their attention to legislative activities. Considerable debate ensued and in 1976 Congress enacted the Federal Land Policy and Management Act (FLPMA). This was widely known as BLM's organic act, putting into place the multiple-use management scheme coveted by agency officials. Much to the disdain of traditional constituency groups, the new law amended the Taylor Grazing Act by replacing the provision identifying livestock grazing as the predominant use of public rangelands with a much broader set of policy goals. It requires that: "Public lands be managed in a manner that will protect the quality of scientific, scenic, historical, ecological, environmental, air and atmospheric, water resource, and archeological values; that, where appropriate, will preserve and protect certain public lands in their natural condition; that will provide food and habitat for fish and wildlife and domestic animals; and that will provide for outdoor recreation and human occupancy and use."

This statute also required incorporation of planning requirements into resource-allocation decisions and an opportunity for public participation through testimony on resource management plans and judicial review (Coggins 1983).

While these sections were clearly welcomed by environmental groups, other parts of FLPMA were designed to allay the fears of traditional constituencies by reaffirming the need for extractive uses of the public lands. The law abolished neither the permit system nor the grazing advisory boards. In addition, an additional moratorium on fee increases was mandated. However, environmentalists were generally satisfied by the removal of structural advantages embedded within the Taylor Grazing Act (such as the dominant use clause) that had proven to be beneficial to livestock producers (Cawley 1993).

The dust had scarcely cleared with the passage of FLPMA when Congress enacted yet another policy affecting BLM's administration of public rangelands in 1978. The Public Range Improvement Act (PRIA), like FLPMA, contained sections to satisfy divergent constituencies. Environmentalists generally applauded a key section assigning greater management priority to the improvement of range conditions. This goal was to be achieved through a series of actions including continuous monitoring of rangeland quality and use of this information in the preparation of allotment management plans (AMPs), increased funding for the rejuvenation of damaged lands, and an experimental stewardship program designed to offer incentives or rewards to permittees who demonstrated sound resource management (Congressional Quarterly 1979, 716–18).

While these program changes were well received by reform advocates, it was equally evident that a substantial gap remained between the promise of better rangeland management practices and the likelihood of effective implementation. For example, the new law was not accompanied by a corresponding increase in funds or personnel needed to make a sizeable dent in rangeland improvement projects (Durant 1992; Hamilton 1987). In addition, ranchers were placated with policy provisions such as an adjusted grazing fee formula that kept fees lower than the amount charged on comparable private lands by factoring in livestock prices and production costs (Backiel and Rogge 1985) and by assurances that permittees would receive security of tenure, a promise that enhanced the property value of private ranches adjacent to public lands (Borman and Johnson 1990). Finally, Congress accepted a last-minute amendment by Senator James McClure (D-ID) calling for a "phased-in approach" to any reductions in livestock deemed necessary for the reconstruction of healthy rangelands.

POLITICAL RESISTANCE TO RANGE CONSERVATION

Perhaps the most visible form of discontent over public land-use changes occurred in the late 1970s when Interior Secretary Cecil Andrus began to implement FLPMA through a combination of intensive management initiatives and livestock reduction plans. Irate ranchers contacted friendly state lawmakers in western states to propose legislation calling for the transfer of BLM and Forest Service lands to the states, a legally questionable but symbolically powerful message that became popularly known as the "Sagebrush Rebellion" (Francis and Ganzel 1984).

The Sagebrush Rebellion epitomized the clash in values between ranchers and other traditional beneficiaries of public lands policy and environmentalists (with an occasional assist from ideological conservatives). In 1980, a self-proclaimed Sagebrush rebel, Ronald Reagan, was elected president, and he promptly rewarded his sizeable core of western supporters by selecting James Watt to become the new Interior Secretary and Robert Burford as the new BLM director. Both men were determined to reverse the direction of range policy by moving away from the "environmental excesses" of the Carter administration to a "good neighbor" policy that placed greater emphasis on the economic health of ranching and other extractive industries (Fairfax 1984).

Early policy initiatives such as privatization of public lands and land swaps between BLM and the Forest Service set off fire alarms in Congress and were subsequently rebuffed. Thereafter, Secretary Watt (and his successors William Clark and Donald Hodel) essentially wrote off the possibility of attaining desired changes within the legislative arena and sought to influence policy through administrative decision-making. BLM's budget was repeatedly slashed and a pro-grazing orientation was maintained through personnel policies that eliminated or transferred environmental positions (such as wildlife biologists) in order to increase the number of positions devoted to commodity production (Durant 1992).

Despite a philosophical orientation toward land management that was quite compatible with the policy preferences of the traditional range policy subsystem, there was relatively little legislative activity during Reagan's two terms in office or during the administration of President George Bush from 1989 to 1993. An executive order issued by President Reagan in 1986 continued the grazing fee formula established under PRIA for an indefinite period of time. And President Bush's Interior Secretary, Manuel Lujan, continued along the same policy path although BLM director Cy Jamieson did tilt policy slightly in the direction of increased recreational use on public lands.

RENEWAL OF RANGE REFORM EFFORTS

A renewed effort to revamp public range laws was launched in the late 1980s within the House Interior Committee. Bills calling for a dramatic increase in grazing fees were advanced by Representatives Mike Synar (D-OK) and Buddy Darden (D-GA), with considerable support from other non-western legislators. Members of the range reform coalition, including the NRDC and the National Wildlife Federation, sought to enfold range policy in the larger issue of deficit politics, arguing that an end to grazing subsidies made sense on both economic and ecological grounds. A move toward fair market value would not only eliminate unfair advantages enjoyed by public land permittees but would produce additional fee revenue that could be used for rangeland improvement projects. Reform advocates also directed attention to such environmental quality problems as the loss of habitat for wildlife (other than coyotes) and the damage to riparian areas from overgrazing on public rangelands.

Supporters of the status quo, including the Bush administration and members of the pro-grazing coalition, were vehemently opposed to these bills, suggesting that the true purpose of the legislation was not "true reform" but the virtual elimination of livestock grazing on public lands. Moreover, they argued, a careful analysis of non-fee costs incurred by ranchers operating on public lands indicated that the characterization of grazing fees as a subsidy was misleading since the amount and quality of forage on public rangelands was not comparable to more lush pastures associated with privately owned ranches. In addition, more expensive private sector leases often included fences, stock ponds, and other improvements not found on BLM or Forest Service lands (Obermiller 1991). Several western legislators, led by Representative Ben Campbell (D-CO), cosponsored a rival bill that called for a much smaller fee increase and maintained the basic formula established under PRIA.

Reform advocates received a political boost in 1992 with the election of Bill Clinton as president. Environmentalists were elated when Clinton selected Bruce Babbitt as Interior Secretary and Jim Baca as BLM director. Both men had held elective office in a western state, had wrestled with the details of public land issues, and were known to favor change which would overturn entrenched resource development privileges held by the "lords of yesterday" (Wilkinson 1992). Proposed legislation was soon developed that combined substantially higher grazing fees, as in the Synar and Darden proposals, with a partial rebate for ranchers who thereafter practiced good environmental management. As before, the new proposal encountered fierce resistance from western senators, led by Pete Domenici (R-NM).

Under pressure, the Clinton administration dropped the grazing fee proposal from the 1994 budget act when several western Democrats threatened to vote against the closely contested package unless it was deleted (Knickerbocker 1993). The proposal was then introduced as a separate piece of legislation. Once again, the pro-grazing coalition held firm against the bill. In an effort to break legislative gridlock, Secretary Babbitt then threw his support to a compromise bill sponsored by Senator Harry Reid (D-NV) that maintained most reform provisions but called for a lower ceiling on fee increases. Once again, their efforts were unsuccessful. The bill was defeated in November 1993 after the Senate waged a successful filibuster.

Conceding that a legislative solution was unlikely to work, Secretary Babbitt turned to administrative options. One initiative was the promulgation of regulations aimed at strengthening the hands of BLM administrators attempting to implement FLPMA. Another was an attempt to build consensus among differing constituencies to achieve desired policy goals (Kenworthy 1994). The product of these efforts was a package of regulations titled *Rangeland Reform '94* that went into effect in August 1995. The new regulations did not include the fee increases sought by Secretary Babbitt. What did emerge were several changes in legal definitions that had implications for permittees' security of tenure and BLM administrators' decision-making authority. Another part of the regulatory package was the replacement of rancher-dominated grazing advisory boards with resource advisory councils (RACs) comprising members representing diverse constituencies within the community. Secretary Babbitt argued that public land managers should give considerable weight to advice offered by these newly constituted councils in developing individual allotment plans; for example, recommendations on how permittees might take steps to mitigate livestock impacts on riparian areas (Babbitt 1994a).

Supporters of the traditional grazing coalition were unhappy with these programmatic shifts and took action in both Congress and the federal courts to reverse these decisions. In a Republican-controlled Congress, Senator Pete Domenici (R-NM) introduced legislation in May 1995 that would have designated livestock grazing as a dominant use of the public lands, increased the tenure of grazing permits from ten to twelve years, and made it more difficult for BLM administrators to reduce the number of livestock on public rangelands to achieve ecological benefits (Bryner 1998; Donahue 1999). The bill narrowly passed the Senate and the House Resources Committee but did not progress any further in the House of Representatives. Subsequent efforts to achieve similar policy goals in 1997 also failed to elicit majority support in Congress (Cody and Baldwin 1998).

ABOUT FACE: PRESIDENT BUSH
AND THE GRAZING POLICY COMMUNITY

The election of George W. Bush to the presidency in 2000 produced a shift away from a more ecologically sensitive range management program for federal lands to one more sympathetic to the ranchers' goals. A different tone was established at the outset with the appointment of pro-industry officials, notably Gale Norton as Interior Secretary and Mark Rey as Undersecretary of Agriculture with the charge of overseeing Forest Service activities. Both had prior ties to organizations with a history of supporting commodity producers. Norton had been a senior attorney for the Mountain States Legal Foundation, a Colorado-based law firm that often challenges environmental policies and regulations in the courts. Rey was a former vice president of the American Forest and Paper Association. Policy decisions adopted to date focus on the economic and social benefits of public lands ranching within a DOI initiative termed "Sustaining Working Landscapes."

The Public Lands Council and other organizations representing the interests of the western livestock industry were hopeful that the new regime would take strides to overturn or alter Clinton-era regulations that ranchers holding federal grazing permits found to be particularly onerous. After reviewing the details of *Public Lands Council v. Babbitt* (2000), Secretary Norton announced in December 2003 that the Bush administration would seek a major rule change aimed at giving ranchers "more flexibility to run their ranches and protect the land" (U.S. Department of the Interior, Bureau of Land Management 2003). Proposed changes "allow BLM to share title with permittees of permanent range improvements such as fences or wells; allow a more realistic timeframe (24 months rather than the current 12 months) for deciding on grazing-related actions needed to achieve rangeland health standards; eliminate . . . existing regulatory provisions that allow the BLM to issue a long-term 'conservation-use' grazing permit; and make clear how the BLM will authorize grazing if a Bureau decision affecting a grazing permit is postponed pending administrative appeal" (U.S. Department of the Interior, Bureau of Land Management 2003). Opposition from environmental groups such as the NRDC stems from the belief that these changes collectively reduce incentives to comply with policies to prevent overgrazing and the resulting rangeland deterioration (Benke 2003).

EVALUATING CHANGE IN FEDERAL GRAZING POLICIES

How can we evaluate the likelihood of change in federal grazing policy decisions using the punctuated equilibrium model? Some policies are more stable than others because of structural characteristics that inhibit efforts to alter their image or to expand the scope of conflict. One key factor here is the ability of the subsystem to restrict access to outside participants over time (Ripley and Franklin 1987). On the other hand, policy equilibrium can be jeopardized by a shift in the attitudes of subsystem participants or in the expansion of organized interests with stakes in the program.

GRAZING SUBSYSTEM PARTICIPANTS

The range policy subsystem has historically been quite dominant, working to preserve program benefits such as low grazing fees and to suppress major policy reform efforts. Key subsystem partners included BLM and Forest Service officials, livestock associations, and federal legislators and governors representing western states. Prior to the mid-1960s, BLM administrators held an unenviable reputation as the archtypical "captured agency" that catered to the interests of ranchers, miners, loggers, and energy companies with little regard for the environmental consequences of extractive land-use activities. However, as Culhane noted in *Public Lands Politics* (1981), agency officials sought greater administrative independence (like the Forest Service) through the attainment of a multiple-use mandate for range management programs. This goal was achieved by the enactment of the Federal Land Management and Policy Act of 1976, a statute that also provided legislative authorization for the agency. Since then, BLM has remained close to traditional constituencies but has also made some effort to accommodate environmental and recreational interests as well (Cubbage et al. 1993; Davis and Davis 1988). While Forest Service officials have traditionally exhibited a greater willingness than BLM to balance the preferences of livestock operators with the "carrying capacity" of forage areas within national forests (Graf 1990), it is likely that between-agency differences have narrowed over the past decade. One factor is the increasing institutionalization of environmental concerns within BLM. Another factor is the decision by Congress to standardize grazing fee levels across the two agencies.

Congressional support for subsystem policy goals remains high. The House Resources Committee (formerly the Interior Committee) has retained sole jurisdiction over federal grazing policies, thus reinforcing a policy monopoly for the pro-grazing coalition. The membership base continues to be more representative of the western United States, i.e., from 1964 through 2002 it averaged around 50 percent. Legislators from this region have consistently voted to reject changes in the grazing laws. A strong regional base of support was particularly important in defending coalition goals against efforts to reform grazing policies from the late 1980s through the early 1990s. During this period, pro-reform legislators such as Morris Udall and George Miller chaired the House Natural Resources Committee and pushed for change in grazing policies—thanks, in part, to the willingness of nonwestern legislators on the committee and in the parent chamber to disregard western interests in favor of national economic and resource conservation objectives. Bills calling for an increase in grazing fees were adopted by the House of Representatives annually between 1990 and 1994 but each time the Senate refused to follow suit. After the midterm congressional elections of 1994, Republicans gained control over the committee and the House of Representatives and have espoused policy positions favorable to organizations representing livestock operators.

A similar pattern of geographical representation is found within the Senate Energy and Natural Resources (formerly Interior) Committee. The average proportion of western state members declined from approximately 70 percent for the 1960 to 1972 period to 50 percent from 1976 to 2002. However, unlike their House counterparts, committee leaders have steadfastly maintained a pro-development philosophy. The temporary rift between the reform-minded House of Representatives of the early 1990s and the Senate dissipated after the 1994 congressional elections. Since then, Congress as a body has remained wedded to the preservation of grazing program benefits. However, it is noteworthy that a large enough bloc of reform advocates exists among Democrats and moderate Republicans to prevent passage of laws adding new benefits or repealing environmental requirements in existing laws.

The expansion of participants in either the pro-grazing or pro-grazing re-form camps could conceivably alter the balance of political influence and change political outcomes. The dominant grazing policy subsystem has re-tained the traditional livestock groups and related organizational participants who work closely with the staff of relevant legislative committees, but their pol-icy network has expanded to meet political challenges from environmentalists and nonwestern fiscal conservatives. Congressional testimony in support of federal grazing programs is now offered not only by ranchers but also by state and local officials, bankers, university range management researchers, umbrella organizations like the Public Lands Council, and, on occasion, western gover-nors.

However, the number of grazing reform advocates also increased signifi-cantly during the environmental era. Original members included wildlife or-ganizations and staff agencies (the Bureau of the Budget) as well as Interior Secretary Stewart Udall, whose tenure spanned the Kennedy and Johnson ad-ministrations. By the end of the 1960s, environmental organizations such as the Sierra Club, the Wilderness Society, and the NRDC had joined the Na-tional Wildlife Federation in pushing for change. Other participants within the coalition include pro-environmental members of Congress and, to a lesser ex-tent, Interior Department and Forest Service officials whose support for range reform is largely tied to the policy preferences of differing presidential adminis-trations. This increase is reflected in the sizeable growth in the number of envi-ronmental organizations offering testimony in congressional hearings from the early 1960s through the early 1990s (Davis and Ellison 1996). Public partici-pation in the management of federal range programs also increased because of requirements spelled out under NEPA, FLPMA, and the Wilderness Act. More recent organizations such as Southwest Center for Biological Diversity and Forest Guardians also advocate reform but tend to operate independently of other groups, using more aggressive tactics to achieve their policy goals.

POLICY IMAGE

Baumgarter and Jones (1993) suggest that an important precursor of policy change is the ability of would-be reformers to shift the prevailing views of exist-ing programs from positive to negative. If a program is portrayed in a different light, the media and eventually the public may well react in a negative fashion, resulting in pressures for reform. The emergence of new organizations with an interest in federal grazing policies accompanied the increasing visibility of range policy issues within the media, thanks to key focusing events such as the Sagebrush Rebellions that surfaced in the late 1970s and mid-1990s (Davis 2001) and increasing demands for recreation on BLM lands. Previously, very little media attention covered range policy issues, and such coverage was restricted to ranchers' concerns.

Strategic efforts to redefine how a policy issue is perceived require new information or, at minimum, the recasting of available data to emphasize different points. How an issue is redefined is important to gain the attention not only of print or electronic media but also of policy brokers as well (Kingdon 1984). Within the context of federal policymaking, an emphasis on "economic efficiency" often plays very well within the deliberative process and can be deployed as a means of diverting attention away from the capture of benefits by a particular constituency to issues such as "government waste" or "unwarranted subsidies." Administrators within the Bureau of the Budget (BOB), the Forest Service, and the Interior Department advocated an increase in grazing fees in the early 1960s but recognized the need to bolster their case with technical analyses that revealed the magnitude of existing program subsidies. A pair of reports, the 1964 BOB study and the 1966 survey of public land permittees, was designed to move the policy debate in the direction of an economically rational grazing fee formula based on fair market value and were relied upon heavily by the authors of the USDA/DI task force in their proposed fee increase of 1968 (Backiel and Rogge 1985).

Since that time, USDA/DI researchers have conducted comprehensive studies in 1977 and again in 1985, 1992, and 1993 to assess range management costs and to evaluate fee alternatives other than the PRIA-based formula (Backiel and Rogge 1985; Cody 1993). These studies, along with a series of reports issued by the U.S. General Accounting Office (GAO) over the past fifteen years, have frequently been cited by members of the grazing reform coalition in congressional hearings as evidence justifying the need for policy change (U.S. House of Representatives 1991). Indeed, many of the proposals contained within Secretary Babbitt's *Rangeland Reform '94* report were drawn from a 1993 study, *Incentive-Based Grazing Fee System* (U.S. Departments of Agriculture and Interior BLM 1993). While the technical materials were clearly aimed at policy brokers, reform advocates sought to attract media attention through the use of colorful metaphors or catchy phrases such as "cow free in ninety-three" or "welfare cowboys."

Not surprisingly, members of the pro-grazing coalition were prepared to respond on both fronts. To the technical arguments put forward by reform advocates, spokespersons for the livestock industry argued in a Senate hearing that allegations of undue subsidies were flawed because of a failure to consider key differences in privately owned ranches and those which operate on a combination of public and private lands. This was bolstered by testimony from consultants brought in by western legislators to challenge the methodology used by GAO in reaching conclusions about the need for reform (U.S. Senate Committee 1992). Moreover, status quo advocates were also ready to use public relations arguments of their own, suggesting that the net result of grazing policy changes would be the conversion of healthy rangelands to "condos" and "latte bars." Another phrase used repeatedly in testimony by a variety of groups was the need "to preserve the western way of life" (Donahue 1999, 268–72).

A glance at the visibility of grazing policy issues within the media reveals considerable variation between 1960 and 1993. The annual number of articles as measured by a content analysis of *Reader's Guide* under the topics "grazing fees" or "grazing on public lands" was typically quite low, except for a couple of spikes occurring in 1981 (the height of the Sagebrush Rebellion) when sixteen stories were published and a half-dozen years with five or six articles published (Davis and Ellison 1996). An updated content analysis of this source showed that interest was bolstered once more in 1995 (ten articles) when Interior Secretary Babbitt revealed the details of his rangeland reform program. Thereafter, grazing policy virtually disappeared from view as a story line. Under these conditions, the task of successfully redefining grazing policy issues is decidedly uphill—only the emergence of a major focusing event is likely to spark the interest of most media outlets other than trade journals.

VENUE SHOPPING

While changes in policy image represent an important precondition for amending existing policies or formulating new ones, a dominant policy subsystem with key supporters in positions of authority makes it exceedingly difficult for policy change advocates to obtain their goals in a legislative setting. This was the situation confronting supporters of grazing fee increases in the 1970s after Congress imposed four consecutive moratoria on proposals to move fees closer to fair market value. A state of gridlock for a given policy topic will often lead to a search for a more favorable decision-making venue; that is, some goals that are unattainable within a sharply divided legislative process can be realized through alternative institutional arrangements. For federal grazing programs, the principal alternative for advocates of change is the federal courts.

Access to the federal courts as a strategic option for environmental groups was made possible by the passage of several laws by Congress in the 1960s and 1970s such as the Wilderness Act, NEPA, and FLPMA, among others, that incorporated citizen participation requirements allowing lawsuits. A particularly important example of how NEPA was used to affect the administration of federal grazing programs is exemplified by the case of *NRDC v. Morton* (1973), discussed in an earlier section, where environmentalists successfully challenged BLM's use of an area-wide EIS in a minimalist effort to meet NEPA requirements. The short-term effect of Judge Flannery's decision was to change BLM's administrative practices, requiring site-specific EISs for all resource management plans. This raised questions about agency authority and resource commitments that could not be resolved by the court; hence, Congress took action in 1976 with the enactment of FLPMA. Other laws that have been frequently utilized by environmental groups to obtain industry or agency compliance with environmental quality requirements include the Clean Water Act, the National Forest Management Act, and the Endangered Species Act (ESA).

Livestock groups have not been able to achieve the same level of success in meeting their policy goals within the federal courts as within Congress. But they too have options. Litigation has been utilized in an effort to restrict the ability of federal land management agencies' discretion in the issuance, modification, or denial of grazing permits generally as well as in such specific management actions as reducing the number of livestock to improve rangeland health. One legal approach that was more commonly utilized from the 1980s to the present is based on the "takings clause" from the Fifth Amendment to the U.S. Constitution, which prohibits government actions that unduly restrict private property rights without providing just compensation. Ranchers have contended that a permit constitutes a "property right" since it typically increases the monetary value of ranch properties adjacent to federal lands (Cody and Baldwin, 1998).

How have grazing policy advocates and would-be reformers fared in the courts? I scanned federal district court cases within the Lexis-Nexis database from 1990 through 2003 for all cases involving disputes over grazing permits involving the Forest Service or BLM. A total of twenty-seven cases were identified and evaluated. Eleven were initiated by environmental groups on the basis of NEPA or the ESA; for example, more recent cases involved successful efforts by Forest Guardians and the Southwest Center for Biological Diversity to block the issuance of grazing permits by the Forest Service because agency officials had failed to consult with the U.S. Fish and Wildlife Service about the effects of livestock grazing on threatened or endangered species habitat. Six cases were initiated by firms representing livestock interests, using property rights or "takings" as the primary legal argument, but none of these lawsuits were successful. Remaining cases dealt with attempts by individual ranchers to overturn decisions by BLM or Forest Service officials to deny, revoke, or modify permits, basing these cases on such legal rationales as the failure to give ample notice before action was taken or the charge that administrators had exceeded their legal authority to undertake disciplinary actions of this magnitude. On these grazing permit cases, courts have generally upheld the application of environmental laws to resource management decisions, rejected industry claims that grazing permits constituted a legally defensible property right, and deferred to agency judgment on questions involving the alleged abuse of discretionary authority.

Grazing cases rarely involve points of law that are sufficiently critical to warrant a hearing by the U.S. Supreme Court. An exception is the landmark case of *Public Lands Council v. Babbitt* (2000), a case that challenged the constitutionality of several regulations forming the basis of Secretary Babbitt's rangeland reform package unveiled in 1995. In particular, Public Lands Council attorneys took issue with the BLM definition of "grazing preference," which referred to rangeland forage allocated on the basis of land-use plans rather than seniority and historic patterns of use. Other major concerns included regulations allowing a grazing permit to be issued to organizations for conservation purposes (that is, no grazing) rather than the continuation of livestock grazing, a definition allowing permits to be issued to people "engaged in the livestock business" rather than "stock owners" (a more inclusive phrase), and a rule affirming that BLM shall retain title to permanent range improvements made upon federal lands by permittees unless specified otherwise in a cooperative agreement.

Because the U.S. District Court in Cheyenne, Wyoming, and the 10th Circuit Court of Appeals had differing interpretations on three of the four regulations, the stage was set for an appeal to the U.S. Supreme Court. Both courts ruled that the regulation allowing permit holders to substitute conservation or non-use of range resources for livestock grazing was invalid, a decision that Secretary Babbitt chose not to contest in the higher court. The remaining issues were resolved by the U.S. Supreme Court in *Public Lands Council v. Babbitt* (2000). In a rare unanimous decision, the justices decided to uphold the remaining regulations, thereby affirming the circuit court decision. The immediate public policy impact was to bring closure to the long simmering debate over the property rights issue associated with DOI's administration of grazing permits. The livestock industry was also disappointed with the decision allowing the federal government to retain ownership of range improvement structures made by ranchers while environmentalists were generally displeased with the demise of the rule allowing conservation as a legitimate permit use.

CONCLUSIONS

Federal grazing programs rank quite low among environmental policy issues characterized as ripe for significant policy change. Programs lack visibility within the media except for occasional acts of political protest or major administrative decisions made by DOI or Forest Service officials. Moreover, grazing programs are geographically limited to the western United States, affect a relatively small number of people and involve the use of land resources with less political appeal than national forests or national parks. Thus, it has become difficult for change advocates to get the media or policymakers to pay attention to the issue, quite apart from the task of creating a more negative political image. The grazing policy subsystem also benefits from a de facto policy monopoly that allows legislators chairing the House Resources Committee and the Senate Energy and Natural Resources Committee to control the agenda, aided, in part, by the fact that half the membership of both committees typically represents western districts or states. The pro-grazing coalition has succeeded in preventing major policy shifts on grazing fee issues, a top priority for livestock operators.

Range reform advocates have nevertheless been able to build a political base with sufficient clout to become a player to be reckoned with in the policymaking process. They have done so by identifying officials within more favorable policymaking venues willing to consider their programmatic concerns. For example, environmental groups succeeded in using the federal courts to not only compel administrative changes within BLM in the *NRDC v. Morton* case but to use that decision as a catalyst for the attainment of policy goals within the legislative process. Organizations representing ranchers are equally adept at venue shifts. A common reaction to losses in federal court for industry groups is to overturn the decision in Congress through the attachment of policy riders to appropriations bills. A different route was taken by organizations still smarting over the judicial outcome in *Public Lands Council v. Babbitt.* The new venue of choice is the executive branch within the current Bush administration. DOI Secretary Gale Norton recently proposed a new regulation effectively reversing

Clinton-era rules dealing with government ownership of improvements made on federal rangelands by permit-holding ranchers.

What does this issue tell us about policy change and the punctuated equilibrium model? Federal grazing programs remind us that there are low-stakes programs that offer apt characterizations of dominant subsystems and distributive policymaking. This is especially challenging for advocates of change since the structure of decisional bias is difficult to crack and the ability to redefine program issues is limited by indifferent media sources. Under these conditions, it is essential for analysts to recognize the importance of smaller-scale non-legislative policy change, including regulatory shifts, court cases, program decentralization leading to the empowerment of state and local policy actors, and courses of actions recommended under the auspices of collaborative decision-making arrangements.

What would it take for fundamental policy changes to occur within the federal grazing policy arena? One possibility raised by William Brock is that slow-moving demographic shifts in the interior western states might transform the politics of grazing through urban growth patterns that raise the importance of land for the construction of new residential subdivisions at the expense of land uses that are less economically rational—for example, livestock grazing. For example, DOI officials recently approved the sale of BLM lands to the City of Las Vegas, Nevada, for residential expansion purposes. Moreover, new residents within Las Vegas and other western cities are more likely to favor using nearby public lands for recreation than for traditional uses such as grazing, mining, logging, or energy development. However, given the prevalence of pro-grazing forces in positions of authority, it remains unlikely that these changes alone could tilt the political status quo without additional preconditions such as the breakup of the policy monopoly, the election of pro-change candidates to Congress and the presidency, the emergence of a well-positioned policy entrepreneur to push for change, and a crisis or focusing event that raises the visibility of grazing policy issues. Taken together, that is a very tall order.

References

Acheson, James. 1992. Capturing the commons: Legal and illegal strategies. In *The political economy of custom and culture,* ed. Anderson and Simmons. Lanham: Rowman and Littlefield Publishers.

Agliardi, Elettra. 1998. *Positive feedback economics.* London: MacMillan.

Alliance of Automobile Manufacturers. 2000. *Vehicle manufacturers call for sulfur-free fuels.* http://www.autoalliance.org/pressreleases/pr042700.htm

Alston, Lee. 1996. *Empirical studies in institutional change,* ed. Eggertson and North. Cambridge: Cambridge University Press.

Alston, Lee, and B. Mueller. 2002. *Property rights, violence and the state.* Institute for Behavioral Studies. Boulder: University of Colorado.

Alston, Richard. 1984. Organizational values and political power: Review article. *Journal of Forestry* 82 (June): 374.

Alverson, Robert. 2000. Fishing vessel owner's association. Testimony to the U.S. Senate, Committee on Commerce, Subcommittee on Oceans and Fisheries, 18 January.

Amaro de Matos, J., and J. Perez. 1991. Fluctuations in the Curie-Weiss version of the random field Ising model. *Journal of Statistical Physics* 62:587–608.

American Automobile Manufacturers Association. 1997. *Automobile Facts and Figures.* Washington, D.C.: AAMA.

American Forest and Paper Association. 1993. *American Forest and Paper Association: Representing a vital national industry.* Washington, D.C.

American Petroleum Institute. 2000. *Reducing sulfur in gasoline.* http://lobby.la.psu.edu/024_ Low-Sulfur_Gasoline/Organizational_Statements/American_Petroleum_Institute/ API_Reducing_Sulfur_in_Gasoline.HTM (accessed September 28, 2000; page now discontinued); http://www.api.org/consume/reducesulfur.htm.

Anderson, S., A. de Palma, and J. Thisse. 1992. *Discrete choice theory of product differentiation.* Cambridge: MIT Press.

Anderson, Terry, and Peter Hill. 1975. The evolution of property rights: A study of the American West. *Journal of Law and Economics* 18 (1): 163–79.

Anderson, Terry, and Donald Leal. 1991. *Free market environmentalism.* San Francisco: RIPP.

Ansolabehere, Stephen, and John Deutch. 2003. *The future of nuclear power.* Cambridge: MIT Press.

Arnason, Ragnar. 1997. Property rights as an organizational framework in fisheries: The case of six fishing nations. In *Taking ownership: Property rights and fisheries management on the Atlantic coast,* ed. B. L. Crowley. Halifax: Atlantic Institute for Market Studies.

Arnason, Ragnar, and H. Gissurarson, eds. 1999. *Individual transferable quotas in theory and practice.* Reykjavik: University of Iceland Press.

Arnold, Douglas. 1990. *The logic of congressional action.* New Haven: Yale University Press.

Arthur, W. Brian, S. Durlauf, and D. Lane. 1997. *The economy as an evolving complex system.* Reading: Addison-Wesley.

Auerbach, Alan, and Laurence Kotlikoff. 1995. *Macroeconomics: An integrated approach.* Cincinnati: South-Western College Publishing.

Austin, Duncan, et al. 2003. *Changing drivers: The impact of climate change on competitiveness and value creation in the automotive industry.* Washington, D.C.: World Resources Institute.

Axelrod, Robert. 1984. *The evolution of cooperation.* New York: Basic Books.

———. 1997. *The complexity of cooperation: Agent-based models of competition and collaboration.* Princeton: Princeton University Press.

Babbitt, Bruce. 1994a. Remarks to the Society of Range Management. *Land and Water Law Review* 29 (2).

———. 1994b. The Endangered Species Act and "takings": A call for innovation within the terms of the act. *Environmental Law* 24 (2): 355–67.

Babiker, Mustafa, Gilbert Metcalf, and John Reilly. 2000. *Tax distortions and global climate policy.* MIT Joint Program on the Science and Policy of Global Change. Cambridge, Massachusetts.

Backiel, Adela, and Lee Ann Rogge. 1985. Federal grazing fees administered by the Bureau of Land Management and the Forest Service. *Congressional Research Service,* 21 February. Washington, D.C.

Bak, Per. 1996. *How nature works.* New York: Springer-Verlag.

Baltimore, Chris. 2003. U.S. EPA says it won't regulate CO_2 emissions from autos. *Environmental News Network.* http://www.enn.com/news/2003–08–29/s7886asp (page now discontinued).

Barrett, Scott. 2003. *Environment and statecraft: The strategy of environmental treaty-making.* New York: Oxford University Press.

Baumgartner, Frank. 2003. Punctuated equilibrium models of policy change and stability. Discussion paper, Department of Political Science, Pennsylvania State University.

Baumgartner, Frank, and Bryan Jones. 1991. Agenda dynamics and policy subsystems. *Journal of Politics* 53 (4): 1044–74.

———. 1993. *Agendas and instability in American politics.* Chicago: University of Chicago Press.

———, eds. 2002. *Policy dynamics.* Chicago: University of Chicago Press.

Baumgartner, Frank, Bryan Jones, and Michael MacLeod. 2000. The evolution of legislative jurisdictions. *Journal of Politics* 62 (2): 321–49.

Baumgartner, Frank, and Beth Leech. 1998. *Basic interests: The importance of groups in politics and in political science.* Princeton: Princeton University Press.

Bay Institute of San Francisco. 2001. *The First Annual State of the Environmental Water Account Report.* September. http://www.bay.org.

Bayer, P., and C. Timmins. 2001. Identifying social interactions in endogenous sorting models. Discussion paper, Yale University.

Becker, Gary. 1992. A note on restaurant pricing and other examples of social influences on price. *Journal of Political Economy* 99 (5): 1109–16.

Begley, Sharon. 1993. The birds and the trees: Clinton convenes a summit on the spotted owl. *Newsweek,* 5 April, 53–54.

Behr, Peter. 2003. Senate rejects tougher fuel economy standard. *Washington Post.* 30 July, sec. E, p. 1.

Bell, Frederick. 1972. Technological externalities and common property resources: A study of the U.S. northern lobster fishery. *Journal of Political Economy* 80:148–58.

Benedick, Richard. 1998. *Ozone diplomacy: New directions in safeguarding the planet.* Cambridge: Harvard University Press.

Benford, Robert, and David Snow. 2000. Framing processes and social movements: An overview and an assessment. *Annual Review of Sociology* 26:611–39.

Benke, Richard. 2003. Proposed grazing rules will enhance ranchers' flexibility, Norton maintains. *Fort Collins Coloradoan.* 6 December.

Berry, Jeffrey M. 1999. *The new liberalism: The rising power of citizen groups.* Washington, D.C.: The Brookings Institution.

Berry, Jerry M. 1984. *The interest group society.* Boston: Little, Brown & Co.

Bewley, Truman. 1986. Knightian decision theory: Part 1, Cowles Foundation Discussion Paper. No. 897. Yale University.

Bikhchandani, Sushil, David Hirshleifer, and Ivo Welch. 1992. A theory of fads, fashion, custom and cultural change as informational cascades. *Journal of Political Economy.* 100 (5): 992–1026.

Blatter, Joachim, Helen Ingram, and Suzanne Levesque. 2001. Expanding perspectives on transboundary water. In *Reflections on water,* ed. Blatter and Ingram. Cambridge: MIT Press.

Bohi, Douglas, and William Quandt. 1984. *Energy security in the 1980s: Economic and political perspective.* Washington, D.C.: The Brookings Institution.

Borman, Michael, and Douglas Johnson. 1990. Evolution of Grazing and Land Tenure Policies on Public Lands. *Rangelands* 12 (August).

Bosso, Christopher. 1987. *Pesticides and politics.* Pittsburgh: University of Pittsburgh Press.

Bradsher, Keith. 2002. *High and mighty: SUVs—the world's most dangerous vehicles and how they got that way.* New York: Public Affairs.

Brock, William. 1993. Pathways to randomness in the economy: Emergent nonlinearity and chaos in economics and finance. *Estudios Economicos* 8 (1): 3–55.

———. 2001. Economics for ecologists: A reader's guide," *SSRI Working Paper.* http://www.ssc.wisc.edu/~wbrock.

Brock, William, and Steven Durlauf. 1999. A formal model of theory choice in science. *Economic Theory* 14:113–30.

———. 2001a. Discrete choice with social interactions. *Review of Economic Studies* 68: 235–60.

———. 2001b. Interactions-based models. In *Handbook of Econometrics V,* ed. Heckman and Leamer. Amsterdam: North-Holland.

———. 2002. A multinomial choice model of neighborhood effects. *American Economic Review* 92 (2): 298–303.

Brock, William, Steven Durlauf, and Kenneth West. 2003. Policy evaluation in uncertain economic environments. *Brookings Institution Papers on Economic Activity* (1): 235–322.

Brock, William, and Scott Taylor. 2003. Economic growth and the environment: Matching the stylized facts. *SSRI Working Paper.* http://www.ssc.wisc.edu/~wbrock.

Brown, Courtney. 1994. Politics and the environment: Nonlinear instabilities dominate. *American Political Science Review* 88:293–303.

———. 1995. *Serpents in the sand.* Ann Arbor: University of Michigan Press.

Brown, Lee, and Helen Ingram. 1987. *Water and poverty in the Southwest.* Tucson: University of Arizona Press.

Browne, William. 1988. *Private interests, public policy and American agriculture.* Lawrence: University of Kansas Press.

———. 1995. *Cultivating Congress: Constituents, issues and interests in agricultural policymaking.* Lawrence: University of Kansas Press.

Bryner, Gary. 1998. *U.S. land and natural resources policy.* Westport: Greenwood Press.

Bryson, John, et al. 1996. Critical incidents and emergent issues in managing large-scale change. In *The State of Public Management,* ed. D. Kettl and H. B. Milward. Baltimore: Johns Hopkins University Press.

Busby, Josh, and Alexander Ochs. 2003. From Mars and Venus down to earth: Understanding the transatlantic climate divide. In *Climate policy for the 21st century: Meeting the long-term challenge of global warming,* ed. David Michel. Washington, D.C.: Center for Transatlantic Relations.

Business Daily Update. 2003. China's energy demand set to double by 2020. http://www.wbcsd.org/includes/getTarget.asp?type=DocDet&id=3114 (page now discontinued).

Cahn, Mathew. 1995. *Environmental deceptions: The tension between liberalism and environmental policymaking in the United States.* New York: State University of New York Press.

Caldwell, Lynton, Charles Wilkinson, and Margaret Shannon. 1994. Making ecosystem policy: Three decades of change. *Journal of Forestry* 92 (4): 7–11.

California Bay-Delta Environmental Program. 2001. *First Annual EWA Science Review Panel Report.* December. http://www.calfed.ca.gov (site now discontinued).

California Department of Water Resources. 2002. *Information to Parties Interested in Making Water Available to the Environmental Water Account or the State's 2002 Dry Year Water Purchase Program.* 8 March. http://www.calwater.ca.gov.

California Environmental Protection Agency. 2003a. *Climate change emissions regulation workshop: standards and economics. http://*www.arb.ca.gov/cc/ 091803workshop/091803attacha. pdf (page now discontinued).

———. 2003b. *Vehicle manufacturers, dealers and the state of California resolve litigation impacting zero emission vehicle regulation.* Exhibit C. http://www.arb.ca.gov/msprog/zevprog/ zevlitigation/exhibitc.pdf.

———. 2003c. ARB Modifies Zero Emission Vehicle Regulation. *Air Resources Board.* News Release. http://www.arb.ca.gov/ newsrel/nr042403.htm (page now discontinued).

Calthorpe, Peter. 1993. *The next American metropolis: Ecology, community, and the American dream.* New York: Princeton Architectural Press.

Carpenter, Daniel, Kevin Esterling, and David Lazer. 1998. The strength of weak ties in lobbying networks: Evidence from health care politics. *Journal of Theoretical Politics* 10:417–44.

———. 2004. Friends, brokers, and transitivity: Who informs whom in Washington politics. *Journal of Politics* 66 (1): 224–46.

Cashore, Benjamin. 1997a. Governing Forestry: Environmental Group Influence in British Columbia and the U.S. Pacific Northwest. Ph.D. diss., University of Toronto.

———. 1997b. A tale of two journeys: Environmentalism and the politics of forest policy change in the U.S. Pacific Northwest. Paper read at the University of British Columbia, Forest Economics and Policy Analysis Research Unit (FEPA) edited book conference, *An International Comparison of Forest Institutions,* 23 January.

———. 1999. U.S. Pacific Northwest. In *Forest policy: International case studies,* ed. Wilson et al., 47–80. Oxon: CABI Publications.

Cashore, Benjamin, and Graeme Auld. 2003. The British Columbia environmental forest policy record in comparative perspective. *Journal of Forestry* 101 (8): 42–r7.

Cater, Douglass. 1964. *Power in Washington.* New York: Random House.

Cawley, McGreggor. 1993. *Federal land, western anger: The sagebrush rebellion and environmental politics.* Lawrence: University of Kansas Press.

Chang, Ching-Cheng, Robert Mendelsohn, and Daigee Shaw. 2003. *Global warming and the Asian Pacific.* Northampton: Edward Elgar Publishing.

Chanin, Rachel. 2003. California's authority to regulate mobile source greenhouse gas emissions. *New York University Annual Survey of American Law* 58. http://web.lexis-nexis. com/universe/document?.

Christensen, Tom, and Kjell Arne Rovik. 1999. The ambiguity of appropriateness. In *Organizing political institutions: Essays for Johan P. Olsen,* ed. Egeberg and Laegreid, 159–80. Oslo: Scandinavian University Press.

Christy, F. 1978. *The costs of uncontrolled access in fisheries: Limited entry as a fishery management tool.* Seattle: University of Washington Press.

———. 1996. The death rattle of open access and the advent of property rights regimes in fisheries. *Marine Resource Economics* 11:287–304.

Clarke, Jeanne, and Daniel McCool. 1996. *Staking out the terrain.* Albany: SUNY Press.

Cody, Betsy. 1993. Grazing fees: A primer. *Congressional Research Service,* November. Washington, D.C.

Cody, Betsy, and Pamela Baldwin. 1998. Grazing fees and rangeland management. *Congressional Research Service,* December 4. Washington, D.C.

Coggins, George Cameron. 1983. The law of Public Rangeland Management IV: FLPMA, PRIA and the multiple use mandate. *Environmental Law* 14 (1).

Cohen, Linda, and R. Noll. 1991. *The technology pork barrel.* Washington, D.C.: The Brookings Institution.

Colander, D., ed. 1984. *Neoclassical political economy: The analysis of rent-seeking and dup activities.* Cambridge: Ballinger Publishing Company.

———, ed. 2000. *The Complexity vision and the teaching of economics.* Cheltenham: Edward Elgar.

Congressional Budget Office. December 2003. *The economic costs of fuel economy standards versus a gasoline tax.;* http://www.cbo.gov/showdoc.cfm?index=4917&sequence=0

Congressional Quarterly. 1975. Text of Ford's State of the Union address. *Congressional Quarterly Weekly Report,* 140–43.

———. 1979. *1978 Congressional Quarterly Almanac.* Washington, D.C.

Cowan, Robin, and Philip Gunby. 1996. Sprayed to death: Path dependence, lock-in, and pest control strategies. *Economic Journal* 106:521–42.

Crandall, Robert, H. Gruenspecht, T. Keeler, and L. Lavel. 1986. *Regulating the automobile.* Washington, D.C.: The Brookings Institution.

Crandall, Robert, et al. 2002. Fuel economy standards: Do they work? Do they kill? http://www.heritage.org/Research/EnergyandEnvironment/WM85.cfm

Crandall, Robert, and John Graham. 1989. The effect of fuel economy standards on automobile safety. *Journal of Law and Economics* 32:94–118.

Crenson, Matthew. 1987. The private stake in public goods: Overcoming the illogic of collective action. *Policy Sciences* 20:259–76.

Crutchfield, James. 1979. Marine resources: The economics of U.S. Ocean Policy. *American Economic Review.* 69:260–71.

Cubbage, Frederick, and Paul Ellefson. 1980. State forest practice laws: A major policy force unique to the natural resources community. *Natural Resources Lawyer* 13 (2): 463–8.

Cubbage, Frederick, Jay O'Laughlin, and Charles Bullock. 1993. *Forest resource policy.* New York: John Wiley and Sons.

Culhane, Paul. 1981. *Public lands politics.* Baltimore: Johns Hopkins University Press.

Dale, Reginald. 2003. European Union, properly construed. *Policy Review* 122.

Daugbjerg, Carsten. 1997. Policy networks and agricultural policy reforms: Explaining deregulation in Sweden and regulation in the European Community. *Agricultural Policy* 1.

Davis, Charles. 1995. Public lands policy change: Does Congress support it? *Journal of Forestry* (June): 8–11.

———, ed. 2001. *Western public lands and environmental politics.* 2nd ed. Boulder: Westview Press.

Davis, Charles, and Brian Ellison. 1996. Change on the range. *Society and Natural Resources* 9 (June).

Davis, Charles, and Sandra Davis. 1988. Analyzing change in public lands politics. *Policy Studies Journal* 17 (Fall).

———. 1988. Analyzing change in public lands policymaking: From subsystems to advocacy coalitions. *Policy Studies Journal* 17 (Fall): 3–24.

Davis, Jacquelyn. 2003. *Reluctant allies and competitive partners: U.S.-French relations at the breaking point?* Cambridge: Institute for Foreign Policy Analysis.

Davis, Sandra. 2001. Fighting over public lands: Interest groups, states, and the federal government. In *Western public lands and environmental politics,* 2nd ed., ed. Charles Davis. Boulder: Westview Press.

De Alessi, Michael. 1998. *Fishing for solutions.* London: Institute of Economic Affairs.

Deeg, Richard. 2001. Institutional change and the uses and limits of path dependency: The case of German finance. Discussion paper 01/6. Koln: Max Planck Institute fur Gesellschaftsforschung.

Demsetz, Harold. 1967. Towards a theory of property rights. *American Economic Review* 57(2): 347–59.

Dennen, R. Taylor. 1976. Cattlemen's associations and property rights in the American West. *Explorations in Economic History* 13:423–36.

DiMaggio, Paul, and W. Powell. 1991. Introduction to *The New Institutionalism in Organizational Analysis.* Chicago: University of Chicago Press.

Donahue, Debra. 1999. *The western range revisited.* Norman: University of Oklahoma Press.

Doremus, Holly. 1997. Listing decisions under the Endangered Species Act: Why better science isn't always better policy. *Washington University Law Quarterly* 75.

Doyle, Jack. 2000. *Taken for a ride: Detroit's big three and the politics of pollution.* New York: Four Walls Eight Windows.

Duffy, Robert. 1997. *Nuclear politics in America.* Lawrence: University Press of Kansas.

Dunn, James. 1998. *Driving forces: The automobile, its enemies and the politics of mobility.* Washington, D.C.: The Brookings Institution.

Durant, Robert. 1992. *The administrative presidency revisited: Public lands, the BLM and the Reagan administration.* Albany: SUNY Press.

Durlauf, Steven. 2002. On the empirics of social capital. *Economic Journal* 112 (483): 450–79.

Durlauf, Steven, and M. Fafchamps. 2003. Empirical studies of social capital: A critical survey. *SSRI Working Paper,* 12. http://www.ssc.wisc.edu/econ/archive.

Durlauf, Steven, and P. Young, eds. 2001. *Social dynamics.* Cambridge: MIT Press.

Edelman, Murray. 1985. *The symbolic uses of politics.* Chicago: University of Illinois Press.

Eggertson, Thrainn, 1990. *Economic behavior and institutions.* Cambridge: Cambridge University Press.

Eldredge, Niles. 1985. *Time frames: The evolution of punctuated equilibrium.* Princeton: Princeton University Press.

Eldredge, Niles, and Stephen Gould. 1972. Punctuated equilibria: An alternative to phyletic gradualism. In *Paleobiology,* ed. T. Schopf, 82–115. San Francisco: Freeman, Cooper.

Ellefson, Paul, and Antony Cheng. 1994. State forest practice programs: Regulation of private forestry comes of age. *Journal of Forestry* 92 (5): 34–7.

Ellefson, Paul, Antony Cheng, and Robert Moulton. 1995. *Regulation of private forestry practices by state governments.* Station Bulletin 605. St. Paul: University of Minnesota.

———. 1997a. State forest practice regulatory programs: An approach to implementing ecosystem management on private forest lands in the United States. *Environmental Management* 21 (3): 421–32.

———. 1997b. Regulatory programs and private forestry: State government actions to direct the use and management of forest ecosystems. *Society and Natural Resources* 10 (2): 195–209.

Ellefson, Paul, Robert Moulton, and M. Kilgore. 2002. An assessment of state agencies that affect forests. *Journal of Forestry* 100 (6): 35–41.

Ellis, R. S. 1985. *Entropy, large deviations, and statistical mechanics.* New York: Springer-Verlag.

Energy Future Coalition. 2004. About the coalition. http://www.energyfuturecoalition.org/preview.cfm?catID=2

Energy Futures, Inc. 2003. The clean fuels and electric vehicles report 15: 20.

Energy Information Administration. International energy outlook. 2002. Washington, D.C.: U.S. GPO. March.

Environmental Protection Information Center. 2002. Hundreds flock to Sacramento for public hearing: Board of forestry fails to ban old-growth logging. Press release. 12 January. http://www.wildcalifornia.org/press_releases/2000/pr000112.html (accessed May 10, 2002).

Euell, Elliott, and L. D. Kiel, 1999. *Nonlinear dynamics, complexity and public policy.* Commack: Nova Science Publishers.

European Environment Agency. 2001. *Late lessons from early warnings: The precautionary principle, 1896–2000.* Copenhagen.

EWA Science Review Board. 2003. Statement of a panel of stakeholders to the third annual Science Review Board, October.

Fairfax, Sally. 1984. Beyond the sagebrush rebellion: The BLM as neighbor and manager in the Western states. In *Western Public Lands,* ed. John Francis and Richard Ganzel. Totowa: Rowman and Allanheld.

Ferguson, Niall, and Laurence Kotlikoff. 2003. Going critical: American power and the consequences of fiscal overstretch. *The National Interest* 73 (Fall): 22–32.

Foss, Phillip. 1960. *Politics and grass: The administration of grazing on the public domain.* Seattle: University of Washington Press.

Francis, John. 1984. Environmental values, intergovernmental politics, and the Sagebrush Rebellion. In *Western Public Lands,* eds. John Francis and Richard Ganzel. Totowa: Rowman and Allanheld.

Francis, John, and Richard Ganzel, eds. 1984. *Western public lands.* Totowa: Rowman and Allanheld.

Frankel, David, and P. Young. 2000. Resolving indeterminancy in dynamic settings: The role of shocks. *Quarterly Journal of Economics* 115:285–304.

Frankel, Glenn. 2004. U.S. mulled seizing oil fields in 1973. *Washington Post.* 1 January.

Franklin, Jerry. 1988. Old growth: Its characteristics and its relationship to Pacific Northwest forests. Paper read at Old Growth Conference, 25 August, Corvallis, Oregon.

————. 1993. The fundamentals of ecosystem management with applications in the Pacific Northwest. In *Defining sustainable forestry*, eds. G. Aplet et al. Washington, D.C.: Island Press.

Freeman, J. Lieper. 1965. *The political process*, rev. ed. New York: Random House.

Friedman, David. 2003. A comprehensive approach to oil dependency and climate change. Presentation at AECS Workshop on Climate Change and Transportation, Washington, D.C.

Fullerton, David. 1993. California water policy: Adjusting to new realities. *California Water Reporter: Law and Policy* 9 (10).

Fulton, William, and Paul Shigley. 2003. Future's water is down on the farm: The agricultural sector will provide a key resource for continuing urban prosperity. *Los Angeles Times*. 9 February, sec. M, p. 2.

Gamson, William. 1975. *The strategy of social protest*. Homewood: Dorsey Press.

Gavious, Arieh, and S. Mizrahi. 2000. Information and common knowledge in collective action. *Economics and Politics* 12:297–319.

Genschel, Philipp. 1997. The dynamics of inertia: Institutional persistence and change in telecommunications and health care. *Governance* 10 (1): 43–66.

George, Alexander. 1979. Case studies and theory development: The method of structured, focused comparison. In *Diplomacy: New approaches in history, theory and policy*, ed. P. G. Lauren, 43–68. New York: Free Press.

Gersick, Connie. 1991. Revolutionary change theories: A multilevel exploration of the punctuated equilibrium paradigm. *Academy of Management Review* 16 (1): 10–36.

Gilmour, John. 1990. Bargaining between congress and the president: The bidding up phenomenon. Paper read at the annual meeting of the American Political Science Association.

Gilpin, Kenneth. 2003. S&P cuts Ford's debt rating to lowest investment grade. *New York Times*. 12 November.

Gitlin, Todd. 1987. *Years of hope, days of rage*. New York: Bantam Press.

Giuliano, Genevieve. 1999. Land use policy and transportation: Why we won't get there from here. Paper presented at the Conference on Policies for Fostering Sustainable Transportation Technologies, Monterey, California.

Gokhale, Jagadeesh, and Kent Smetters. 2003. *Fiscal and generational imbalances: New budget measure for new budget priorities*. Washington, D.C.: The American Enterprise Institute.

Goldstone, Jack. 1998. Initial conditions, general laws, path dependence, and explanation in historical sociology. *American Journal of Sociology* 104 (3): 829–45.

Gordon, H. Scott. 1954. The economic theory of a common-property resource: The fishery. *Journal of Political Economy* 62:124–42.

Gordon, Philip. 2003. Bridging the Atlantic divide. *Foreign Affairs* 82 (1): 70–83.

Gould, Stephen, and Niles Eldredge. 1972. Punctuated equilibria: An alternative to phyletic gradualism. In *Models in Paleobiology*, ed. Thomas Shopf, 82–115. San Francisco: Freeman, Cooper and Co.

————. 1977. Punctuated equilibria: The tempo and mode of evolution reconsidered. *Paleobiology* 3:115–51.

Graf, William. 1990. *Wilderness preservation and the sagebrush rebellions.* Lanham: Rowman and Littlefield.

Grafton, Quentin R., , D. Squires, and K. J. Fox. 2000. Private property and economic efficiency: A study of a common pool resource. *Journal of Law and Economics* 43:679–713.

Granovetter, Mark. 1973. The strength of weak ties. *American Journal of Sociology* 78:1360–80.

———. 1978. Threshold models of collective behavior. *American Journal of Sociology.* 83 (6): 1420–43.

Grant, Wyn. 1995. *Autos, smog, and pollution control: The politics of air quality management in California.* Aldershot: Edward Elgar.

Greene, David, Daniel Sperling, and Barry McNutt. 1998. *Transportation energy in the year 2020: A look ahead.* Transportation Research Board. Washington, D.C.

Gregg, Frank. 1989. Public land policy: controversial beginnings for the third century. In *Government and environmental politics: Essays on historical developments since World War Two,* ed. M. J. Lacey, 144–46. Washington, D.C.: The Woodrow Wilson Center Press and the Johns Hopkins University Press.

Griffith, Ernest. 1939. *The impasse of democracy.* New York: Harrison-Hilton Books.

Gross, Tom. 2003. The case for transportation energy diversity. Presentation and handout on behalf of the office of energy efficiency and renewable energy, U.S. Department of Energy, Michelin 2003 Challenge Bibendum. Sonoma, California.

Grossman, Gene, and E. Helpman. 2001. *Special interest politics.* Cambridge: MIT Press.

Gunderson, Lance, and C. Holling, eds. 2002. *Panarchy: Understanding transformation in human and natural systems.* Washington, D.C.: Island Press.

Haddock, Mark. 1995. *Forests on the line: Comparing the rules for logging in British Columbia and Washington state.* Vancouver and New York: Sierra Legal Defense Fund and the Natural Resources Defense Council.

Hakim, Danny. 2003a. California/motor city: Pollution fight turns from smog to global warming. *New York Times.* 22 October.

———. 2003b. Ford chairman, now confident of turnaround, expects a profit. *New York Times.* 27 November.

Hall, Peter. 1993. Policy paradigms, social learning and the state: The case of economic policy making in Britain. *Comparative Politics* 23 (3): 275.

Hamilton, Michael. 1987. Deregulation and federal land management in the 1980s. In *Federal Lands Policy,* ed. Phillip O. Foss. New York: Greenwood Press.

Hansen, James. 2004. Defusing the global warming time bomb. *Scientific American* (March): 290–303.

Hansen, Lars, and Thomas Sargent. 2003. Robust control and model uncertainty in macroeconomics. Departments of Economics, the University of Chicago and New York University.

Hartley, P. 1997. Conservation strategies for New Zealand. New Zealand Business Roundtable, The Terrace, Wellington, New Zealand.

Heclo, Hugh. 1978. Issue networks and the executive establishment. In *The New American Political System,* ed. Anthony King. Washington, D.C.: American Enterprise Institute.

Heller, Peter. 2003. *Who will pay? Coping with aging societies, climate change, and other long-term fiscal challenges.* Washington, D.C.: International Monetary Fund.

Herzberg, Roberta. 1986. Blocking coalitions and policy change. In *Congress and policy change,* eds. Wright, Rieselbach, and Dodd. New York: Agathon Press.

Higgs, Robert. 1982. Legally induced technical regression in the Washington salmon fishery. *Research in Economic History* 7:82–95.

Hirt, Paul. 1994. *A conspiracy of optimism.* Lincoln: University of Nebraska Press.

Hoberg, George. 1992. *Pluralism by design: Environmental policy and the American regulatory state.* New York: Praeger.

———. 1993a. From logroll to logjam: Structure, strategy, and influence in the old growth forest conflict. Paper read at annual meeting of the American Political Science Association, Washington, D.C.

———. 1993b. Regulating forestry: A comparison of institutions and policies in British Columbia and the U.S. Pacific Northwest. *Forest Economics and Policy Analysis Research Unit.* University of British Columbia.

———. 1997. From localism to legalism: The transformation of federal forest policy. In *Western public lands and environmental politics,* ed. Charles Davis. Boulder: Westview Press.

———. 2003a. Science, politics, and U.S. forest law: The battle over the Forest Service planning rule. *Resources for the Future.* Washington, D.C.

———. 2003b. The optimal choice of regulatory approach: Concepts and case studies from forestry. Paper read at annual meeting of the Law and Society Association, 5–8 June, at Pittsburgh, Pennsylvania.

Hoffert, Martin, et al. 2002. Advanced technology paths to global climate stability: Energy for a greenhouse planet. *Science* 298 (November): 981–87.

Hoffman, Peter, and Robert Rose. 2003. Toward tomorrow's energy: Speeding the commercial use of fuel cells and hydrogen. *Progressive Policy Institute Report.* 22 January. http://www.ppionline.org.

Hogwood, Brian, and Guy Peters. 1983. *Policy dynamics.* New York: St. Martin's Press.

Hojnacki, Marie, and Frank Baumgartner. 2003. *Symbols and advocacy.* Paper read at Midwest Political Science Association Meeting, 3–6 April, Chicago, Illinois.

Homer-Dixon, Thomas. 2002. Environmental changes as causes of acute conflict. In *Conflict after the cold war: Arguments on causes of war and peace,* ed. Richard Betts. New York: Longman.

Humphrey, Hubert. 1976. In the courts, or in the woods? *American Forests* 82 (1): 14–15, 62.

Hungerford, Andrea. 1994. Changing the management of public land forests: The role of the spotted owl injunctions. *Environmental Law* 24:1395–1434.

Huntington, Samuel. 1996. *The clash of civilizations and the remaking of world order.* New York: Simon and Schuster.

Huntsman, Archibald G. 1949. *Research on the use and increase of fish stocks.* Proceedings of the United Nations Scientific Conference on the Conservation and Utilization of Resources, Lake Success, New York.

Immergut, Ellen. 1990. Institutions, veto points, and policy results: A comparative analysis of health care. *Journal of Public Policy* 10 (4): 391–416.

———. 1992. The rules of the game: The logic of health policy-making in France, Switzerland, and Sweden. In *Structuring politics: Historical institutionalism in comparative analysis,* ed. Steinmo, Thelen, and Longstreth, 57–89. Cambridge: Cambridge University Press.

Independent Multidisciplinary Science Team. 1999. Recovery of wild salmonoids in Western Oregon forests: Technical report. http://www.fsl.orst.edu/imst/reports/forestry.html

Ingram, Helen. 1990. *Water policy: Continuity and change.* Albuquerque: University of New Mexico Press.

International Council for the Exploration of the Sea. 1997. *Report of the study group on the management performance of individual quota (ITQ) systems.* Copenhagen, Denmark.

Interwies, Eduard, et al. 2002. Ökosteuer—Stand der Diskussion und der Gesetzgebung in Deutschland, auf der EU-Ebene und in den anderen europaischen Staaten. *Ecologic* (May).

Jenkins-Smith, Hank, Gilbert St. Clair, and Brian Woods. 1991. Explaining change in policy subsystems. *American Journal of Political Science* (November).

Jensen, Cheryl. 2004. Growth trend: Big pickups. *New York Times.* 18 January, sec. 12, p. 18.

Johnston, James. 1997. *Driving America: Your car, your government, your choice.* Washington, D.C.: American Enterprise Institute.

Johnson, Ronald, and Gary Libecap. 1995. Contracting problems and regulation: The case of the fishery. *American Economic Review* 12:1005–22.

Jones, Bryan. 2001. *Politics and the architecture of choice: Bounded rationality and governance.* Chicago: University of Chicago Press.

Jones, Bryan, and Frank Baumgartner. 2005. *The evolution of American politics.* Forthcoming.

Jones, Bryan D., Frank R. Baumgartner, and James L. True. 1998. Policy Punctuations: U.S. Budget Authority, 1947&45; 95. *Journal of Politics* 60:1–33.

Jones, Bryan, Tracy Sulkin, and Heather Larsen. 2003. Policy punctuations in American political institutions. *American Political Science Review* 97 (1): 151–69.

Jones, Charles, and Randall Strahan. 1985. The effect of energy politics on congressional and executive organization in the 1970s. *Legislative Studies Quarterly* 10 (May).

Jones, Philip, and John Cullis. 2003. Key Parameters in policy design: The case of intrinsic motivation. *Journal of Social Policy* 32 (4): 527–47.

Kagan, Robert. 2002. Power and Weakness. *Policy Review* 113 (June/July).

Kahn, Helen. 1981. Thirty-four auto regulations shot down. *Automotive News* 2.

Kareiva, Peter, et al. 2000. Using science in habitat conservation plans. National Center for Ecological Analysis and Synthesis, American Institute of Biological Sciences NCEAS HCP working group. University of California, Santa Barbara.

Kaufman, Herbert. 1967. *The forest ranger: A study in administrative behavior.* Baltimore: Johns Hopkins University Press.

———. 1976. *Are government organizations immortal?* Washington, D.C.: The Brookings Institution.

Keeler, Andy. 2004. An evaluation of state carbon dioxide reduction policies. *Climate Policy Center Working Paper* (January).

Kempton, Willett, James S. Boster, and Jennifer A. Hartley. 1999. *Environmental values in American culture.* Cambridge: MIT Press.

Kenworthy, Tom. 1994. For love of the land. *Washington Post National Weekly Edition.* February 21–27.

Kerry, John. 2003. John Kerry's comprehensive vision for a cleaner environment, a stronger economy, healthier communities. http://www.johnkerry.com/pdf/longenviro.pdf (site now discontinued).

Kiely, Kathy. 2003. Former adversaries combine their energies. *USA Today.* www.usatoday.com/news/nation/2003–09–93-energies-usat_x.htm (page now discontinued).

King, Gary, Robert Keohane, and Sidney Verba. 1994. *Designing social inquiry: scientific inference in qualitative research.* Princeton: Princeton University Press.

Kingdon, John. 1984. *Agendas, alternatives and public policies.* Boston: Little, Brown.

———. 1995. *Agendas, alternatives and public policy.* 2nd ed. New York: Harper Collins.

Kirman, Alan. 1993. Ants, rationality, and recruitment. *Quarterly Journal of Economics* (February): 137–56.

Kline, D. 2001. Positive feedback, lock-in and environmental policy. *Policy Sciences.* 34:95–107.

Klyza, Christopher McGory. 1996. *Who controls public lands?* Chapel Hill: University of North Carolina Press.

Knickerbocker, Brad. 1993. Babbitt wades into the debate on western land. *Christian Science Monitor,* 4 May.

Knill, Christoph, and Andrea Lenschow. 2001. Seek and ye shall find! Linking different perspectives on institutional change. *Comparative Political Studies.* 34 (2): 187–215.

Knoll, Bob. 2004. From the birthplace of Godzilla, Japan's first monster truck. *New York Times.* 18 January, sec.12, p.1.

Kohm, Kathryn, and Jerry Franklin. 1997. *Creating a forestry for the 21st century: The science of ecosystem management.* Washington, D.C.: Island Press.

Kugler, Jacek, and Douglas Lemke. 2003. The power transition research program: Assessing theoretical and empirical advances. In *Handbook of War Studies II,* ed. Manus Midlarsky. Ann Arbor: University of Michigan Press.

Kuran, Timur. 1989. Sparks and prairie fires: A theory of unanticipated political revolution. *Public Choice* 61:41–74.

———. 1991. Now out of never: The element of surprise in the East European revolution of 1989. *World Politics.* 44:7–48.

Lach, Denise, Steve Rayner, and Helen Ingram. Taming the waters: Strategies to domesticate the wicked problems of water resource management. *International Journal of Water.* Forthcoming.

Ladd, Everett, and Karlyn Bowman. 1995. *Attitudes toward the environment: Twenty-five years after Earth Day.* Washington, D.C.: The American Enterprise Institute.

Lee, Jennifer, and Andrew Revkin. 2003. Senate defeats climate bill but proponents see silver lining. *New York Times.* 31 October.

Lee, Kai. 1993. *Compass and gyroscope: Integrating science and politics for the environment.* Washington, D.C.: Island Press.

Leman, C. K. 1988. A forest on institutions: Patterns of choice on North American timberlands. In *Land rites and wrongs: The management, regulation and use of land in Canada and the United States,* ed. Elliot Feldman and Michael Goldberg. Cambridge: Lincoln Institute of Land Policy.

Libby, Ronald T. 1998. *Eco-wars: Political campaigns and social movements.* New York: Columbia University Press.

Libecap, Gary. 1978. Economic variables and the development of the law: The case of western mineral rights. *Journal of Economic History* 38 (2): 399–458.

Lieberman, Joseph. 2003. U.S. Senate. Summary of Lieberman/McCain Draft Proposal on Climate Change.

Lieberman, Robert. 2002. Ideas, institutions and political order: Explaining political change. *American Political Science Review* 96 (4): 697–712.

Liebowitz, Stanley J., and Stephen Margolis. 1995. Path dependence, lock-in, and history. *Journal of Law, Economics and Organization* 11 (1): 205–25.

Lindblom, Charles, and E. Woodhouse. 1980. The policymaking process. Englewood Cliffs, N.J.: Prentice-Hall.

Lindner, Johannes. 2003. Institutional stability and change: Two sides of the same coin. *Journal of European Public Policy* 10 (6): 912–35.

Lohmann, Susanne. 1996. Demosclerosis, or special interests "R" us: An information rationale for political gridlock. In *The political economy of conflict and appropriation,* ed. Garfinkel and Skaperdas. Cambridge: Cambridge University Press.

Loughlin, John. 2004. The "transformation" of governance: New directions in policy and politics. *Australian Journal of Politics and History* 50 (1): 8–22.

Lowi, Theodore. 1964. American business, public policy, case studies and political theory. *World Politics* 16 (June).

———. 1969. *The end of liberalism.* New York: Norton.

Lowry, William. 2003. *Dam politics: Restoring America's rivers.* Washington, D.C.: Georgetown University Press.

Maas, Arthur. 1951. *Muddy waters: The army engineers and the nation's rivers.* Cambridge: Harvard University Press.

MacLeod, Michael. 2002. The logic of positive feedback: telecommunications policy through the creation, maintenance, and destruction of a regulated monopoly. In *Policy dynamics,* ed. Baumgartner and Jones. Chicago: University of Chicago Press.

Magee, S., William Brock, and L. Young. 1989. *Black hole tariffs and endogenous policy theory: Political economy in general equilibrium.* Cambridge: Cambridge University Press.

Mahoney, James. 2000. Path dependence in historical sociology. *Theory and Society* 29 (4): 507–48.

March, James, and Johan Olsen. 1989. *Rediscovering institutions: The organizational basis of politics.* New York: The Free Press.

Mashaw, Jerry, and David Harfst. 1990. *The struggle for auto safety.* Cambridge: Harvard University Press.

Maynard, Micheline. 2003. *The end of Detroit: How the big three lost their grip on the American car market.* New York: Currency Doubleday.

McAdam, Douglas. 1982. *Political process and the development of black insurgency, 1930–1970.* Chicago: University of Chicago Press.

McAdam, Douglas, J. McCarthy, and M. Zald, eds. 1996. *Comparative perspectives on social movements*. Cambridge: Cambridge University Press.

McConnell, Grant. 1966. *Private power and American democracy*. New York: Knopf.

McCool, Daniel. 1987. *Command of the waters*. Berkeley: University of California Press.

———. 1990. Subgovernments as determinants of political viability. *Political Science Quarterly* 105 (Summer).

Mead, Walter Russell. 2003. Why do they hate us? Two books take aim at French anti-Americanism. *Foreign Affairs* 82 (3): 139–42.

Mearsheimer, John J. 1994–95. The False Promise of International Institutions. *International Security* 19 (3).

———. 2001. *The tragedy of great power politics*. New York: Norton & Company.

Melnick, Shep. 1985. The politics of partnership. *Public Administration Review* 45 (November).

Mendelsohn, Robert, and James E. Neumann, eds. 1999. *The impact of climate change on the United States economy*. Cambridge: Cambridge University Press.

Meyer, David, Valerie Jenness, and Helen Ingram, eds. 2005. *Routing the opposition: Social movement in public policy and democracy*. Minneapolis: University of Minnesota Press, forthcoming.

Meyer, David, and Sidney Tarrow. 1998. *The social movement society: Contentious politics for a new century*. Lanham: Rowman and Littlefield Publishers.

Michaels, Patrick. 2003. PowerPoint presentation. CATO Forum. 12 December.

Micklethwait, John, and A. Wooldridge. 2004. *The Right Nation: Conservative Power in America*. New York: Penguin Press.

Milgrom, Paul, and J. Roberts. 1992. *Economics, organization and management*. Englewood Cliffs, N.J.: Prentice-Hall.

Mintrom, Michael. 1997. Policy entrepreneurs and the diffusion of innovation. *American Journal of Political Science* 41 (November).

———. 2000. *Policy entrepreneurs and school choice*. Washington, D.C.: Georgetown University Press.

Mintrom, Michael, and S. Vergari. 1996. Advocacy coalitions, policy entrepreneurs and policy change. *Policy Studies Journal* 24:420–34.

MIT Laboratory for Energy and the Environment. 2003. Hydrogen fuel-cell vehicle won't reduce greenhouse gas emissions by 2020; Diesel and gasoline hybrids are a better bet, concludes an MIT study. News Release. http://lfee.mit.edu/features/ hydrogen_vehicles (page now discontinued).

Montgomery, David. 1992. Economics of Conservation. In *Technologies for a greenhouse-constrained society*, ed. Kuliasha, Zucker, and Ballew. Michigan: Lewis Publishers.

Morrill, Calvin. 1993. Institutional change through interstitial emergence: The growth of alternative dispute resolution in American law, 1965–1995. In *How institutions change*, ed. Powell and Jones. Chicago: University of Chicago Press.

Moyer, Bill. 2001. *Doing democracy*. British Columbia: New Society Publishers.

Müller, Friedemann. 2003a. Energiepolitische Neuordnung am Persischen Golf; Erweiterte U.S.-Handlungsspielräume. Berlin: Deutsches Institut für Internationale Politik und Sicherheit.

———. 2003b. *Kyoto-Protokoll vor dem Aus? Deutsches Institut für Internationale Politik und Sicherheit.* Berlin: Forschungsgruppe Globale Fragen. October.

National Academies. 2004. Hydrogen economy offers major opportunities but faces considerable hurdles. News release. http://www4.nationalacademies.org/news.nsf/isbn/0309091632?OpenDocument.

National Commission on Energy Policy. 2004. About the commission. http://www.energycommission.org/about.

National Intelligence Council. 2000. *Global trends 2015: A dialogue about the future with nongovernment experts.* National Foreign Intelligence Board with the Central Intelligence Agency, December.

National Research Council. 1998. *Striking a balance.* Washington, D.C.: National Academy Press.

———. 1999. *Sharing the fish: Toward a national policy on individual fishing quotas.* Ocean Studies Board. Washington, D.C.: National Academy Press.

———. 2002. *Effectiveness and impact of corporate average fuel economy (CAFE) standards.* Washington, D.C.: National Academy of Sciences.

Nawi, David, and Alf Brandt. 2002. CALFED Bay-Delta Program: From conflict to collaboration. Paper read at University of Miami Law School Conference on Adaptive Management, December.

Nelson, Robert. 1985. *NRDC v. Morton:* The role of judicial policy-making in public rangeland management. *Policy Studies Journal* 14 (December).

Newell, Richard, J. Sanchirico, and S. Kerr. 2002. Fishing quota markets. Discussion paper. Washington, D.C.: Resources for the Future.

Newman, Peter, and Jeffrey Kenworthy. 1999. *Sustainability and cities: Overcoming automobile dependence.* Washington, D.C.: Island Press.

Nivola, Pietro. 1986. *The politics of energy conservation.* Washington, D.C.: The Brookings Institution.

Nivola, Pietro, and Robert Crandall. 1995. *The extra mile: Rethinking energy policy for automotive transportation.* Washington, D.C.: The Brookings Institution.

Noecker, Robert, and Lynne Corn. 1997. The Red-cockaded Woodpecker: Federal protection and habitat conservation plans. Congressional Research Service. Washington, D.C.

Nordhaus, William. 1992. Lethal model 2: The limits to growth revisited. *Brookings Papers on Economic Activity* 2:1–59.

———. 2002. Prepublication version of *Modeling induced innovation in climate change policy.* Washington, D.C.: Resources for the Future.

Nordhaus, William, and Joseph Boyer. 2000. *Warming the world: Economic models of global warming.* Cambridge: MIT Press.

North, Douglass. 1990. *Institutional Change and Economic Performance.* Cambridge: Cambridge University Press.

North, Douglass, and Robert Thomas. 1970. An economic theory of the growth of the western world. *Economic History Review* 23 (1): 1–17.

Obermiller, Frederick. 1991. Elements of the 1991 federal grazing (fee) debate. Testimony presented to the U.S. House Committee on Agriculture in Burns, Oregon, August 19.

Olson, Mancur. 1965. *The logic of collective action: Public goods and the theory of groups.* Cambridge: Harvard University Press.

Oregon Natural Resources Council. 1993. Why ONRC doesn't (usually) do advisory committees. Portland, Oregon.

Orski, Kenneth. 2003. The end of the road for the electric vehicle. *Innovation Briefs* 14.

Ostrom, Elinor. 1990. *Governing the commons: The evolution of institutions for collective action.* Cambridge: Harvard University Press.

Ostrom, Elinor, R. Gardner, and J. Walker. 1994. *Rules, games, and common-pool resources.* Ann Arbor: University of Michigan Press.

Parry, Ian. 2002a. Is gasoline undertaxed in the United States? *Resources.* Summer: 28–33.

———. 2002b. *Adjusting carbon cost analyses to account for prior tax distortions.* Washington, D.C.: Resources for the Future.

———. 2002c. Are tradable emissions permits a good idea? *Americans for Equitable Climate Solutions* 33.

Pautzke, Clarence, and C. Oliver. 1997. Development of the individual fishing quota program for sablefish and halibut longline fisheries off Alaska. *North Pacific Fishery Management Council.* Presented to the National Research Council's Committee to Review Individual Fishing Quotas, 4 September. Anchorage, Alaska.

Pierce, John, et al. 2000. *Only a border apart? Political culture and public policy in Canada and the United States.* Lewiston: The Edwin Mellen Press.

Pierson, Paul. 2000. Increasing returns, path dependence, and the study of politics. *American Political Science Review* 94 (2): 251–268.

Porter, Richard. 1999. *Economics at the wheel: The costs of cars and drivers.* New York: Academic Press.

Portney, Paul, et al. 2003. The economics of fuel economy standards. *Journal of Economic Perspectives* 27 (4): 203–17.

Powell, Walter. 1991. Expanding the scope of institutional analysis. In *The new institutionalism in organizational analysis,* ed. Powell and DiMaggio, 183–233. Chicago: Chicago University Press.

Public Citizen. 2004. *California water: A primer.* http://www.citizen.org/california/water/articles.cfm?ID=13054

Rae, John. 1984. *The American automobile industry.* Boston: Twayne Publishers.

Rao, Hayagreeva, Calvin Morrill, and Mayer Zald. 2000. Power plays: How social movements and collective action create new organizational forms. *Research in Organizational Behavior* 22:237–81.

Rao, Hayagreeva. 1998. The construction of nonprofit consumer watchdog organizations. *American Journal of Sociology* 103:912–61.

Rathmell, Andrew, Theodore Karasik, and David Gompert. 2003. *A new Persian Gulf security system.* Santa Monica: RAND Corporation.

Rayner, Steven, et al. 2002. *The use of climate forecast information in decision-making processes.* Final Report, Office of Global Programs, National Oceanographic and Atmospheric Administration, 29.

Reisner, Marc. 1993. *Cadillac desert: The American West and its disappearing water.* New York: Penguin Books.

Repetto, Robert. 2001a. A natural experiment in fisheries management. *Marine Policy* 25:251–64.

———. 2001b. *Yes, Virginia, there is a double dividend.* The Tim Wirth Chair in Environmental Policy, Graduate School of Public Affairs. Denver: University of Colorado.

Repetto, Robert, and Duncan Austin. 1997. *The costs of climate protection: A guide for the perplexed.* Washington, D.C.: World Resources Institute.

Reuther, Alan. 2001. Statement on Reforming Corporate Average Fuel Economy (CAFE) Standards. U.S. Senate Committee on Commerce, Subcommittee on Science and Transportation. 6 December.

Revkin, Andrew. 2003. No crisis, no bill? At 1,200 pages, the energy plan weighs itself down. *New York Times.* 23 November, sec. 4, p. 3.

Rieke, Elizabeth Anne. 1966. The Bay-Delta Accord: A stride toward sustainability. *University of Colorado Law Review* 67:341.

Rieser, Alison. 1999. Prescription for the commons: Environmental scholarship and the fishing quota debate. *Harvard Environmental Law Review* 23:393–421.

Ripley, Randall, and Grace Franklin. 1987. *Congress, the bureaucracy and public policy.* 4th ed. Homewood: Dorsey Press.

Ris, Howard. 2003. Senate vote on McCain-Lieberman changes political climate on global warming. *Union of Concerned Scientists.* http://www.ucsusa.org/news/press_release.cfm?newsID=365 (page now discontinued).

Robertson, Dale. 1992. Policy directive on ecosystem management of the national forests and grasslands. U.S. Department of Agriculture, National Forest Service. Washington, D.C.

Robinson, Scott. 2004. Punctuated equilibrium, bureaucratization and budgetary changes in schools. *Policy Studies Journal* 32 (1): 25–40.

Rosser, J. Barkeley. 2000. *From catastrophe to chaos: A general theory of economic discontinuities.* 2nd ed. Boston: Kluwer Academic Publishers.

Rowland, Melanie. 1994. Bias undermines Forest Practices Board. *Seattle Times.* 15 July, B5.

Rowley, William. 1985. *U.S. Forest Service grazing and rangelands: A history.* College Station: Texas A&M University Press.

Saad, Lydia. 2003. Giving global warming the cold shoulder. *The Gallup Organization.* www.gallup.com.

Sabatier, Paul. 1988. An advocacy coalition framework of policy change and the role of policy oriented learning. *Policy Sciences* 21.

Sabatier, Paul, and H. Jenkins-Smith. 1993. *Policy change and learning: An advocacy coalition approach.* Boulder: Westview Press.

Scheffer, Marten, F. Westley, and William Brock. 2000. Socioeconomic mechanisms preventing optimum use of ecosystem services: An interdisciplinary theoretical analysis. *Ecosystems* 3:451–71.

———. 2003. Slow response of societies to new problems: Causes and costs. *Ecosystems* 6:493–502.

Schelling, Thomas. 1971a. On the ecology of micromotives. *The Public Interest* 25 (Fall): 59–98.

———. 1971b. Dynamic models of segregation. *Journal of Mathematical Sociology* 1 (1): 143–86.

———. 1972. A process of residential segregation: Neighborhood tipping. In *Discrimination in economic life,* ed. A. Pascal, 157–84. Lexington: D. C. Heath.

———. 1978. *Micromotives and macrobehavior.* New York: Norton.

———. 2002. What makes greenhouse sense? Time to rethink the Kyoto Protocol. *Foreign Affairs* 31 (3): 2–9.

Schneider, Anne, and Helen Ingram. 1997. *Policy design for democracy.* Lawrence: University of Kansas Press.

Sending, Ole. 2002. Constitution, choice and change: Problems with the "logic of appropriateness" and its use in constructivist theory. *European Journal of International Relations* 8 (4): 443–70.

Shabecoff, Philip. 2003. *A fierce green fire.* Washington, D.C.: Island Press.

Sher, Victor. 1993. Travels with strix: The spotted owl's journey through the federal courts. *The Public Land Law Review* 14:41–79.

Shnayerson, Michael. 1996. *The car that could: The inside story of GM's revolutionary electric vehicle.* New York: Random House.

Shotton, Ross, ed. 2000. Use of Property Rights in Fisheries Management. Proceedings of the Fish Rights 99 Conference, Fremantle, Australia, 11–19 November 1999. Fisheries Technical Paper T404/1. *United Nations Food and Agricultural Organization.* Rome.

Sierra Club. 2002. *Battle of the Bigs.* http://www.sierraclub.org/sierra/199903/l012.htm (page now discontinued).

Simmons, Wendy. 2002. Despite dire predictions of global warming, Americans have other priorities. *The Gallup Organization.* www.gallup.com.

Smith, Adrian. 2000. Policy networks and advocacy coalitions: Explaining policy change and stability in U.K. industrial pollution policy. *Environment and Planning C: Government and Policy.* 18:95–114.

Smith, Anne. 2003. Cost of carbon control with and without CAFE standards. Presentation at AECS Workshop on Climate Change and Transportation. Washington, D.C.

Smith, Anne, and Martin Ross. 2002. *Allowance allocation: Who wins and loses under a carbon dioxide control program?* Center for Clean Air Policy. February.

Smith, Anne, Martin Ross, and David Montgomery. 2002. Implications of trading implementations design for equity-efficiency trade-offs in carbon permit allocations. Working paper, Charles River Associates. December.

Smith, Anne, Margaret Moote, and Cecil Schwalbe, 1993. The emerging triumph of ecosystem management: The transformation of federal forest policy. In *Western public lands and environmental politics,* ed. C. Davis, 1038–9. Boulder: Westview Press.

Snow, David, and Robert Benford. 1992. Master frames and cycles of protest. In *Frontiers in social movement theory,* ed. Morris and Mueller. New Haven: Yale University Press.

Sorge, Marjorie. 1980. 31-MPG Fleet Average Seen for GM by 1985. *Automotive News* (July 14): 1.

Special Edition. 2002. California's AB 1493: Trendsetting or setting ourselves up to fail? *UCLA Journal of Environmental Law & Policy* 21. http://web.lexis-nexis.com/universe/document.

Sperling, Daniel. 2001. Public-private technology R&D partnerships: Lessons from the U.S. partnership for a new generation of vehicles. *Transport Policy* 8 (4): 247–56.

————. 2003. Freedom CAR and fuel cells: Toward the hydrogen economy? *Progressive Policy Institute Report.* 22 January. http://www.ppionline.org.

Speth, J. Gustave. 2004. *Red sky at morning.* New Haven: Yale University Press.

Squires, Dale, et al. 1995. Individual transferable quotas as a fisheries management tool. *Reviews in Fisheries Science* 3:141–69.

Stanford Law School Case no. 039–99. *Environmental Law and Natural Resources Law and Policy Program.* http://casestudies.stanford.edu.

Stewart, Richard, and Jonathan Wiener. 2003. *Reconstructing climate policy: beyond Kyoto.* Washington, D.C.: The American Enterprise Institute.

Swope, Christopher. 2003. Made in Sacramento. *Governing* (July). http://www.governing. com/articles/7calif.htm (page now discontinued).

Tarrow, Sidney. 1978. *Power in movement: social movements and contentious politics.* Cambridge: Cambridge University Press.

Teahan, John. 2004. 2003 a good year? Not for the Big 3. *Automotive News* (January 12): 51.

Tellus Institute. 2003. Analysis of the Climate Stewardship Act: A study for the Natural Resources Defense Council. Boston, Massachusetts.

Temples, James. 1980. The politics of nuclear power: A sub-government in transition. *Political Science Quarterly* 95 (Summer).

Thelen, Kathleen, and Sven Steinmo. 1992. Historical Institutionalism in Comparative Politics. In *Structuring politics: Historical institutionalism in comparative analysis,* ed. Steinmo, Thelen and Longstreth. Cambridge: Cambridge University Press: 1–32.

Thomas, Jack, et al. 1990. A conservation strategy for the northern spotted owl. *Interagency Scientific Committee,* Portland, Oregon.

Thurber, James. 1991. Dynamics of policy subsystems in American politics. In *Interest Group Politics,* ed. Cigler and Loomis. 3rd ed. Washington, D.C.: Congressional Quarterly Press.

Tilly, Charles. 1978. *From mobilization to revolution.* Reading: Addison-Wesley.

Townsend, Ralph. 1990. Entry restrictions in the fishery: A survey of the evidence. *Land Economics* 66:359–79.

True, James. 2000. Avalanches and incrementalism: Making policy and budgets in the United States. *American Review of Public Administration* 30 (1): 3–18.

True, James, Frank Baumgartner, and Bryan Jones. 1999. Explaining stability and change in American policymaking: The punctuated equilibrium model. In *Theories of the policy process,* ed. Paul Sabatier, 97–115. Boulder: Westview Press.

True, James, Bryan Jones, and Frank Baumgartner. 1999. Punctuated-equilibrium theory: Explaining stability and change in American policymaking. In *Theories of the policy process,* ed. Sabatier. Boulder: Westview Press: 97–115.

Twight, Ben. 1983. *Organizational values and political power.* University Park: Pennsylvania State University Press.

Twight, Ben, and Fremont Lyden. 1989. Measuring Forest Service bias. *Journal of Forestry* 87 (5): 35.

U.S. Department of Agriculture, Forest Service and U.S. Department of the Interior, Bureau of Land Management. 1993. *Incentive-Based Grazing Fee System.* A report from the Secretaries of Interior and Agriculture. Washington, D.C.: GPO.

U.S. Department of Energy. 2003a. Energy Information Administration. Annual Energy Review 2002. http://www.eia.doe.gov/emeu/aer/contents.html.

———. 2003b. Energy Information Administration. Analysis of S. 139, the Climate Stewardship Act of 2003: Highlights and summary. http://www.eia.doe.gov/oaif/servicerpt/ml/pdf/summary.pdf (page now discontinued).

———. 2003c. Office of Energy Efficiency and Renewable Energy. President's Hydrogen Fuel Initiative FAQ. Washington, D.C.: USDOE.

U.S. Department of the Interior, Bureau of Land Management. 1984. *50 years of public land management: 1934–1984.* Washington, D.C.: GPO.

———. 2003. Interior secretary announces proposed grazing rule that would improve grazing management. http://www.blm.gov/nhp/news/releases/pages/2003/pr031205_grazing.html (page now discontinued).

U.S. Forest Service. 1994. Establishment of Intergovernmental Advisory Committee, Implementation of the President's forest plan. U.S. Department of Agriculture.

U.S. House of Representatives. 1991. Committee on Interior and Insular Affairs. *BLM Reauthorization and Grazing Fees.* Hearings held on 12 March. Washington, D.C.: GPO.

U.S. Office of Technology Assessment. 1992. Forest Service planning: Accommodating uses, producing outputs, and sustaining ecosystems. Washington, D.C.: GPO.

U.S. Senate. 1992. Committee on Energy and Natural Resources. *Grazing Management and Grazing Fee Issues.* Hearings held on 3 September. Washington, D.C.: GPO.

University of Michigan. 2003. Economic contributions of the automotive industry to the U.S. economy: An update. *Center for Automotive Research.* http://www.cargroup.org.

Verbrugge, Randall. 2003. Interactive-agent economics: An elucidative framework and survey of results. *Macroeconomic Dynamics* 7 (3): 424–72.

Vogel, David. 1993. Representing diffuse interest in environmental policy making. In *Do institutions matter?,* ed. Weaver and Rockman. Washington, D.C.: The Brookings Institution.

Voigt, William, Jr. 1976. *Public grazing lands: Use and misuse by industry and government.* New Brunswick: Rutgers University Press.

Wald, Mathew. 2004. Report questions Bush plan for hydrogen-fueled cars. *New York Times.* 6 February.

Warner, Jens. 1983. On rent of fishing grounds. Translated by Peder Anderson. *History of Political Economy* 15:3.

Washington Department of Natural Resources. 1998. Forest Practices Board adopts a new emergency rule to protect listed bull trout. New rules go into effect today, Nov 18. http://access.wa.gov/news/news1140.asp (accessed September 2000; page now discontinued).

Washington Forest Protection Association. 1999. Forests & Fish Forever Press Releases. http://www.forestsandfish.com (accessed September 9, 2000).

Weaver, Kent. 1994. Domestic political structures and the management of complex interdependence. Revised version of a paper read at a conference of the Centre for Trade Policy and Law, October, Ottawa, Ontario.

Wenner, Lettie. 1993. The courts in environmental politics: The case of the spotted owl. In *Environmental politics and policy in the West,* ed. Zachary Smith. Dubuque: Kendall-Hunt.

Wilkinson, Charles. 1992. *Crossing the next meridian: Land, water and the future of the West.* Washington, D.C.: Island Press.

Wilsford, David. 1994. Path dependency, or why history makes it difficult but not impossible to reform health care systems in a big way. *Journal of Public Policy* 14 (3): 251–84.

Wilson, James. 1980. *The politics of regulation.* New York: Basic Books.

———. 1995. *Political organizations.* Princeton: Princeton University Press.

Wirth, Timothy, C. Boyden Gray, and John Podesta. 2003. The future of energy policy. *Foreign Affairs* 82:4.

Wood, Dan, and Alesha Doan. 2003. The politics of problem definition: Applying and testing threshold models. *American Journal of Political Science* 47 (4): 640–53.

Worster, Donald. 1985. *Rivers of empire: Water, aridity, and the growth of the American West.* New York: Pantheon Books.

Wright, Patrick. 2001. Fixing the Delta: The CALFED Bay-Delta Program and water policy under the Davis administration. *Golden Gate University Law Review* 31:331.

Yaffee, Steven. 1994. The wisdom of the spotted owl: Policy lessons for a new century. Washington, D.C: Island Press.

Yang, Zili, and Henry Jacoby. 1997. *Necessary conditions for stabilization agreements.* Cambridge: MIT Press.

Yergin, Daniel. 1979. Conservation: The key energy resource. In *Energy future: Report of the energy project at the Harvard Business School,* ed. Stobaugh and Yergin. New York: Random House.

Yergin, Daniel, and Michael Stoppard. 2003. The next prize. *Foreign Affairs* 82 (6): 103–14.

Contributors

Richard B. Allen, a resident of Rhode Island, has more than thirty years of experience as a commercial fisherman and fisheries consultant. He was a member of the New England Fishery Management Council for nine years and was a commissioner on the Atlantic States Marine Fisheries Commission for ten years. He is also a former member of the National Sea Grant Review Panel and served one term as its chairman. He is currently a member of the National Marine Fisheries Service's East Coast Advisory Panel on Individual Fishing Quotas. In 1998 he was selected as a Pew Fellow in Marine Conservation.

Frank R. Baumgartner (Ph.D., University of Michigan, 1986) is professor and head of the Political Science Department at Penn State University, where he has taught since 1998. He previously taught at the University of Iowa (1986–87), Texas A&M University (1987–98), and Caltech (1998–99). He has been a visiting scholar at the Universities of Michigan, Washington, Bergen (Norway), and Aberdeen (Scotland), as well as the Institute for Public Management (Paris). His work on public policy, agenda-setting, and interest groups in American politics has appeared in such journals as the *American Political Science Review, American Journal of Political Science, The Journal of Politics, Comparative Politics, and Legislative Studies Quarterly.* His most recent book, *Policy Dynamics* (co-edited with Bryan D. Jones) was published in 2002 by the University of Chicago Press.

An earlier book, *Agendas and Instability in American Politics* (with Bryan Jones) (University of Chicago Press, 1993) was a pioneering application of punctuated equilibrium theory to policy change.

William A. Brock is a professor of economics at the University of Wisconsin at Madison. He has also been a professor of economics at Cornell and the Universities of Chicago and of Rochester. He is a Fellow of the Econometric Society, the American Academy of Arts and Sciences, and is a Member of the National Academy of Sciences. Among his many prizes and awards is the Sherman Fairchild Distinguished Scholar Award at the California Institute of Technology. His many publications have dealt with economic dynamics, game theory, political economy, economy-ecology interactions and other topics.

Benjamin Cashore is an associate professor at the Yale School of Forestry and Environmental Studies. He was a Fulbright Scholar at Harvard University during 1996–97. He has held positions as a legislation/policy adviser to the leader of the Canadian New Democratic Party (1990–93); postdoctoral fellow, Forest Economics and Policy Analysis Research Unit, University of British Columbia (1997–98); and assistant professor, School of Forestry and Wildlife Sciences, Auburn University (1998–2001). Cashore's publications include articles in *Policy Sciences, Governance,* the *Canadian Journal of Political Science, Canadian Public Administration, Canadian-American Public Policy,* and *Forest Policy and Economics* and several book chapters. He is co-author of *In Search of Sustainability: The Politics of Forest Policy in British Columbia in the 1990s.*

Charles Davis is a professor of political science and head of the department at Colorado State University. He received his Ph.D. from the University of Houston in 1977. His fields include environmental politics and policy, and public administration. He was the editor of *Western Public Lands and Environmental Politics,* 2nd ed. (2000), author of *The Politics of Hazardous Waste* (1993), and co-editor of *Dimensions of Hazardous Waste Politics and Policy* (1988). He has also authored or co-authored numerous book chapters and articles appearing in *American Politics Quarterly, Policy Studies Review, Society and Natural Resources, Western Political Quarterly, Environmental Law, Polity, Industrial* and *Labor Relations Review, Environmental Management, Policy Studies Journal, Journal of Forestry,* and other sources.

James A. Dunn, Jr., is professor of political science and public administration at Rutgers University-Camden. He was a member of the U.S. research team on MIT's International Automobile Program and he served as chairman of the South Jersey Transit Advisory Committee. He is the author of *Driving Forces: The American Automobile and Its Enemies* (1998), and *Miles To Go: European and American Transportation Policies* (1981).

Leah Fraser is a Ph.D. candidate in the Department of Political Science and was a Warmington Public Policy Fellow in the School of Social Ecology in 2002–03. In 2003, Leah was awarded the Eckstein Scholar Award in recognition for excellence in her graduate studies program since candidacy. She recently co-authored with Helen Ingram "Changing the Policy Paradigm," in *Moving Waters: The Colorado River and the West,* ed. Max Oelschlaeger and Peter Friederici (forthcoming).

Michael Howlett is Burnaby Mountain Professor of Political Science at Simon Fraser University in British Columbia, Canada. He is co-author of *Studying Public Policy: Policy Cycles and Policy Subsystems* (2003 and 1995), *In Search of Sustainability: British Columbia Forest Policy in the 1990s* (2001), *The Political Economy of Canada: An Introduction* (1999 and 1992), and *Canadian Natural Resource and Environmental Policy: Political Economy and Public Policy* (1997). He has edited *Canadian Forest Policy: Adapting to Change* (2001). His articles have been published in numerous professional journals in Canada, the United States, Europe, Brazil, New Zealand and Australia. Dr. Howlett is currently the English language co-editor of the *Canadian Journal of Political Science* (2002–05).

Helen Ingram is Warmington Professor of Social Ecology at the University of California at Irvine. Her research has dealt with transboundary national resources, particularly on the U.S./Mexican border, water resources policy, public policy design and implementation, and the impact of policy upon democracy and public participation. Professor Ingram has helped elucidate self-reinforcing policy subsystems in such publications as *Policy Design for Democracy* (1997); "Interest Groups and Environmental Policy," chapter 5 in *Environmental Politics and Policy: Theories and Evidence,* ed. James Lester (1995); and Helen Ingram and Steven R. Smith, *Public Policy for Democracy* (1993).

Lee Lane is the executive director of Americans for Equitable Climate Solutions, a nonprofit environmental organization in Washington, D.C. Lane previously served as vice president for research with the CSX Corporation and from 1994 to 1998 was president of Policy Services Inc., a Washington consulting firm specializing in corporate strategy. Earlier Lane had held the position of vice president for policy at the Association of American Railroads. In the 1970s Mr. Lane had been the executive director of the Coalition to Tax Pollution, an organization advocating the implementation of sulfur emission taxes.

Robert Repetto is a professor in the practice of sustainable development at the Yale School of Forestry and Environmental Studies. He was formerly vice president of the World Resources Institute in Washington, D.C., and an associate professor of economics and public health at the Harvard School of Public Health. In 1998 he was selected as a Pew Fellowship in Marine Conservation. His publications have explored the interface between economic and environmental policy.

James Gustave Speth is dean of the Yale School of Forestry and Environmental Studies. He was formerly administrator of the United Nations Development Programme and is a founder of both the Natural Resources Defense Council and the World Resources Institute, which he led as president from 1983 to 1996. He is a recipient of the Blue Planet Award for leadership service to the global environment. Dean Speth recently wrote the book *Red Sky at Morning,* an overview of global environmental problems and solutions.

Index